Achieving your Diploma in Teaching (FE & Skills)

Achieving your Diploma in Teaching (FE & Skills)

Putting theory into practice for the qualification or apprenticeship

Ann Gravells
Gavin Lumsden

LM Learning Matters

Learning Matters
A Sage Publishing Company

1 Oliver's Yard
55 City Road
London EC1Y 1SP

2455 Teller Road
Thousand Oaks
California 91320

Unit No 323-333, Third Floor, F-Block
International Trade Tower
Nehru Place, New Delhi – 110 019

8 Marina View Suite 43-053
Asia Square Tower 1
Singapore 018960

Editor: Amy Thornton
Senior project editor: Chris Marke
Project management: Westchester Publishing
Marketing manager: Lorna Patkai
Cover design: Wendy Scott
Typeset by: C&M Digitals (P) Ltd, Chennai, India
Printed in the UK

Library of Congress Control Number: 2024939702

British Library Cataloguing in Publication Data

A catalogue record for this book is available from the British Library

ISBN 978-1-5296-9049-1
ISBN 978-1-5296-9048-4 (pbk)

CONTENTS

ACKNOWLEDGEMENTS

We would like to give a special thanks to the following people who have helped with the production of this book. They have freely given their time, knowledge, and advice, which has resulted in some excellent contributions and additions to the content, and we are truly grateful. We would also like to thank our social media followers who gave us some great ideas regarding other aspects which we could include.

Daniel Scott-Purdy – Digital Curriculum Manager https://danielscott86.blogspot.com

Holly Saunders – Education Consultant and IQA at Essential Teaching UK

Jeminiyi Ogunkoya – Managing Director – AASOG Education and Training

Joey Greenwood – Training Director at Smart Training Solutions (UK) Ltd

Lisa Morris – Director at Educating UK, and Lead External Quality Assurer at TQUK

Matt Griffin – Advanced Practitioner/Vocational Assessor at CST Training

Rick Mills – Technical Training Specialist, United Utilities Water Limited

Robert Milligan – Education Consultant and Teacher/Assessor at Essential Teaching UK

Simon Linard – Director at SL Training and Development

Gavin would also like to personally thank his wife, Louise Lumsden, who has given him outstanding support, and for the endless amounts of proofreading she has carried out. He would also like to thank his co-author Ann Gravells, for her excellent mentoring and support during the writing of this book.

We would both like to thank our Senior Commissioning Editor (Education) Amy Thornton for her continued support and guidance.

Every effort has been made to trace the copyright holders and to obtain their permission for the use of copyright material. The publisher and authors will gladly receive any information enabling them to rectify any error or omission in subsequent editions.

Ann Gravells

Gavin Lumsden

Ann Gravells

Ann Gravells

Ann has been teaching in the FE and Skills sector since 1983. She is an experienced teacher educator, and has delivered events nationally and internationally.

She is a well-respected author, having been writing, co-writing, and editing text books for the sector since 2006.

Ann holds a Masters in Educational Management, a PGCE, a Degree in Education, and a Medal of Excellence for teaching. She is a Fellow of the Society for Education and Training, and holds QTLS status.

You can find out more about Ann here: www.anngravells.com

Gavin Lumsden

Gavin Lumsden

Gavin has been teaching in the FE and Skills sector since 2007 and is an inspiring figure in the field of education, specialising in coaching. As the Director of Education at Essential Teaching UK, he brings a wealth of experience and passion to the realm of teaching.

Gavin holds a Degree in Education and a Certificate in Education. He is a Member of the Society for Education and Training, and holds QTLS status. He is an active member of the SET Practitioner Advisory Group, and speaks at conferences and events.

You can find out more about Gavin here: www.essentialteaching.uk/the-teacher-coach

INTRODUCTION

Congratulations on purchasing this book which we hope will help you on your journey towards achieving the Level 5 Diploma in Teaching (Further Education and Skills) or the Learning and Skills Teacher apprenticeship. Both are based on the Occupational Standards for the FE sector, and each chapter in this book is cross-referenced to them. The qualification is also offered at higher levels, and sometimes referred to as the CertEd or PGCE/PGDE.

The book should help you to gain the knowledge you need to begin to put theory into practice. Although this book will be a good foundation for your learning, you will need to refer to other relevant text books to demonstrate wider reading. At the back of this book is a list of books for further reading, along with useful references and websites.

The chapters can be read according to what you need to know at any given time. You can refer to the index at the back of the book to locate relevant topics, or just look in the contents list. If you have an electronic copy, you should be able to carry out searches.

There are *activities* in every chapter to help you work towards relevant aspects in the qualification or apprenticeship. There are also *theory into practice* activities which are designed to help you with your job role as a teacher. *Helpful hints* are included in each chapter, along with *examples* of relevant teaching scenarios.

There are many aspects in this book which have previously appeared in Ann Gravells' other text books. They have been updated and included here as they are still relevant. As the saying goes: *'If it ain't broke, don't fix it'!*

Ann Gravells and Gavin Lumsden wish you great success with your teaching career and hope that you find the content of this book helpful. The illustrations were created by Gavin using www.canva.com, a really useful online tool for teachers to use.

1

Teaching in the Further Education and Skills sector

Putting theory into practice to become a professional teacher

Introduction

Being a teacher can be a really rewarding career. You will be helping many learners to achieve their goals by gaining the knowledge, skills, understanding, and behaviours they need at a given point in time. However, you also need to be a learner yourself in order to become a teacher for your particular subject specialism.

There are currently two routes to gain recognition as a professional teacher in the Further Education (FE) and Skills sector (at level 5 and above in England). One is to obtain the qualification known as the Diploma in Teaching (sometimes referred to as CertEd/PGCE/PGDE), and the other is through a Learning and Skills Teacher apprenticeship programme.

This chapter will introduce you to the following topics:

- The Diploma in Teaching (FE and Skills)
- Occupational Standards
- The Learning and Skills Teacher apprenticeship
- Teaching in the Further Education and Skills sector
- Evidence-based practice
- Education for sustainable development

Occupational Standards covered in Chapter I

Duties	Knowledge	Skills	Behaviours
D1, D3, D8	K5	S1, S6, S7, S16, S21	B2, B3, B4, B6

The Diploma in Teaching (FE and Skills)

The Diploma in Teaching (FE and Skills) is the qualification for practitioners in England who teach learners aged 14 and above in various locations and contexts. For example, this could be in: a college, a prison, a private training provider, the uniformed services, the workplace, outdoor environments, or in community organisations and the voluntary sector. You will learn how to teach, how to assess that learning has taken place, how to plan courses, how to devise resources for your subject specialism, and how to evaluate and improve your practice. Being a teacher involves an ongoing commitment to supporting your learners, as well reviewing and updating your practice. This includes keeping up to date with your teaching skills (pedagogy), as well as developments with the subject you will teach.

The qualification is available at level 5 (usually via further education colleges and training providers) and up to level 7 (usually via higher education institutions [HEIs] such as universities). The content will still be the same at higher levels, but the amount and level of study and research required and the difficulty and complexity of assessment activities will differ. The qualification might be called something different by HEIs, for example, Certificate in Education (CertEd) at level 5, Professional Graduate Certificate in Education (PGCE) at level 6, or Post Graduate Certificate/Diploma in Education (PGC/DE) at level 7. These, and the Diploma in Teaching (DiT), are all recognised as the full teaching qualification for practitioners in the FE and Skills sector. The qualification will be offered in different ways, for example, one year full-time, two years part-time, in-person, online, or a blended learning approach.

If you are currently teaching, this is known as *in-service*, if you are not yet in a teaching role, this is known as *pre-service* and you will be required to carry out teaching practice in a work placement. You might also deliver short lessons to your peers, known as micro-teaching (in Chapter 7).

You will need to meet certain application criteria, such as holding relevant maths and English qualifications at level 2 (level 3 if you will be teaching these as your subject specialism). You might also need to hold a qualification which is a level above that which you wish to teach, for example, holding a level 3 to teach level 2, or to have a degree in your subject specialism if you are teaching academic subjects. If you are teaching in professional or vocational contexts, you are usually expected to have a professional or trade qualification as well as experience of working in that area, for example, hairdressing or construction. In some vocational areas this may be problematic, but a reasonable expectation is that you hold the highest level trade qualification available, unless you have substantial professional experience. The qualification specification or relevant Occupational Standards for the subject you wish to teach will state what is required.

Example

Lisa is an experienced hairdresser who owns and manages a salon. She would like to teach part-time in her local college but still continue to work. She has found out that she needs to be qualified at level 3 to teach hairdressing at level 2, and she needs to have experience of working in a salon. She meets both of these requirements, as well as holding maths and English qualifications at level 2. However, she might also need to hold an assessment qualification, but she can achieve this while training to be a teacher. She decides to apply to a local college to teach evening classes. If successful, they will offer her a place to work towards the Diploma in Teaching over two years part-time.

The content of the DiT qualification is based on a set of standards known as *Occupational Standards*, which are explained later in this chapter. You will be assessed to ensure that you have met the required knowledge aspects, for example, by completing assignments. You will also be observed in your work placement (in Chapter 8) to ensure that you have met the required skills and behaviours. If you don't pass a certain aspect, you should be referred, usually with the opportunity to resubmit your work or to be re-observed within a set timescale. Your course tutor (who might also be known as your assessor and/or your observer) will give you more information regarding this. However, you must successfully meet all of the Occupational Standards to achieve the DiT qualification.

Activity

If you haven't yet applied to work towards the DiT qualification, find out where it is offered locally, or if it's possible to do some or all of it online. Take a look at this link for tips to find a legitimate training provider: https://tinyurl.com/FindTrainingProvider.

Units

The DiT qualification will be made up of several units which relate to different areas of the Occupational Standards. The units will have different titles depending upon which awarding organisation (AO) your training provider has registered you with. An AO is a body who creates qualifications and issues certificates, and there are many in existence. Each unit has a *credit value*, which again might differ between AOs. You must successfully achieve a total of 120 credits to gain the DiT qualification.

Example unit titles (in alphabetical order):

- Action research
- Assessment principles and practices
- Coaching and mentoring
- Curriculum development
- Developing and using resources
- Digital and online pedagogies
- Educational practice
- Equality, diversity and inclusion

- Learners and learning
- Managing behaviour
- Professional practice
- Subject specialist teaching
- Teaching and learning
- Teachers and teaching
- Teaching my subject

Work placements/teaching practice

Your work placements are where you will carry out your teaching practice and will include teaching hours and non-teaching hours. If you are in-service, this will be at your current place of work. If you are pre-service, a placement might be arranged for you by your training provider, or you might have to find your own. You should find out what your roles and responsibilities will be, along with your hours of work, your teaching timetable, and anything else such as who your contact will be, any travel arrangements, and if you can be on first name terms with your learners. The work placement must be with learners aged 14 and above, and not based on one-to-one teaching, but with groups of learners (usually at least ten).

You will need to evidence your practice in more than one location. This is in order to improve the breadth of your experience. Your first location might be where you carry out your teaching practice. Your second location might be where you carry out administration duties. Ideally, it should be in a separate department, site, or building. It might even be at a different organisation, perhaps if you are employed part-time by more than one provider, or have two work experience placements.

You must spend at least 250 hours in your work placement locations, with a minimum of 150 teaching hours in your first location. This will consist of:

- a minimum of 100 hours teaching your subject specialism, with a further 50 hours teaching your subject specialism or another subject (total 150 hours)
- a minimum of 20 hours of the 150 hours should be remote live teaching
- a minimum of 80 hours of the 150 hours should be in-person teaching.

Non-teaching hours must include a minimum of 100 hours (at least 20 hours of this should be in your second location). This might involve: observing other teachers, attending meetings, interviewing learners, and carrying out other activities such as administration, standardisation activities, preparation, and planning. You will need to clarify all this with your course tutor.

Assessment for the qualification

Depending upon which awarding organisation you have been registered with, the assessment methods might differ. However, they are all designed to assess your achievement of the duties; knowledge, skills and behaviours (KSB) of the Occupational Standards (explained later in this chapter).

Some assessment methods which might be used to assess your KSBs are listed in Table 1.1 and are explained here.

Table 1.1 Examples of assessment methods for the DiT qualification

Knowledge	Skills	Behaviours
• assignments • case studies/research projects/reports • essays • professional discussions • questions (oral/written/online) • reflective accounts/journals	• teaching practice observations • professional discussions • reflective accounts/journals • witness testimonies	• teaching practice observations • professional discussions • reflective accounts/journals • witness testimonies
All three areas cover the duties and will be assessed by a viva based around your professional practice portfolio. A viva is a face-to-face oral assessment.		

Assignments

An assignment is a way of ensuring that certain criteria can be met through various tasks, questions, and/or problem-solving activities. The assignment will assess your knowledge and how you apply it, perhaps by: answering questions, holding group discussions, giving presentations to peers, and providing evidence of your teaching practice. You will be given a target date for completion, and possibly a word count. Your assessor should provide you with ongoing developmental feedback, and if you don't fully meet certain criteria, you should be given the opportunity to resubmit by a certain date.

Assignments often use process words (active verbs) such as analyse, explain, identify, and evaluate. When you are given an assignment, you will need to ensure that you fulfil the requirements of the process word in the question, as well as meeting the relevant assessment criteria and/or Occupational Standards.

Helpful hint

It's worth finding out in advance what the process words mean in relation to the question. For example, analyse means that you need to give a methodical, detailed and logical explanation or criticism regarding why the teaching approaches you used did or did not work.

You will need to take a systematic approach when answering questions, and make sure that you read the question carefully to ensure that you meet all the requirements, as in Figure 1.1. You must be able to demonstrate theory into practice by applying your knowledge to your job role. This will involve reading and referring to quotes from what is already available, perhaps from relevant journals and books. You should then relate it to your own practice, stating what worked (or not) and why. Any quotes used should be referenced in an academic style. Referencing your work gives credit to the original author (if you don't reference them, you are plagiarising their work) and it shows that you have carried out relevant wider reading.

Alternatively, you could devise a research activity to find the answers to a particular theory of your own. All research should be ethical i.e. follow a process which is morally and socially responsible. Your course tutor will be able to give you advice regarding academic writing, referencing, and how to carry out research.

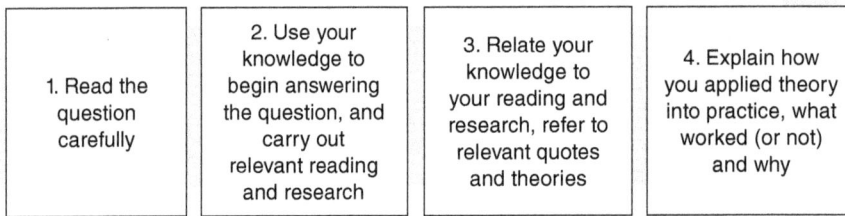

1. Read the question carefully	2. Use your knowledge to begin answering the question, and carry out relevant reading and research	3. Relate your knowledge to your reading and research, refer to relevant quotes and theories	4. Explain how you applied theory into practice, what worked (or not) and why

Figure 1.1 A systematic approach to answering questions

Case studies/research projects/reports

A case study usually consists of a hypothetical or an imaginary event for you to consider and analyse. You can then make suggestions regarding how you would deal with the event. Alternatively, you could produce your own research project or report regarding a real situation that you have encountered, and how you dealt with it, relating your response anonymously to the relevant criteria.

Essays

Essays are formal pieces of writing which should address a particular question. The structure should include: an introduction, main body, conclusion, and a reference list. There will usually be a word count to ensure you remain focused and specific. You will have a target date for submission and if you can't meet this for any reason, you will need a legitimate reason to ask for an extension.

Essays often include citing from relevant text books, websites and journals. The *Harvard* system is the style that is generally used and there are many books and websites available which you can refer to. However, your course tutor should give you guidance as to the system they expect you to use.

Professional discussions

A professional discussion is a conversation with your assessor rather than questions and answers. It gives you the opportunity to justify how you have achieved certain criteria. For example, your assessor could verbally explore your knowledge and understanding of your teaching role. Having a professional discussion with your assessor is a good way to demonstrate how you have met certain criteria, perhaps if you are having difficulty expressing yourself through written work.

A professional discussion can be used as a *holistic* assessment method, meaning several criteria can be assessed at the same time. Your assessor will prompt you to explain how you have met the criteria, and ask to see documents (known as evidence) which confirm this. Prior to the professional discussion, you should agree with your assessor the nature of the content of the conversation to enable you to prepare. You may need to bring along examples of teaching materials you have prepared and used. When you are taking part in the professional discussion, try and remain focused, don't digress but be specific with your responses. At the end of the discussion, your assessor should confirm which criteria you have met and which you still need to work towards.

A final professional discussion will also take place based around your professional practice portfolio (in Chapter 8), called a *viva*. This will usually be carried out by your assessor and your placement provider to decide if you have met the Occupational Standards.

Questions – oral/written/online

You may need to produce answers to written or oral questions which will be based around certain criteria. These could be part of a written test, or asked orally by your assessor, or be completed online. If it's the latter, the online program could give you the results immediately, but it might not tell you which questions were answered correctly or not.

If you have answered written questions and met most but not all of the criteria, your assessor might follow this up with some oral questions or a professional discussion. This is to ensure that you have the relevant knowledge and understanding.

Reflective account/journals

A reflective account or journal is a way of helping you to formally focus upon your learning, progress and achievements. You might be given a template or an online document to complete, or you could write in a diary, a notebook, or word-process your accounts. If you are handwriting, make sure your work is legible as your assessor will need to be able to read and understand it. Try and reflect upon your experiences by analysing as well as describing them (in Chapter 9). Be as specific as possible as to how your experiences have met the criteria which you are being assessed towards. Try and note which of these you feel you have met, as this will help your assessor when they read your account. Don't just write a chronological account of events; consider what worked well, or didn't work well (and why), what theories have influenced you, and how you could do something differently given the opportunity.

Teaching practice observations

As you progress through the DiT qualification, you will be observed on at least ten occasions, for a minimum of 45 minutes each, to groups (not individuals). The observations will be by your course tutor/assessor, and subject specialist mentor. Earlier observations will focus on your development, whereas later observations will focus on how you have met the Occupational Standards. Observations and teaching practice are covered further in Chapter 8.

A maximum of two observations can be of live remote teaching (where you and your learners are online at the same time but in different locations). One other lesson can be observed remotely (where your observer is not present in the room with you). However, recorded lessons cannot be used for formal observations, but could be used as a learning tool. For example, you could record one of your lessons and play it back to your mentor for their feedback. Or you could watch it yourself to reflect on your practice, and evaluate what went well, what didn't and why.

Please check with your course tutor as to the requirements for observed practice. It could differ depending upon which awarding organisation you are registered with, and if you teach in a prison, or with learners who have special educational needs and disabilities (SEND).

Witness testimonies

A witness is usually someone who is an expert in your subject specialism or an area of your practice. A witness testimony from your mentor can confirm which criteria you have met, and can be used towards your professional practice portfolio. You could also obtain witness testimonies from colleagues or other practitioners you work with.

Professional practice portfolio

This is a file which contains evidence of your practice to prove that you have met the Occupational Standards. It can be electronic or paper-based and is covered in detail in Chapter 8. A professional discussion will take place between you and your assessor which will be based around the contents.

Viva

A viva is a face-to-face oral assessment usually carried out by two qualified teachers. This might be your course tutor/assessor, and your placement provider. The session will typically last around half an hour to an hour. It is carried out once you have successfully completed all your coursework, teaching practice, and observations. The viva will consist of questions based around your professional practice throughout your time working towards the qualification. Your professional practice portfolio will be used as a basis for this.

Throughout the session, you will need to satisfy your assessors that you have met the required Occupational Standards. It's a great opportunity for you to explain what you have learnt and achieved in support of the documents in your portfolio. This will be the final judgement which will inform you if you have or haven't met the Occupational Standards.

If you haven't met them, you will need to talk to your assessor as to whether you can be reassessed for the areas you haven't met.

Mentors

You will need to have the support of two mentors at your work placements, in addition to the support of your course tutor/assessor. They should partake in mentoring training which will be arranged by your DiT training provider.

The first mentor is known as your *subject specialist mentor* who must be competent in, and currently teaching in, the same subject area as yourself. This is so that they can provide you with subject-specific support as well as guidance regarding teaching, learning, and assessment. They should be able to support you on a weekly basis, and it would be useful to keep a log of this support. This could include the date and time, what was discussed, and how you have met any identified action points.

You could observe your mentor when they are teaching, to see how they work. They will also observe you teaching, provide you with developmental feedback, and complete an observation report and/or witness testimony for your professional practice portfolio.

The second mentor is a *pastoral support mentor* (or *professional mentor*) who will be able to give you general advice and support regarding your teaching role. They should be able to meet you on a weekly basis, and it would be useful to keep a log of this support. This could include the date and time, what was discussed, and how you have met any identified action points.

They should liaise with your course tutor/assessor and update them regarding your progress. However, they cannot carry out any formal lesson observations, but could carry out informal ones to provide developmental feedback.

Theory into practice

Who could be your two mentors to support your teaching role? If you are already in a teaching position, approach at least two colleagues to ask if they would be prepared to carry out the roles (subject and pastoral). If so, find out how they can partake in relevant training from the organisation you are registered with for the DiT qualification.

Occupational Standards

The Occupational Standards for FE and Skills teachers in England are taken from the Learning and Skills Teacher apprenticeship programme (explained later). They are developed by employers and experts from the sector. They include *duties* which are mapped to *knowledge, skills* and *behaviours* (KSBs). Each aspect is given a reference and it's these which you will use to cross-reference your evidence to in your professional practice portfolio. An Occupational Standard sets out the KSBs required to be competent in a particular occupation e.g. a teacher, an electrician or a customer service practitioner. The term *pedagogy* is used in the teaching Occupational Standards and relates to the way knowledge and skills are imparted in an educational context. For example, the methods and activities which teachers use with their learners for their subject specialism.

Helpful hint

The chapters in this book have been cross-referenced to the Occupational Standards. An online link to the Standards is at the end of this section. You could use them like a checklist of your achievements as you progress through the DiT course.

Duties

Duties describe what someone in the occupation usually does in the workplace, and are sometimes called competences or activities. They are similar to what you would find listed in a job description, and are referenced to the KSBs.

Example

Duty 1: Promote a passion for learning and set high expectations of all students, and support their personal and skills development (K5, K9, S10).

Duty 2: Maintain a focus on outcomes for all students, so that they recognise the value of their learning and the future opportunities available to them (K5, K6, K8, K9, A1, S3, S10, S11).

Knowledge

This relates to the information and technical details that someone needs to know and understand to successfully carry out the duties. Some knowledge will be occupation-specific, whereas some may be more generic.

Skills

This is the practical application of knowledge which is needed to successfully undertake the duties.

Behaviours

These are attitudes and/or approaches needed for competence in a particular occupation. Behaviours tend to be transferable to other contexts and situations. They may be more similar across occupations than knowledge and skills.

Each of the KSBs have a reference; the first few are in Table 1.2. Please note, these might differ if they have been updated since publication of this book.

Table 1.2 Examples of the Occupational Standards for FE and Skills teachers

Knowledge	**K1**: The pedagogical theory and how to apply this theory to practice **K2**: How to support contextualised opportunities to develop English and maths **K3**: The principles of designing, planning, and organising the curriculum **K4**: Methods for creating and adapting inclusive learning resources
Skills	**S1**: Integrate subject and pedagogic research into teaching activity to enhance teaching and support changes of practice **S2**: Identify, consider, and take steps to minimise the impact of barriers to learning **S3**: Contextualise English and maths in a way that promotes understanding of key topics **S4**: Use a variety of teaching and assessment methods depending on the learning environment and learners' needs
Behaviours	**B1**: Be resilient and adaptable when dealing with challenge and change, maintaining focus and self-control **B2**: Underpin their practice by reference to professional standards and evidence-based teaching and learning **B3**: Committed to continuous professional development **B4**: Act in a professional manner, and in a way that builds and maintains positive relationships with colleagues, students and stakeholders

Activity

Carry out an online search to find the Occupational Standards for the particular subject you will teach. Take a look at the duties and KSBs, as they will provide a good foundation of the topics you will use when teaching your subject.

Occupational Standards are not just parts of apprenticeship programmes, but are also used in the development of Technical (T) Level qualifications, and underpin other qualifications. This means that Occupational Standards can also form the basis of a technical qualification, for example, the Diploma in Teaching (DiT).

Theory into practice

Take a look at the Occupational Standards for teachers in the FE and Skills sector. See how the duties, knowledge, skills and behaviours relate to the role of a teacher. If you are currently teaching, compare them to your job description. http://tinyurl.com/LSTTeacher. If the link is no longer live, just search for Occupational Standards for teachers in the FE and Skills sector.

The Learning and Skills Teacher apprenticeship

The Learning and Skills Teacher (LST) apprenticeship programme is a great way for you to demonstrate your professional practice to meet the Occupational Standards while working as a teacher in the FE sector. You will partake in paid on-the-job work experience, as well as attending off-the-job training to develop your knowledge, skills and behaviours. The apprenticeship programme lasts around 18 months full-time. You will need to have a subject specialist mentor who can support your progress and development in the workplace. You must achieve English and maths qualifications to at least level 2 prior to your final assessment (known as end-point assessment). However, an apprenticeship is not a formal qualification, but it has a level equal to one, for example, the Diploma in Teaching at level 5. Please read the previous section regarding the DiT qualification as it is very similar to the apprenticeship programme.

Example

Mira has been teaching information technology for a year on a part-time basis at a large college. They have now been offered a full-time position on an apprenticeship basis. They will earn a salary and have the opportunity to attend day-release classes to learn how to put the Occupational Standards into practice. Although Mira has some knowledge and experience already, this is a chance for them to learn much more to improve their role and gain recognition as a professional teacher.

Assessment for the apprenticeship

Assessments and teaching practice observations will be carried out by at least one independent assessor from an end-point assessment organisation (EPAO). Your employer will liaise with them regarding your progress and achievement, as well as liaising with your off-the-job training provider to ensure that you are ready to be assessed.

Assessment will be by:

- observations

- professional discussion and portfolio of evidence

- end-point assessment.

You might also need to complete some case studies or assignments to evidence your knowledge, which can also go into your portfolio.

Observations

An assessor will observe your practice (simulation is not permitted) with groups of learners. They will then carry out a professional discussion with you to ascertain how you have met the Occupational Standards. Some of these lessons will be observed by your subject specialist mentor to provide you with developmental feedback, and some by an independent assessor as part of the end-point assessment process.

Activity

Find out how you will be assessed for the apprenticeship programme, how many observed teaching practice lessons you will partake in (and when), and who will conduct them.

Professional discussion and portfolio of evidence

An assessor will hold a professional discussion with you which is a formal conversation based around your teaching practice. It gives you the opportunity to discuss and confirm your competency across the Occupational Standards, which will be cross-referenced to the evidence in your portfolio. This will contain proof of the activities which you have carried out as a teacher.

Helpful hint

Your portfolio of evidence can be started when you commence the apprenticeship programme, and be added to as you progress through it. It's worth showing it to your mentor on a regular basis, to gain their feedback and advice.

Your completed portfolio of evidence must be submitted to the EPAO at the gateway. The gateway is the period of time between completing your training and commencing the end-point assessment (EPA) process. This involves a review meeting with your employer and a representative from the training provider. This is to evaluate your performance against the Occupational Standards and to confirm whether you are ready for end-point assessment.

End-point assessment

The end-point assessment (EPA) process consists of formal observations of your teaching practice, and a discussion based around your completed portfolio of evidence.

Prior to this, you must have met the following requirements which includes:

- completing the minimum duration of the apprenticeship programme

- completing the mandatory off-the-job training

- achieving English and maths to at least level 2

- working at or above the Occupational Standards

- compiling and submitting a portfolio of evidence

- providing the independent assessor (who will observe your practice) with a copy of your lesson plans, and supporting teaching and learning materials.

Once this has been confirmed, the EPA period starts and should be completed within three months. You will be graded fail, pass, or distinction. Your employer and training provider will be able to explain more about how you will be assessed and graded. If you fail one or more assessments, you will be offered the opportunity to take a resit or a re-take if appropriate (at your employer's discretion). A resit does not require further training, whereas a re-take does. An action plan will be agreed for this, and it cannot be taken with the intention of increasing the original grade from a pass to a distinction.

Theory into practice

Take a look at the assessment plan for the Learning and Skills Teacher apprenticeship programme at http://tinyurl.com/FETeacherApprenticeship. Make a note of anything you are unsure of. It would be useful to ask any relevant questions well before you are assessed. If the link is no longer live, just search for **FE Teacher Apprenticeship**.

Teaching in the Further Education and Skills sector

The Further Education and Skills sector is for learners who are aged 14 and above. Courses can be academic i.e. theoretical (knowledge and understanding of a subject) or vocational (skills and behaviours for a job), and it can take place in any context or environment such as indoors, outdoors, or online. The opportunity for people to take further education often gives them chances to do new things. It also gives people the opportunity to improve their knowledge, skills and behaviours for personal as well as professional reasons.

Your job role within the sector might be called something other than a teacher. For example, instructor, lecturer, professor, supervisor, trainer, or tutor. Whatever you are called, your purpose will be to educate someone to ensure that learning takes place. Your learners should then be able to put their newfound learning into practice, demonstrating their knowledge and skills, along with a change in their behaviour.

In the FE and Skills sector there are many acronyms, some of which you will already be familiar with, but they often change. An acronym is an abbreviation formed from the initial letters of words e.g. DiT for Diploma in Teaching. It's useful to become familiar with them as you will no doubt talk to people who use them.

Activity

Take a look at the Appendix at the back of this book. This is a list of educational abbreviations and acronyms. Choose five you are not familiar with, find out what they mean, and identify how relevant they are to you at this time.

The teaching, learning, and assessment cycle

Your teaching role will usually be based around the teaching, learning, and assessment cycle, as in Figure 1.2. It is a systematic process which helps to prepare your learners for their transition through education into employment, or to achieve their chosen goal. The process can start at any stage of the cycle and keep on going. However, all stages should be addressed for learning to be effective. Don't worry if what follows doesn't make sense at the moment; it will be covered throughout the book.

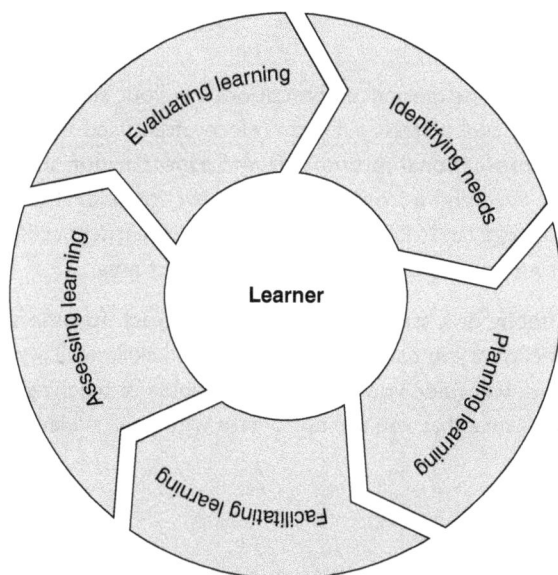

Figure 1.2 The teaching, learning, and assessment cycle

All aspects of the cycle focus around the learner, and will briefly involve:

- identifying needs: finding out what your organisation's, your own, and your potential learners' needs are, finding out why learners are taking the course and what their expectations are, carrying out initial and diagnostic assessments, ensuring learners are capable of achieving their goals and progressing towards their chosen destination

- planning learning: preparing schemes of work, lesson plans, and teaching and learning resources, liaising with others such as those providing support or work experience

- facilitating learning: promoting a passion for learning, teaching your subject in a confident and professional manner, using a variety of approaches and activities in a safe environment, using resources and technology to motivate, engage, and inspire your learners

- assessing learning: checking your learners have gained the necessary knowledge, skills and behaviours at all stages throughout their time with you, using formal and informal types and methods of assessment, providing feedback, maintaining records

- evaluating learning: obtaining feedback in order to make improvements, reflecting on your role and all aspects involved with the teaching, learning, and assessment process, partaking in relevant continuing professional development (CPD), and carrying out relevant research.

There are many variations of this cycle which you might come across as you progress through your teacher training journey. Reflecting on your teaching role, as well as your subject pedagogy, can relate to all aspects of the cycle. If something doesn't work, or if you make a mistake, reflect as to why this happened, and how you can get it right next time.

Dual professionalism

As a teacher, you will be an experienced practitioner in your *subject*, and also be a professional *teacher*. The term *dual professional* is therefore often used to denote your role. This is because you are a professional in two different aspects: your subject, and teaching it. Often, teachers in FE have come from a vocational background. This is ideal, as they have the experience, knowledge, and skills to pass on to their learners, along with lots of anecdotes of what works and what doesn't work in the subject area.

Perhaps you have a hobby or a trade you would like to teach to others, you know you are good at it and you feel that you have the knowledge and skills which you could pass on to others. While this book will guide you through the process of teaching, learning, and assessing, it is up to you to ensure that you are up to date with your subject knowledge.

Example

Peter works full-time as a plumber and has been considering teaching part-time. The local college is advertising for experienced plumbers to teach an evening class. Peter feels he has the necessary knowledge and skills and would like to apply. The advertisement states that the successful applicant will be able to take a teaching qualification part-time which will be paid for by the college. If Peter is successful, he can continue with his plumbing job, teach the evening class, and work towards a teaching qualification. Peter will therefore be a dual professional. A professional plumber and a professional teacher.

Government policy

In 2013, the government (in England) removed the requirement for teachers in the FE and Skills sector to be qualified. It's currently the responsibility of the individual employer, college or university to make the decision as to what qualifications their staff should hold. Most people in a teaching role will want to hold a qualification, and organisations will want to give a quality service to their learners by having qualified staff. However, this might change at some point in the future if further regulation is introduced.

In January 2021, the government published a White Paper entitled *Skills for Jobs: Lifelong Learning for Opportunity*. This paper outlined the intention that the future of the technical education system will be based on employer needs, with the substantial majority of post-16 technical and higher technical education and training aligned to Occupational Standards (OS). This system will lead to a common set of employer-led standards that define the content of technical courses, qualifications, and apprenticeships. If there is no qualification available in a particular subject, the OS can be used as a basis for teaching it.

The *Skills and Post-16 Education Act* (2022) underpins the government's transformation of post-16 education and skills as set out in the White Paper, and will help level up and drive growth. The legislation will also give more people the opportunity to get jobs in their local areas, by requiring employers and colleges to work together to identify the skills needed within communities.

Helpful hint

While working towards your qualification or apprenticeship, you may need to research government policy and its impact upon FE over the years. Make sure that you check the latest publications and news sources, as policies can evolve over time. The impact can also vary, as evaluations of their effectiveness may differ between various stakeholders in the sector.

There is often a particular body responsible for your subject specialism. In the UK, it's the Federation for Industry Sector Skills and Standards and you can access their website at: http://fisss.org. They, along with the AO who accredit and certificate the qualification, will decide what is required by teachers to deliver and assess in a particular subject area. AOs all differ, and although they might offer a qualification with a particular title, such as the *Diploma in Teaching (FE and Skills)*, the unit titles within their qualification specification may differ. However, they will all have the same aim of meeting the Occupational Standards for a particular sector.

Professional standards

Professional standards are created for particular work areas, they can take many forms, and are either mandatory or voluntary. In England, the Education and Training Foundation (ETF) has a set of Professional Standards for teachers and trainers to follow, which were launched in 2014 and updated in 2022. They are not mandatory, but they can give teachers something to aspire to, and will guide your practice and development. They can also be used as a form of self-assessment once you have achieved your teaching qualification and are a practising teacher. At the time this book was produced, the ETF were considering a name change; therefore they might now be known as something different.

Professional teaching status

Gaining a professional teaching status confirms your commitment to your role as a teacher and to your subject specialism. In England, it's possible to apply for Qualified Teacher Learning and Skills status (QTLS) once you have achieved a level 5 teaching qualification. This is based on the ETF Professional Standards. QTLS status is currently a voluntary process which demonstrates your commitment to being a professional teacher. Gaining QTLS status gives parity with *Qualified Teacher Status* (QTS), and you will automatically receive a Teacher Reference Number (TRN). This will help if you wish to make the transition from FE to a school or an academy.

After you have been teaching for four years (and hold QTLS) you can apply for Advanced Teacher Status (ATS). This is currently a voluntary process and is the badge of advanced professionalism and mastery in further education and training. It's a chance to present research and influence change, as well as demonstrating your knowledge, skills and behaviours.

There are other teaching statuses, such as Chartered Teacher Status (CTeach) from the Chartered College of Teaching. It's worth finding out which professional bodies you can join, and whether they offer a teaching status which you could work towards.

Theory into practice

Take a look at the ETF Professional Standards at http://tinyurl.com/ETFPSTeachers. Decide which areas you feel you already excel in, and which areas you may need to develop further. This will be useful if you wish to progress to gaining your professional teaching status. If the link is no longer live, just search for ETF Professional Standards.

Evidence-based practice

Evidence-based practice can help you to make effective decisions and improve your role as a teacher. It's about using tried and tested theories, models and principles (evidence), and putting them into practice with your learners. Having something to refer to is better than starting with nothing.

Example

Jemmy has been teaching an evening class in communication skills to a group of 20 learners for three months. Whenever she places them in small groups to complete an activity, she notices that the learners go through a process. This includes firstly introducing themselves to each other, and then working out what will be done and by whom, before they even start the activity. She decided to research what was happening and she found out there's a theory called Tuckman's Group Formation (in Chapter 2). After reading more about this, she now understands how to put this theory into practice with her learners, for group work to be effective.

Evidence is confirmation or proof of something, but how do you know what works best if you are a new teacher? You could try the following:

- talking to other teachers, experts and your mentors. Discussing what you have done and why it did or did not work. Finding out what they do, why they do it, and why what they do works

- researching what has been done before e.g. theories, models and principles. There are many journal papers and books written by educational experts who have tried and tested different ways of doing things over the years. However, there might equally be other experts who contradict them

- trying something out with your learners, for example, from the research you have carried out, testing if it works or not, and considering why. However, what works with one learner or group might not work with another. Don't be put off trying; you can adapt and keep experimenting. You can even be honest with your learners and tell them that you are trying something new, and that you would like their feedback if it worked or not

- creating a research model yourself. For example, creating your own theory about how to do something, testing it out and reflecting on the process

- reviewing what you do and why you do it, and reflecting upon each experience you have, comparing it to theories and research which currently exists.

Activity

Research what evidence-based practice involves. You could use the internet by keying in 'evidence-based practice' into an online search engine. Alternatively, you could read relevant text books and/or journal articles.

If you are a new teacher, you might not really have anything on which to base the teaching approaches you will use, other than your past experiences as a learner yourself. These experiences might have been positive, for example, a college course with a friendly and helpful teacher. Alternatively, they could have been negative, for example, a class in a school where you had a domineering or unhelpful teacher. You will know what worked and did not work for you. However, you can't base how you will teach on how you were taught, as all situations are different.

Helpful hint

Whatever you do, sometimes things will go wrong, or something you had planned to do just doesn't work. Don't panic, just be honest with yourself and your learners, and don't bluff your way out of something.

It's useful to make a note of what went well after each lesson you teach, and what didn't go well. You can then use this to help you evaluate your practice and reflect on how you could do things differently next time (in Chapter 9). You will develop your own strategies as time progresses, and you will also learn from your own experiences and mistakes, as well as from relevant theories.

Education for sustainable development

Your role as a teacher will require you to embed aspects of Education for Sustainable Development (ESD) within your subject. One of the Department for Education's (2024, page 6) strategic aims is: *Excellence in education and skills for a changing world: preparing all young people for a world impacted by climate change through learning and practical experience.*

Wherever possible, you should embrace the above statement by discussing and/or carrying out relevant activities with your learners, which relate to your subject. It's important for you to do what you can to help the environment, as well as empowering your learners. You and your learners can help make a real difference to the health of the planet, and improve the quality of life for future generations.

It will depend upon your subject specialism as to which topics and areas are relevant to carry out with your learners, and whether they can occur naturally during lessons or need to be taught separately. Topics which you could use for discussions, or to create activities around, include the following (in alphabetical order):

- accountability of own actions
- adverse effects of non-native flora and fauna
- biodiversity
- carbon footprint/reduction
- clean energy/energy efficiency
- clean water and sanitation
- climate change

- conservation

- consumerism i.e. throw-away society, food waste

- corporate social responsibility ('polluter pays' principle)

- deforestation

- disaster risk reduction

- environmental impact of intensive farming practices

- food security

- green economy

- greenhouse gas emissions

- health and wellbeing of people and animals

- how to verify what is real and fake news regarding sustainability and the environment

- long-term global consequences of poor government policies and practices

- pesticide use and the effects on bee and insect populations

- plastic waste in the oceans

- pollution: air, sea, land, rivers

- poverty and hunger

- reducing, reusing, recycling, repairing, regifting

- renewable energy

- responsible production and packaging

- social responsibility

- sustainable consumption

- waste disposal and management.

No matter how minor you think the change might be, small steps can lead to big changes in the long term. The discussions and activities will help to prepare your learners to contribute to a more sustainable and equitable world. This can be done by fostering an understanding of environmental issues, social justice, and economic considerations.

Example

Ajay was explaining the assignment process for his subject to his new group of learners, all aged between 19 and 24. He asked them how they could contribute to reducing the use of paper throughout the course. To his surprise, they all asked him to send the assignments via email, and that they would also submit

(Continued)

(Continued)

them that way. A few also suggested that handouts and other course documents be issued electronically, and any paper which was used during the lessons should be written on both sides. Ajay decided to create an online platform to upload the assignments and course materials to, which learners could access at any time. This discussion also prompted other ideas based on recycling and reusing items.

You could think of ESD as a way of providing education that meets the needs of the present without compromising the needs of the future. Ideally, your organisation should have an ESD policy which integrates the principles of sustainability throughout the curriculum. Once you are aware of the policy, you can begin to embed various aspects during your lessons. Regular discussions and activities with learners can help them to stay informed, and become more socially aware of the impact their actions have. Projects could be carried out in small groups and be followed by a presentation and discussion regarding their findings. This is a good way to embed ESD into your subject, and to also assess other skills such as teamwork and communication.

Helpful hint

Lead by example by not wasting energy in the classroom. Turn down the heating, turn off lights during the day, recycle and reuse what you can, and don't leave equipment switched on when not in use. Using real examples during the learning process can help to encourage good practice.

If possible, learners could get involved with organisational initiatives such as recycling, or supporting local community groups with environmental projects (perhaps in their own time). This would help to instil a sense of responsibility and a willingness to help others. As part of the learning process for your subject, you could invite guest speakers from local businesses (or arrange a visit to their premises) which have successfully made a difference in some way to their sustainable working practices. Alternatively, you could jointly with your learners design a project which addresses environmental or social issues. If your learners also attend lessons with other teachers, you could work with them to incorporate ESD across multiple subjects.

Embedding sustainable practices is an ongoing process which will require a commitment to staying informed and up to date, and to adapt to evolving challenges.

Theory into practice

Make a list of discussion topics and activities which you could carry out with your learners, which relate to your subject. You could refer to the previous bullet list for ideas. If you are currently teaching, carry out one of them with your learners and evaluate how effective it was. What would you change and why?

Summary

This chapter has explored:

- The Diploma in Teaching (FE and Skills)
- Occupational Standards
- The Learning and Skills Teacher apprenticeship
- Teaching in the Further Education and Skills sector
- Evidence-based practice
- Education for sustainable development

2

Embedding your subject within your teaching role

Putting theory into practice regarding your subject

Introduction

The role of a teacher extends far beyond just imparting knowledge of your subject. Teaching is multifaceted and requires not only a deep understanding of your subject, but the ability to teach it successfully as part of the curriculum.

You therefore need to be an expert in your subject, and an expert in how to teach it, no matter what type of environment you might teach in, or the limited time and resources available to you.

This chapter will introduce you to the following topics:

- The role of a teacher
- Teaching in an educational organisation
- Teaching your subject specialism
- Teaching and learning environments
- Curriculum development
- Working with others

Occupational Standards covered in Chapter 2

Duties	Knowledge	Skills	Behaviours
D2, D3, D4, D5, D6, D7, D8, D9	K1, K10, K11, K12, K14, K15	S1, S2, S7, S13, S15, S17, S19, S21, S23, S24	B1, B4

The role of a teacher

Your main role as a teacher will be to manage and facilitate the learning process. This will be by teaching your subject in a way which actively involves and engages your learners to ensure that learning takes place. Your employment contract should outline your roles and responsibilities, which will include other aspects such as relevant administration and participating in meetings.

Teaching roles might include:

- interviewing learners
- communicating and working with others
- identifying learners' needs
- preparing teaching, learning, and assessment materials
- designing and using resources
- establishing ground rules with learners
- using a variety of inclusive teaching, learning, and assessment approaches
- managing behaviour
- embedding English, maths, digital skills, and sustainability
- providing feedback to learners
- reflecting on your role.

Teaching responsibilities might include:

- following your organisation's policies and procedures
- following relevant legislation and codes of practice
- creating a scheme of work and lesson plans
- keeping a record of attendance
- maintaining records
- sharing best practice and standardising practice with others
- maintaining own continuing professional development (CPD).

Prior to joining the college as a teacher, Louise received her contract and job description. The supporting letter stated that she would partake in an induction programme when she commenced, which would include an explanation of policies and procedures. As she read through the documents, she also found a list of her teaching roles and responsibilities. The comprehensive details outlined her duties, timetable, assessment expectations, and professional development opportunities. With a newfound clarity, she embraced her roles and responsibilities. Louise's journey at the college commenced with a strong foundation, ensuring a successful and fulfilling term ahead.

Boundaries of teaching

Teachers need boundaries, which will help you to know where your professional role stops. For example, you should not take on tasks which are part of someone else's role, such as a member of the support staff. You should be able to work within the limits of your role but know that it's okay to ask other members of staff for help when necessary. You also need personal boundaries, such as not becoming too friendly with your learners or joining their social media networks. Boundaries are also about the challenges you might face as a teacher.

Examples of challenges include:

- demands from managers e.g. to meet targets and deadlines
- learners whose first language is not English
- a lack of time and/or resources to teach your subject and to fully support the diverse needs of your learners.

Once you start teaching, you will need to find a way to manage the challenges you will be faced with, while remaining professional.

Make a list of the boundaries and challenges which you might face as a teacher. How could you overcome them?

Other boundaries include the things you are bound by, for example, policies and procedures, the amount of administrative work you are expected to complete, or a lack of funding or resources. These boundaries can often be interpreted as the negative aspects of your roles and responsibilities. However, these are a necessary part of your job role, such as maintaining records for audit purposes.

Helpful hint

Always give a professional impression to your learners whenever you are in contact with them, and try and lead by example. They will learn the importance of having the right attitude and how to behave, as your learners will act from watching and listening to you. For example, by arriving early, dressing appropriately, leaving the area tidy and not rushing away at the end of the lesson in case a learner wishes to speak to you. This is often referred to as the hidden curriculum (in Chapter 2) and also relates to Betari's Cycle of Conflict (in Chapter 4).

Legislation

Part of your role will be to understand and follow the relevant legislation which relates to teaching your subject. This will help to ensure that you are remaining current with your knowledge and practice, and to keep doing things right. Examples include:

Health and Safety at Work etc Act (1974)

This Act imposes obligations on all staff within an organisation commensurate with their role and responsibilities. Risk assessments should be carried out where necessary. In the event of an accident, particularly one resulting in death or serious injury, an investigation by the Health and Safety Executive may result in the prosecution of individuals found to be negligent, as well as the organisation.

The Equality Act (2010)

This Act legally protects people from discrimination in schools, colleges and in wider society. It sets out the different ways in which it's unlawful to treat someone or to be treated. The Act replaced all previous anti-discrimination and disability legislation.

Safeguarding Vulnerable Groups Act (2006)

This Act introduced a vetting and barring scheme to make decisions about who should be barred from working with children and vulnerable adults. Teachers may need to apply to the Disclosure and Barring Service (DBS) to have a criminal records' check. The purpose of the DBS is to help employers prevent unsuitable people from working with children and vulnerable adults.

Data Protection Act (2018)

This Act gives rights to individuals with regards to the processing and storage of their personal data. It confers rights to the individual to obtain information, and to require inaccurate personal data to be rectified, or data to be erased. The Act incorporates the General Data Protection Regulation (GDPR).

Copyright, Designs and Patents Act (1988)

This Act relates to the copying, adapting, and distributing of materials, which includes materials found via the internet. Organisations may apply for a licence to enable the photocopying of small amounts from books or journals. All copies should have the source acknowledged.

Regulatory requirements

Teachers must follow various regulations, whether these are external or internal to the organisation. Regulations are often called rules and they specify mandatory requirements which must be met. There will also be specific regulations which relate to your subject specialism and you will need to find out what these are.

Examples include:

- Control of Substances Hazardous to Health (COSHH) Regulations (2002)

- Food Safety and Hygiene Regulations (2013)

- Health and Safety (display screen equipment) Regulations (1992 amended 2002)

- Manual Handling Operations Regulations (1992)

Theory into practice

If you are currently teaching, find out the relevant legislation and regulatory requirements which you will need to follow to teach your subject. How will they impact upon your job role, and the teaching and learning process?

Teaching in an educational organisation

Teaching in an educational organisation, whether it's a college, a university, a private training provider, a prison, or another context, involves understanding how it operates. An organisation should have purposes, values and goals. These are often defined as part of a vision and/or mission statement. A vision statement describes the organisation's aims and where it hopes to be in the future. A mission statement defines the organisation's business strategy, objectives, and how it hopes to reach those objectives. Organisations work within a formal structure to be successful and to support their staff. Teaching involves navigating a structured framework that encompasses various elements, from contracts and policies to codes of practice and guidelines.

Contracts

Contracts in education are legal agreements between the teacher and the organisation, outlining the terms and conditions of employment. This includes details such as salary, working hours, roles and responsibilities, and any other contractual obligations. Educational organisations may offer different types of contracts, such as permanent, fixed-term, or part-time. Each has its implications regarding job security, benefits, and professional commitments.

Helpful hint

It's useful to have a clear understanding of your roles and responsibilities, and any legal and regulatory requirements which you must follow. If there are any areas you are unfamiliar with, make sure you talk to someone about them.

Education policy

Education policy is the legislation which an educational organisation must follow. For example, if an organisation receives government funding for their courses, they will be inspected (usually by Ofsted), and therefore held to account. There are lots of other policies and statutory documents which might apply, such as those relating to health and safety; equality, diversity and inclusion; and teachers' conditions, pay, and pensions. Some private organisations, which do not receive government funding, might not be subject to these policies.

Example

Two government bodies which have an influence, and might impact upon your role, are:

Ofsted - Office for Standards in Education, Children's Services and Skills. They are responsible for inspecting a range of educational institutions.

Ofqual - Office of Qualifications and Examinations Regulation. They regulate qualifications, exams and tests in England.

Legislation changes over time; new legislation is introduced and others are updated. As part of your teaching qualification you may need to research the history of educational policy. A useful document called *Honourable Histories* (1991–2021) by the Further Education Trust for Leadership is available at: https://tinyurl.com/FEHistory.

Organisational policies

An organisation must have its own policies in place to provide guidance to staff, and to ensure compliance. This helps staff to perform their role correctly and to know the lines of accountability. Policies might include:

- confidentiality
- data protection

- safeguarding

- sustainability.

Think of the policy as a statement of intent. There will also be a procedure, which is how the policy will be put into practice. Policies and procedures should be regularly reviewed and updated by the senior management team, and external inspectors may wish to see them.

Codes of practice

A code of practice is a set of written rules regarding how people should behave. They can be mandatory or voluntary, and they help people to perform their role professionally.

Codes of practice might include:

- code of conduct

- conflict of interest

- disciplinary

- lone working

- misconduct.

The impact of not following codes of practice might be disciplinary action i.e. a verbal or written warning, or even dismissal. If you belong to any professional associations or socie-ties, they will usually have a code of practice for you to follow.

Activity

Access the Society for Education and Training's (SET) Code of Ethics and Conduct at http://tinyurl.com/CodeofEthicsConduct. Take a look at the aspects relating to: Professional Responsibility, and Behaviour and Competency. How could you ensure you meet these? If the link is no longer active, just search for SET Code of Ethics and Conduct.

Guidelines

Guidelines help to determine a course of action by advising people how something should be done, and they can help to streamline a task or a routine. While policies are mandatory, guidelines are not always enforceable. They are a *guide* to how something should be done. However, some organisations include them in their policies and procedures to make them enforceable. Guidance from the government is usually statutory and must be followed, for example, the Prevent Duty Guidance: England and Wales (2023). The aim of this guidance is to prevent people from becoming radicalised.

If you are currently teaching, access your organisation's policies, codes of practice, and guidelines. Review them to ensure that you are meeting the requirements of your role. If you have any questions, contact your mentor or manager.

Teaching your subject specialism

You must have an in-depth and up to date understanding of your particular subject specialism in order to pass on the required knowledge, skills and behaviours to your learners. This will come from your vocational experience and qualifications. There will be a qualification specification for your subject which will state the practical experience and formal qualifications which you must have to be able to teach it. You will need to ensure that you are remaining current with any developments and changes to your subject (in Chapter 9).

Activity

If you haven't already found out what the requirements are to teach your subject, search online for a qualification specification for your subject. You might need to have a teaching qualification, an assessment qualification, a subject specialist qualification at a particular level, and/or relevant subject-specific experience.

Your employer might stipulate further requirements such as being a qualified first aider, or holding qualifications which relate to a particular subject such as food hygiene. Continuing professional development (CPD) is also essential to stay well informed regarding evolving knowledge and pedagogical approaches within your subject area (in Chapter 9).

Cultivating specialist knowledge involves a deep understanding of your subject's core concepts and theories, and how to apply them for learning to be effective. You should aim to have a comprehensive and current grasp of your subject, enabling you to impart accurate and up-to-date information to your learners. You might also be required to embed English, maths and digital skills (in Chapter 4) while teaching your subject; therefore you will need to be up to date with your own knowledge in these areas.

Your subject specialism might include recognising the sub-disciplines, branches, or specialised areas within the broader subject. To be a subject specialist, you need to be capable of tailoring your teaching to address the nuances of these areas, ensuring a well-rounded educational experience for your learners.

| Example |

Holly, a physics teacher, may need to navigate between classical mechanics, quantum physics, and astrophysics as part of her subject specialism. An awareness of these distinct areas enables her to provide a more nuanced and contextually relevant education, taking into account the diverse interests and career aspirations of her learners.

Pedagogical content knowledge

Pedagogical content knowledge (PCK) is all about having a thorough understanding of the subject you will teach. It's also about using established and innovative ways of teaching which are built on educational theory. If you just talk to your learners, they might not learn much; if they are active rather than passive, this will help learning to occur. Therefore you will need to use teaching and learning approaches (in Chapter 4) which will ensure that learning takes place.

PCK is a foundational concept in education, created by Lee Shulman in the 1980s. It emphasises the specialised knowledge that teachers must possess for the effective delivery of specific curriculum and subject content to learners. PCK entails the seamless integration of both pedagogical knowledge (teaching and learning approaches) and content knowledge (a deep understanding of the subject). PCK goes beyond a basic understanding of the subject content, and extends to the skilful adaptation of traditional and innovative teaching methods. This should ensure that the subject content is accessible and meaningful to learners.

The components of PCK include:

- a comprehensive understanding of the curriculum and the subject content

- how to sequence the delivery of the curriculum and subject content

- an understanding of various pedagogical teaching and learning approaches

- good classroom and group management techniques

- an awareness of factors which influence teaching and learning, including social, cultural, and organisational aspects

- familiarity with learners' prior knowledge, misconceptions, and individual or additional needs.

An understanding of PCK can empower you to tailor your teaching methods to the needs of your learners, ensuring the accurate conveyance of the subject content. It involves strategic decision making and careful planning about what to teach, how to teach, and how to assess that learning has taken place.

Threshold concepts

Threshold concepts are the basic principles or ideas within subject knowledge that, when learnt, lead to a learner's understanding of that knowledge. These concepts act as a way to deepen the understanding of a subject. Mastering threshold concepts can result in a significant shift in a learner's thinking, enabling them to see the subject in a new light. Concepts can change and develop, and lead to new ways of thinking, or they can challenge existing ways. This can be stimulating for teachers as well as learners. However, once a learner understands a threshold concept, it becomes hard to revert to previous ways of thinking, marking a permanent change in behaviour. Threshold concepts often connect and integrate different aspects of the subject knowledge to provide a holistic view.

Troublesome knowledge

Troublesome knowledge refers to specific concepts or ideas within a subject that learners might find challenging to understand. Think of this as the difficult areas of your subject which could lead to misconceptions, unconscious bias, or errors. You will need to ensure this doesn't occur, perhaps by holding discussions with your learners to check that they have understood the knowledge accurately. Sometimes, the specific concepts could conflict with a learner's beliefs, be difficult for them to understand, or challenge their current way of thinking. Experimenting with imaginative ways of teaching your subject accurately and building up trust with your learners can help with this.

Integration in teaching

Threshold concepts and troublesome knowledge can help you to identify the key aspects of your subject which might be problematic, but which are crucial for understanding to take place. You will need to identify these aspects and consider ways of teaching them to ensure that learning takes place. Using effective teaching and learning approaches, and integrating the troublesome knowledge in a clear and explicit way, can be the key to facilitating the transition from beginner to expert. It will help your learners to master essential ideas and practices to foster a deeper and lasting understanding of the subject.

Considerations for teaching subject content

The subject you teach will help to determine the methods you use i.e. if it's academic or theoretical. However, practical activities, discussions and case studies can help to make any subject more active rather than passive. Developing collaborative learning environments, where learners engage in group projects or research, can also help to foster a sense of community and shared expertise.

Helpful hint

Try to inspire passion, create curiosity, and maintain motivation for your subject. Where possible, use anecdotes and apply your knowledge to current local and world situations. Learners like to know how they can relate the subject to real life examples.

Subject delivery involves tailoring the strategies you will use with your learners to the unique characteristics of your subject. This requires an understanding of your subject's complexity, and the diverse ways learners could use relevant resources to aid the learning process (in Chapter 5). The integration of realistic projects (i.e. setting up a business and creating a website) and stakeholder connections (i.e. a guest speaker from a local company in your subject area) can enhance the relevance of the subject. These collaborations or external visits can all contribute to a more authentic and engaging learning experience.

Theory into practice

Research more about your subject area's sub-disciplines, branches, or specialised areas. This could be via the internet by keying in job role [your subject] into an online search engine. Alternatively, it could be by discussing the topic with colleagues, your subject specialist mentor, or by visiting local employers who work in your subject area.

Teaching and learning environments

Teaching and learning can take place in a variety of environments and locations such as: classrooms, the workplace, training rooms, exercise areas, prisons, outdoors, workshops and online. Although learning can take place almost anywhere, not all locations and environments will be totally suitable. However, it's *how* you ensure that learning takes place that matters (in Chapter 4). The physical aspects of the environment are important, as are the ways that you convey interest, curiosity, enthusiasm, and passion for your subject. It also helps to create a climate which is conducive to learning, maintains motivation, increases confidence, and ensures learners feel equal to their peers. Ideally, you should want your learners to leave your lesson wanting to come back for more. They should feel encouraged, respected, and challenged to reach their potential.

You might be restricted by the availability of particular rooms or resources; therefore you will need to be imaginative with what's available to you. Your learners don't need to know about any organisational problems you might encounter; your professionalism should enable you to teach your subject effectively without them knowing this. However, you do need to take into account any health, safety, and security issues, and let your organisation know if you have any concerns.

The venue, toilets and refreshment areas should all be accessible and appropriate for everyone. It is worth explaining to your learners at the beginning of the course where these are located. If possible, give them a tour of the building when they commence. Having some advance knowledge about your learners will help you to check that everything is suitable and accessible for them. If it's not, you can talk to your learners beforehand to see if any strategies can be implemented or compromises reached. You can find out any particular learner needs from the results of initial assessments (in Chapter 3) or by talking to your learners. If your lesson includes a break, make sure you tell your learners what time this will be, and for how long. If you don't, learners might not be concentrating on their learning, but thinking about when they can go to the toilet or where they can get a drink.

What is on the wall, or what is visible from the windows, could have an impact upon learning. If there are posters on the walls with stimulating pictures and words, your learners will probably look at them, and subconsciously take in the information. If learners have carried out activities which involved them creating posters or writing on flip chart paper, these could be pinned to the walls. Leaving them there as a visual aid could help the learning process. However, you will need to check in advance as to how you can attach things to walls, and whether or not you are allowed to. If there is a view of the landscape or city outside the window, your learners might be more interested in what's happening outside than inside. It might be possible to use blinds or curtains to limit any distraction.

If you are teaching a practical subject, you will need a suitable environment so that you can demonstrate an activity and your learners can practise. If you are teaching a theoretical subject, you may be fine in a room with tables and chairs, but you might need a computer, data projector, and/or an interactive whiteboard. Internet and/or wifi access might not always be available; therefore you will need to check this in advance.

Group sizes could affect the learning process, in both positive and negative ways. If you teach on a one-to-one basis or to a small group, you will be able to get to know your learners well and devote more time to them. If you have a large group, this might be more difficult. You might have no control over group sizes; however, you can try using different teaching and learning approaches and activities (in Chapter 4) to get around this.

Room layouts

An important influence upon the way your lesson progresses and how you and your learners communicate will be the room layout. You may not be able to control this if the furniture is in fixed positions. For example, a room which has computers on benches, or a laboratory with fixed workstations. Hopefully, the chairs can be moved and this might be a way to ensure all your learners can face you to hear what you are saying, see what you are doing, and still communicate with each other. Ideally, you should move around the room regularly and interact with your learners, rather than staying at the front of the room or sitting behind a desk.

Some rooms have a fixed projector with a screen at the front, which all learners will need to be able to see if you are using a visual presentation. However, some rooms might have smaller screens strategically placed. These enable anyone who is not near the front to see the presentation nearer to where they are seated. If this is the case, you may need to seek technical support if you are not familiar with how to operate the system.

If you can choose the layout of the room, you could decide on a furniture arrangement based on the teaching and learning activities to be carried out. For example, placing tables in groups for learner activities, or having tables in rows for a lecture if many learners will be attending.

Table layouts

If possible, you could try different table layouts which will enable learners to work together and to interact during group activities. Grouping learners strategically can encourage positive engagement.

Examples of table layouts include:

- cabaret or café style

- small group or banquet style

- tables in rows or lecture theatre style

- horseshoe or U-shape style

- boardroom style.

You could experiment with other layouts to see how effective they are for the type of teaching and learning activities which will take place for your subject. This can include the teacher as part of the group or not, using tables or not, or a different approach such as chairs in a circle to include all learners as well as the teacher. However, sometimes tables can create barriers; therefore you will need to find what suits you, your learners and your subject. If you need to move the furniture, ideally you should ask a member of staff to help you beforehand and again afterwards. If learners offer to help, you may need to decline their help in case of an accident. You will need to allow space for movement around the room, and for bags and coats, to ensure there are no obstructions where accidents could occur. Always return the room to its original layout at the end of your lesson.

Activity

What's the best room layout for your subject and why? List the strengths and limitations of it. How could you overcome any limitations? You might like to discuss these with your mentor.

The learning environment

The seating arrangements in a room can have a big impact on learning. People like their comfort zones and you may find that learners will sit in the same place each time they are with you. This is often the place they sat during the first lesson and can be useful to help you remember their names. You can sketch a seating plan and note who sits where, as well as who has not participated or who has caused disruption. Your sketch and notes will help you to plan future lessons, for example, to make sure that everyone participates. Remembering and using learners' names will show respect and encourage them to talk to you in confidence if they have any concerns. Some learners like to sit with their friends and might not be happy to work with others in a group situation. If you tell your learners from the start that you will move them around, for example, when carrying out group activities, they will become used to it. If you suddenly decide halfway through a course, they might not take it well.

Group development

The way a group develops in a learning environment can either help or hinder individual learning. Tuckman's theory of group development, also known as Tuckman's Stages, was developed by psychologist Bruce Tuckman in 1965. The theory proposes that there are four stages which groups go through as they develop: forming, storming, norming, and performing. Each stage is characterised by different behaviours, attitudes, and dynamics. Understanding these stages can be useful in managing the environment. This can apply to a new group meeting for the first time, or to small group activities during a lesson.

Forming

This is the initial stage of development, where learners come together and start to get to know each other. At this stage, learners may be polite and cautious, and may be uncertain about their roles and responsibilities within the group. The forming stage can be facilitated by icebreaker activities or team-building exercises. Teachers can also set clear expectations and goals to help establish a sense of purpose and direction.

Storming

This is the stage where conflict and disagreement may arise as learners start to assert their opinions and ideas. This stage can be challenging, but it is also an important part of group development, as it allows for different perspectives and ideas to be shared. The storming stage can be managed by encouraging open communication and providing opportunities for learners to voice their opinions and concerns. Teachers can also help to mediate conflicts and ensure that all learners feel heard and valued.

Norming

This stage is characterised by increased cooperation and collaboration as learners start to develop a sense of shared purpose and common goals. Group norms and expectations may also start to emerge. Teachers can facilitate the norming stage by encouraging learners to work together and to celebrate successes as a group. Setting clear expectations and guidelines for behaviour can also help to establish a sense of cohesion.

Performing

This is the final stage where the learners are able to work together effectively and efficiently towards their shared goals. At this stage, learners have hopefully developed a high level of trust and mutual respect. The performing stage can be supported by giving learners autonomy and responsibility for their work. Teachers can also provide opportunities for the learners to reflect on their achievements and identify areas for Improvement.

Tuckman's theory of group development can be a useful tool for managing and facilitating behaviour. By understanding the different stages of group development and the behaviours and attitudes associated with each stage, you can help to create a positive and productive learning environment for your learners.

Helpful hint

The concept of adjourning is sometimes added as a fifth stage, indicating the dissolution of the group after the completion of its task. However, in the context of

(Continued)

(Continued)

a classroom, especially with learners who have additional needs, the concept of adjourning may not be as straightforward. Thus the concept of adjourning may not fit precisely within the traditional Tuckman model. Adapting it to the unique needs of learners, especially those with additional needs, can involve celebrating achievements, planning for transitions, providing individualised support, and fostering a positive emotional environment during times of change.

Preparing your teaching area

Preparing your teaching area prior to your learners arriving is crucial, not only to help you be organised, but to give a professional impression to your learners. If possible, arrive early to check the area and to prepare any equipment ready for use. You might find that the room hasn't been left in a suitable condition by the previous user and you will need time to rearrange it.

Example

Harry arrived at 10.25 a.m. ready for his lesson which commenced at 10.30 a.m. He found the room was untidy with rubbish on the floor, three chairs were missing, writing was on the board, and the data projector wasn't working. He became very anxious as his learners started arriving. He therefore didn't give a professional impression and was flustered when he commenced the lesson, missing out some vital information as a result.

In this example, the previous occupant of the room had not left it in a fit state for the next person. If this occurs regularly, it might be an idea to talk to someone who can influence those using the rooms to ensure that they are left in a fit state. You will also need to leave your room in an acceptable state at the end of your lesson.

There may be instances when you have no option but to arrive at the time the lesson is due to commence. For example, if another group is timetabled in the room prior to your lesson. When this is the case, you won't know what state the room will be in. You could ask your learners to wait outside the room for a few minutes until you check it's acceptable. Alternatively, you could let your learners in, but tell them you need a few minutes to set up. If this is the case, and depending upon the maturity of your learners, you could ask them to chat among themselves about the topic to be covered.

Theory into practice

If you are currently teaching, identify which stage of Tuckman's theory one of your groups of learners is currently in. Are they still in the forming stage, or have they moved into storming? Understanding this will help you to tailor your teaching and learning approaches. If disruptions persist, address them directly with the learners. Discuss the impact of disruptive behaviour on the learning environment and emphasise the need for cooperation. If this continues and your learners remain in the forming or storming stage, consider rearranging the seating plan to facilitate better interaction and communication.

Curriculum development

Curriculum development within a training provider is a process that plays a pivotal role in shaping what will be offered, as well as the educational experiences of learners. It might not be part of your role to help create the curriculum, but it's useful to understand a little about how it's developed. The term *curriculum* relates to everything which is educational and offered to learners. It is not just a set of standards, a qualification, or a scheme of work. Think of it as everything which an organisation offers. This could include many subject areas as well as additional topics which will benefit learners.

Example

XYZ College has many departments which offer several subjects, Services to Business being one of them. The curriculum offered within this department includes qualifications such as Health and Social Care, Hospitality and Catering, and Retail Skills. The courses for each cover the subject content of the qualification, plus English, maths, digital skills, employability skills, sustainability, and a period of work experience.

This example shows the curriculum can be very broad and that other topics will be covered as part of one of the courses offered. The curriculum should always be fit for purpose. There's no point offering a particular course if there is no demand, or if it does not meet the needs of local employers and learners. English, maths and digital skills are covered in Chapter 4.

Employability and employment skills

Depending upon the requirements of the curriculum, it might be necessary for you to incorporate aspects of employability skills and employment skills during your lessons. Employability skills are the skills which make someone employable, for example, reliability, trustworthiness and honesty. Employment skills are the skills required to perform a job effectively, for example, knowledge and experience of the vocational area, along with English, maths and digital skills. Your learners will benefit from having these skills to help them progress further.

There are also other areas in which you could promote useful knowledge, skills and behaviours with your learners. For example:

- *British values*: researching and discussing what these mean.

- *Citizenship*: discussions based on nationality, politics and the state.

- *Enterprise:* setting up a small business, creating a website and an online ordering system.

- *Personal development, behaviour and welfare (PDBW)*: discussing timekeeping, positive behaviour, and good conduct, acting professionally, having self-confidence, looking after personal health and wellbeing, making decisions, maintaining good attendance, punctuality, staying safe, respecting others, taking responsibility.

- *Sustainability*: how to recycle, reuse, and reduce usage of products (in Chapter 1).

Learners who possess skills in these areas should be able to progress in education, training, and employment, and make a positive contribution to the communities in which they live and work.

Activity

Create a list of employability skills and employment skills related to your subject specialism. Consider which you think are the three most important for each. Discuss with your mentor the advantages and disadvantages of those chosen. Decide on the best ways of achieving them with your learners.

Influences upon the curriculum

The curriculum should be based on offering courses and/or qualifications which fulfil the needs of the potential market. For example, to offer training in particular subject areas due to the type of industry in the local area e.g. farming, shipbuilding, or car manufacturing. Alternatively, it could be to offer employability skills training if there is a high level of unemployment locally. Other factors can also have an influence, for example if funding is available for a particular qualification, or if people are prepared to pay a fee to take a particular course. However, there's no point creating a course unless there is a demand for it.

Courses often require a certain number of learners to make them financially viable. Perhaps some courses could combine staff and resources to share lessons which are the same, for example, when teaching health and safety, or sustainability. Consideration should always be given to the careful timetabling of rooms, staff, and resources to enable the curriculum to be streamlined and effective.

Often there are cultural, political, social, and economic factors which have an influence upon the way an organisation's curriculum is put together. In 2015, David Sainsbury was asked by the government in England to chair a panel of experts to provide clear recommendations for measures that would improve and transform education. *The Report of the Independent Panel on Technical Education* was published alongside the government's White Paper: Skills for

Jobs in January 2021. The latter sets out the government's plan to support young people and adults to secure skilled employment, and to meet the needs of the economy. As a result, young people should be given a choice at the age of 16 between two equally high-quality options: academic and technical. The academic option is based around theoretical subjects and qualifications. The technical option is built around routes to skilled employment. Each route should be available through courses or apprenticeships, so that young people can choose the mode of learning which suits them best. Some routes might also contain vocational qualifications which can be achieved in addition to the demonstration of skills and knowledge.

Expectations upon curriculum practice

The organisation's vision and/or mission statement will have an impact upon the curriculum i.e. what is offered and why. They will also have an impact on your roles and responsibilities, course targets and resource budgets. There will also be internal and external expectations. Internal includes: group sizes on a course, the number of hours allocated to teach and assess a qualification, internal quality assurance activities, and the observations of lessons. External includes: those stakeholders such as Ofsted and inspectors, and awarding organisations who will quality assure the qualifications you teach.

Types of courses and qualifications

Once the curriculum has been established i.e. what will be offered, courses and/or qualifications can be marketed to prospective learners, providing there will be a demand. The content can then be created with appropriate aims and objectives and should be supported with a scheme of work and lesson plans (in Chapter 4). See Figure 2.1 to put this into perspective.

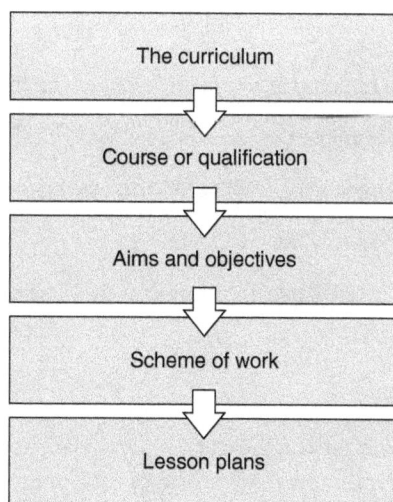

Figure 2.1 The planning process in perspective

Helpful hint

Finding out who the relevant awarding organisation is for your particular subject specialism, and understanding the content of the qualification specification, will help you to interpret the requirements for structuring and teaching your course.

Curriculum models

A curriculum model is a framework which uses a structured approach to prioritise and organise educational content i.e. what must be taught, how, and when. It also helps to align the content with the organisation's educational goals and your learners' needs. It's useful to understand a little about the various models, to help you plan a sequence of logical teaching, learning, and assessment activities for your course.

Course models

Course models are based on how the various aspects of the curriculum will be taught and assessed. For example, a bespoke training course for a local employer, or to meet the requirements of a qualification. They can range from a few hours for a short course, to those taking weeks, months, or years. They could be offered at various times of the day or evening, and at various locations. For example, *on-the-job* (i.e. in the workplace), *off-the-job* (i.e. in a college), *online* (i.e. via an internet connected device), or *near-the-job*. An example of the latter could be where trainee construction workers are undertaking some health and safety training in an onsite building near to the construction site.

Examples of different course models include:

- bespoke training courses for particular employees, either on, off or near to the job at full cost

- blended learning which combines technology with traditional learning in a suitable environment

- classroom or workshop learning in a training provider or the workplace

- conferences, events and seminars in locations such as hotels or specialist centres

- distance and flexible learning via an online or correspondence course

- evening classes in a community centre

- full-time or part-time attendance in a college, training centre, school, academy, or university.

Product and process models

The product and process models of the curriculum relate to how much can be taught effectively within the timeframe, and the way the course content is delivered. The *product* model focuses upon the content of a course to reach a desired outcome. For example, what learners *must* know to pass an exam, a test, and/or to obtain a certificate (known as the *product*). The teacher will just teach what *must* be taught to get the learner through i.e. what is stated in the qualification specification. What *should* and *could* be taught i.e. what is not stated in the qualification specification but would be really helpful to the learner, are not taken into consideration. The product model doesn't add any extra value for the learner. It could be considered a summative model, as it is linked only to the required objectives, outcomes, or tasks which the learner must achieve.

The *process* model focuses on the content of the course *and* other relevant aspects which *should* and *could* be learnt and applied (known as the *process*). This model adds value for the learner, as extra topics can be covered which could help them. Teachers can therefore adapt their courses to include more than is required if there is time available. For example, a cookery teacher might show learners how to present food in an imaginative way on a plate, and how to take photos of it for social media purposes. This would be in addition to teaching them to cook the particular recipes as stated in the qualification specification.

Covering purely what is required to achieve a pass is referred to as the *product* model, whereas including more and/or varying the learning experiences relates to the *process* model. Please see Table 2.1 for some examples of the differences.

Table 2.1 Examples of differences between the product and process models
Adapted from Reece and Walker (2007, page 221)

Product model	Process model
Focuses on the objectives, outcomes, or tasks i.e. the end product such as an exam or a test	Focuses more on the content i.e. extra learning experiences and activities
Content is similar no matter where the learner takes the course	Learning is different as it is tailored towards individual requirements and more content can be added
Learning is just a means to an end i.e. to obtain a pass	Learning is more valuable and meaningful
Teaching and learning activities are limited to meeting the objectives, outcomes, or tasks	Teaching and learning activities can be more imaginative to cover additional topics
Learning can be measured	Not all learning is measurable
Content is fixed	Content can change
Other useful skills and topics are not included	Other skills can be included e.g. problem solving, communication, employability, maths and digital skills
Little opportunity is available to extend learning	Provides the opportunity for extended learning i.e. to stretch and challenge more capable learners

Spiral model

The spiral model, a theory put forward by Jerome Bruner in 1966, spreads the learning out over time, rather than concentrating it into shorter periods. It introduces topics in a simple way and then repeats them with increasing levels of complexity. This helps to reinforce learning, as any issues or concerns can be highlighted early on, with support measures put in place as the learner progresses. Imagine a spiral progressing upwards, which repeats itself as it aims to reach the final outcome, as in Figure 2.2. Bruner felt that the most complex material, if properly structured and presented, can be understood by any learner.

Key features of the spiral model are:

- the topic is introduced

- the topic is revisited several times throughout the learning process, allowing a logical progression from simple to complex ideas

- the complexity of the topic increases each time it is revisited

- new learning is linked to old learning (and vice versa) and put into context.

This repetitive process continues while all the topics are taught and assessed.

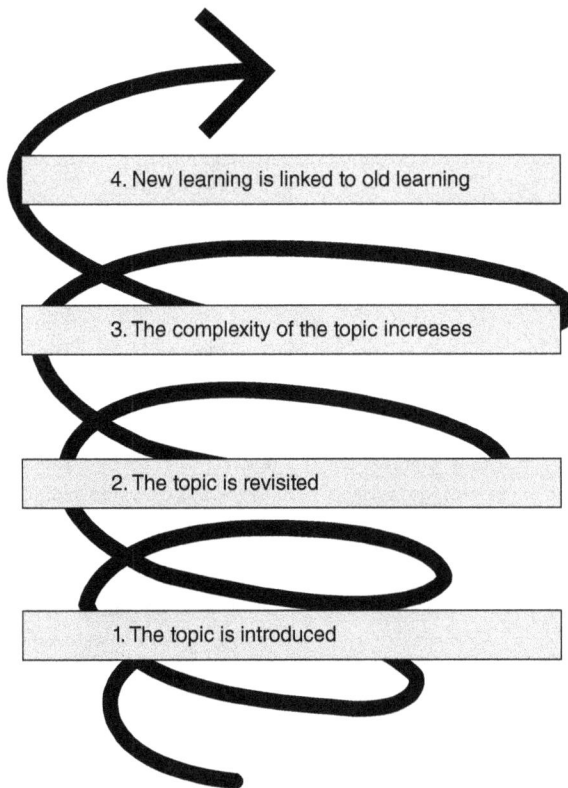

4. New learning is linked to old learning

3. The complexity of the topic increases

2. The topic is revisited

1. The topic is introduced

Figure 2.2 Example spiral curriculum model

Linear model

The linear model, a theory put forward by Ralph W. Tyler in 1949 assumes there is an agreed amount of knowledge that needs to be learnt. This knowledge is not repeated, like the spiral model. The teacher must decide how it will be taught and learnt. Tyler's model proposed that teachers should spend equal amounts of time evaluating their lesson plans, as well as evaluating the learning which is taking place. Imagine a line progressing forwards as it aims to reach the final outcome, as in Figure 2.3.

The linear process goes through four stages:

1. establish the objectives or tasks

2. design teaching and learning activities to achieve them

3. carry out the activities in an effective way to ensure learning takes place

4. assess learners and evaluate the process.

This process starts and finishes without repeating any aspects.

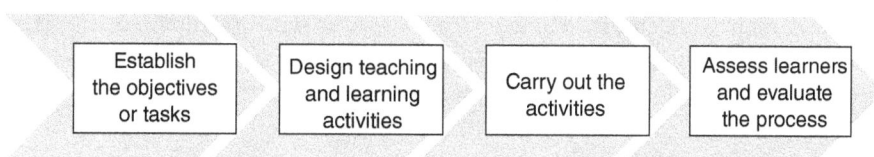

Establish the objectives or tasks	Design teaching and learning activities	Carry out the activities	Assess learners and evaluate the process

Figure 2.3 Example linear curriculum model

The hidden curriculum

The hidden curriculum is a term used to denote aspects of learning which are not explicitly taught i.e. they are *hidden*. They are aspects which are not made obvious, but are demonstrated naturally by teachers. They might not even be mentioned to you at your organisation, but they are important. For example, if a teacher is well dressed in clothing which is suitable for the subject, this could give the message that they take pride in themselves. If rooms and corridors are untidy, with out of date posters on the wall, this could give the message the organisation isn't providing a positive learning environment. If an organisation uses sustainable products and has recycling areas for used paper, plastic, and cardboard, this gives the message they care for the environment. Other hidden aspects can include the policies and procedures of the organisation i.e. how up to date and proactive they are in supporting teaching, learning, and assessment. The rules and routines which a teacher initiates can also have an impact i.e. timekeeping, and marking and returning work on time. If the culture of the organisation and its staff are not of a positive nature, this could impact negatively upon the learners.

However, some aspects can be contradictory. For example, if an organisation offers healthy food and drinks in their refreshment areas, but has vending machines with chocolates and sweets available in other areas. This is giving a mixed message to learners.

Think of the hidden curriculum as the values, attitudes, and behaviours of yourself and others which could influence those of the learners.

Research the cultural, political, social, and economic factors which might have an influence upon the way your organisation's curriculum is put together. Which curriculum model is used at your organisation and how will it impact upon the teaching of your subject? If there is no set model, which of those in this chapter would be best suited for your subject specialism and why?

Working with others

Working with internal members of staff or external contacts will require good communication skills, trust, and honesty. You might need time to build up working relationships with staff such as subject experts and those in support roles, as well as external contacts such as employers and stakeholders. The nature of these relationships can serve as a foundation for innovation, effectiveness, and the overall enhancement of the learner experience. For example, the knowledge and experience which can come from collaborative relationships, such as those with local community groups, can empower teachers to tailor their approaches to address the specific needs of the community or local employers.

Teachers often work in teams, perhaps also team-teaching; therefore effective communication and coordination with colleagues is essential to create a cohesive learning environment. Engaging with your peers can help to foster a supportive professional community of staff who can support each other as well as their learners.

Support roles

Support staff, including administrators, counsellors, and learning support assistants, play a crucial role in creating a supportive learning environment. They help contribute to the effective management, learner wellbeing, and academic success. Externally, partnerships with local businesses can provide additional resources, mentorship courses, and real-world opportunities for learners to engage with.

Helpful hint

It's useful to find out who else can support your job role, such as administration staff, technical support staff, and caretakers. It's also useful to find out if there is a communal rest area for staff use, and whether you need to bring your own drinking mug or contribute to a refreshment fund. It's often the little things that can make your working day much better, like having a cup of coffee during a break.

Collaborative relationships

Collaborative relationships within and beyond your educational organisation can help to:

- create a supportive and enriching learning environment by sharing knowledge and expertise

- support learners' needs by utilising the skills of others

- aid professional growth: collaborating with peers fosters continuous professional development, allowing teachers to learn from each other's experiences and expertise

- share resources: collaborative relationships facilitate the sharing of resources, whether it's teaching materials, best practices, or support services

- lead to innovation: collaborative efforts often lead to innovative teaching methods and approaches, promoting creativity and adaptability in the learning environment

- assist learning support and learner support: if you have a learner requiring support for any reason. There is a difference between *learning support* and *learner support*. Learning support relates to the *subject* and learner support relates to the *person*.

Points of referral

There may come a time when you need to refer a learner to someone else; however, you can't be expected to deal with issues outside of your role. For example, if a learner can't afford to purchase certain resources which are required for the course, then you should not offer to purchase for them. You should refer your learner to someone who might be able to access funding.

Never feel you have to solve any learner's needs, problems, or concerns yourself, and don't get personally involved. Always try and remain professional and impartial. Although you might feel you can help, it's best to seek advice, or refer them to someone who is more suited to help.

Points of referral could be internal i.e. people within your organisation such as first aiders, language interpreters, specialist colleagues; or external such as social workers, caregivers, charities, health centres, police, and agencies such as alcohol, debt, drugs, the Samaritans, and Citizens Advice. It's useful to find out who the internal and external people and organisations are, so that you can contact them quickly if you need to.

Employers and stakeholders

Employers and stakeholders could have an influence on the types of courses offered within an organisation. An employer might wish to support the learning and development of their staff by arranging on- or off-the-job training. If it's part of your role to liaise with apprentices from a local organisation, you would need to communicate with their employer to ensure that you are all working towards the same aim. There might also be stakeholders who support the learning process, perhaps financially, or who have an influence upon the design of a particular course.

Employers

The government and Ofsted want to see how employers have an impact upon education to make sure that skills gaps are being met. Training should therefore be delivered to meet employers' needs where necessary. For example, if you work in a college which is close to several businesses and/or factories, your organisation might be approached to offer training or apprenticeships for them. Alternatively, your organisation could approach them to find out if they have any staff training needs. If local employers are struggling to hire skilled staff, this could be an area where your organisation could collaborate with them.

Activity

If you are currently teaching, find out if your organisation is already providing any training or services, or partnering with local employers, and if so, what they are. If not, what training needs do you think local employers might need? How do you think your organisation could approach them with a view to supporting them and find out whether it's feasible?

Stakeholders

A stakeholder is a person or an organisation who has an interest in something, for example, the progress of learners. Examples are local authorities, councils, employers or companies who your organisation associates with. Stakeholders in the Further Education and Skills sector can include government departments such as Ofqual and Ofsted, who regulate and inspect accredited qualifications in England, and funding agencies who provide finance for training and assessment.

If stakeholders are involved with your organisation, it means you or others will be held accountable in some way, perhaps by supplying information and data. Statistics might be required such as the number of applications, enrolments, achievements and leavers, as well as progression and destination information. You might be responsible for keeping track of this data or it might be someone in a specific department within your organisation.

Demands might be made upon you and others, such as to achieve organisational key performance indicators (KPIs) or to meet certain targets within a timescale. However, the learner is the most important person; therefore try not to get too obsessed with targets. If you feel a learner, or indeed you, cannot meet a certain target, make sure you talk to the stakeholder to keep them informed. The needs of the different stakeholders as well as their learners should be ascertained. This ensures that everyone is clear about what they need to do and when, and are operating transparently.

Partnership working

Partnerships often occur when one organisation isn't able to fulfil a certain activity or course; therefore they decide to work with another organisation to achieve it. Partnerships can be very productive to everyone involved; however, they can also be challenging, as the needs of all partners have to be met. Communication is the key to effective partnership working.

Example

ABC Training has been approached by a local car manufacturing firm to teach and assess a specific off-the-job training course for their staff. While ABC Training have the staff who are capable of doing most of this, they don't have enough staff with the technical expertise required. They have therefore approached a local business who has people capable of this, to partner with them. ABC Training will agree how the two companies will work together for the benefit of the car manufacturer and their staff.

When working in a partnership, it's very important to know who is doing what, by when, and how much money will be involved. Contracts or terms of reference will need to be in place to keep everything legal and professional, and records must be maintained for audit purposes.

Other organisations

There will be other organisations in the wider context of your role, who you will need to communicate with (as follows). They can help to influence the curriculum, enhance the overall learning experience, and ensure compliance. Your role might involve communicating and collaborating with them. There will also be others such as those who could support the organisation financially or with expertise and/or resources. You will need to find out which organisations are relevant to your role and the teaching of your subject, if applicable.

Awarding organisations

Awarding organisations, also known as awarding bodies, provide accreditation for qualifications nationally and internationally. They will supply a qualification specification: sometimes referred to as a syllabus, qualification handbook, or a set of standards. This contains guidance and information regarding the particular qualification offered. Inspections will be conducted by an external quality assurer (EQA), verifier, moderator, or quality consultant, to ensure all the requirements are being met. If everything is satisfactory and the learner successfully achieves the qualification, a certificate will be issued. If you are involved with the teaching, assessment, and/or quality assurance of an accredited qualification, you will be visited at some point by a representative from the awarding organisation.

Department for Education (DfE)

The DfE is the government department responsible for children's services and education, including higher and further education policy, apprenticeships, and wider skills in England.

They are committed to cutting unnecessary burdens and to giving teachers the freedom and autonomy they need to get on with their jobs. Part of this is about making it easier for teachers to understand how to fulfil their legal obligations and exercise their statutory powers, by making guidance and advisory content clearer and more succinct.

Education and Skills Funding Agency (ESFA)

The ESFA is sponsored by the Department for Education (DfE) in England. They are responsible for the funding of education for pupils aged 5 to 16, education and training for those aged 16 to 19, apprenticeships, and adult education.

Institute for Apprenticeships and Technical Education (IfATE)

The IfATE work with employers to develop, approve, review, and revise apprenticeships and technical qualifications. This is to ensure that the courses respond to the needs of business, and give learners the skills and experience they require to succeed.

Office for Standards in Education, Children's Services and Skills (Ofsted)

Ofsted inspects and regulates services in England which care for children and young people, and those providing education and skills for learners of all ages. They were originally established to inspect schools; however, they now inspect provision in the Further Education and Skills sector, including teacher training, according to an Education Inspection Framework (EIF). Ofsted reports directly to Parliament, and they are independent and impartial. The aim of inspections is to promote improvement and value for money in the services inspected and regulated, so that children and young people, parents and caregivers, adult learners, and employers all benefit. You will need to find out if your organisation is inspected by Ofsted. It's possible that they will be if they receive any form of government funding.

Office of Qualifications and Examinations Regulation (Ofqual)

Ofqual is the regulator of qualifications, examinations and assessments in England. They are responsible for maintaining standards, improving confidence in the system, and distributing information about qualifications. Ofqual gives formal recognition to awarding organisations and bodies that offer qualifications. They also monitor their activities, including the fees which are charged.

Sector Skills Councils (SSC)

These are employer-led organisations who gather information and labour market intelligence to influence the development of qualifications and apprenticeship courses in the United Kingdom (UK). Each SSC represents an area of business or industry, of which there will probably be one for the subject you will teach, for example, construction, finance or hospitality. For some subjects they are known as Standard Setting Bodies (SSB). All SSCs are members of the Federation for Industry Sector Skills and Standards (FISSS), and are recognised by the government throughout the UK as the independent, employer-led organisations which ensure that the skills system is driven by employer needs. As a result, they have a major impact on the delivery of publicly and privately funded training through-out the UK. SSCs often produce a set of National Occupational Standards (NOS) for working in a particular sector.

Theory into practice

If you are currently teaching, find out who the relevant stakeholders are which will have an impact upon your job role, how you will be involved, and what the impact will be. If your organisation is inspected by Ofsted, locate and read the last inspection report, and find out if any action has been taken since it took place.

Summary

This chapter has explored:

- The role of a teacher
- Teaching in an educational organisation
- Teaching your subject specialism
- Teaching and learning environments
- Curriculum development
- Working with others

3
Nurturing learner dynamics

Putting theory into practice with a focus on learners

Introduction

Nurturing learner dynamics is all about fostering a suitable environment for your learners to achieve their full potential. You should be able to promote meaningful connections, and create an atmosphere where your learners can embark on a journey of learning and growth.

Getting to know your learners, and understanding their needs and challenges, is an important aspect of your teaching role. This will enable you to help them with their learning, to achieve their chosen goals, and/or to make the transition from education to employment.

This chapter will introduce you to the following topics:

- Getting to know your learners
- Barriers and challenges to learning
- Initial and diagnostic assessment
- Creating and maintaining a safe, supportive, and effective learning environment
- Equality, diversity and inclusion
- Communication with others

Occupational Standards covered in Chapter 3

Duties	Knowledge	Skills	Behaviours
D1, D2, D3, D4, D5, D6, D7, D8, D9	K2, K5, K6, K7, K8, K10, K11, K12, K13, K15, K16	S2, S5, S6, S9, S12, S13, S15, S16, S18, S19, S20	B1, B4, B5

Getting to know your learners

Understanding your learners and their unique learning journey is paramount for effective teaching to take place. Each learner brings a wealth of experience and knowledge to the learning environment. They will also have ambitions and aspirations which will need to be realistically managed. It is essential to cultivate a supportive and inclusive atmosphere where learners feel valued and respected. You should be able to actively engage with your learners, observe their interactions, and support them to overcome any barriers and challenges they may have. Through ongoing dialogue and reflection, you should be able to adjust your teaching approaches (in Chapter 4), resources (in Chapter 5), and assessment activities (in Chapter 7) to cater for the individual needs of your learners. Embracing diversity within the classroom can enrich the learning experience for all involved, fostering a collaborative and dynamic environment where every learner can be confident, motivated, and reach their full potential.

During the first lesson with your group, you will need to allocate time to explain the requirements of the course or qualification, and the facilities, services and support that can be offered within the organisation. This is known as an *induction*. When your learners first commence, you won't want to put them off the course by talking for a long time. Therefore, the first lesson is a good time to introduce learners to each other (if they haven't already met), perhaps with a practical activity known as an *icebreaker*. This will help your learners to feel comfortable and enable them to get to know each other, as well as you. Establishing *ground rules* once your learners have relaxed a little will help underpin appropriate behaviour and respect throughout their time with you.

Induction

The time taken to carry out the induction process might depend upon how much information you need to cover with your learners. It could range from 10–15 minutes as part of the application process beforehand, be at the beginning of the first lesson, or take the whole lesson, perhaps, if initial assessment or diagnostic tests are also included. You will need to carefully plan what you will cover, as you won't want to overload or confuse your learners during the early stage of their course. Don't forget to introduce yourself and tell them about your experiences within the subject/sector; otherwise your learners might be wondering who you are and might not focus on what you are saying.

Activity

Devise an induction checklist regarding the information you will need to cover with your learners i.e. information about the organisation, the course, and the facilities offered. Now add any specific aspects which relate to your particular subject. How can you make the induction process interesting, rather than it becoming a tick list of things to do? If you are currently teaching, obtain a copy of your organisation's induction checklist if there is one, and compare it with yours.

Often, the information you will need to cover during the induction might involve you talking for a long time and your learners might become bored. You could change this by asking your learners to find things out for themselves, perhaps in pairs or small groups, and then report back to the full group. Alternatively, you could create a visual presentation which includes text, pictures, sounds and short videos.

Giving your learners a copy of the induction checklist or making it available electronically will help act as a reminder of what was covered. Often, so much information is given out during the first lesson that learners can easily forget some important points.

Icebreakers

Some learners can be quiet, shy, nervous, or apprehensive when they start a new course or meet strangers. Carrying out an icebreaker is a good way of everyone getting to know each other and encouraging communication to take place. Some learners may already know each other, or have carried out an icebreaker with another teacher they currently have. Knowing this beforehand will help you to decide upon an appropriate and suitable icebreaker to use, and saves repetition. If possible, you could carry out the icebreaker before covering the induction requirements. This will encourage your learners to relax and give them the confidence to speak or ask questions in front of others.

Icebreakers can be quite simple; for example, asking your learners to introduce themselves in front of the group. However, this can be a bit intimidating if none of the learners have met before. A way around this is to form the group into pairs and ask them to talk to each other for five minutes about their interests, reason for attending, how they are feeling, and any expectations they may have. They may find that they have something in common and create a bond. You can then ask each person to introduce the person they have been talking to. People may not feel comfortable talking about themselves to a group of strangers, so another person introducing them might take any anxiety away.

Helpful hint

A good idea to help you remember names is to note these down when the learners introduce each other, perhaps on a rough sketch of a seating plan. It's likely they will return to the same seat next time. You could also make a note of something about them, perhaps a hobby they have mentioned which you could use in a future conversation. This shows that you are taking an interest in each learner as an individual, and using their name when talking to them also helps with this.

More complex icebreakers can involve games or activities, but the outcome should be for your learners to relax and feel comfortable with their peers in a new environment. All learners should be included and you will need to manage the activity carefully to ensure that everyone can take part. For example, it wouldn't be fair to carry out an activity where all the learners have to stand up or jump about if you have a learner who uses a wheelchair.

Energisers

Icebreakers can also be used during an established lesson, perhaps after a break or after lunch to help learners refocus. These are called *energisers* and can be subject-specific such as a quiz, or a fun activity or game which gets learners moving about and working together.

Whichever way you use an icebreaker or an energiser, it should be designed to be a fun and light-hearted activity to:

- build confidence

- create a suitable learning environment

- encourage communication, motivation, interaction, teamwork, and inclusion

- establish trust and respect

- help learners (and you) to remember each other's names.

There are many icebreaker and energiser activities available freely via the internet.

Learners' expectations

Learners often have an expectation of what they want to achieve, or how they expect to learn and be assessed. If you can obtain this information beforehand, perhaps as part of the icebreaker, or by them writing on sticky notes, it will help you match expectations with the course content. If you ask the learners and they state their expectations out loud, you could make a note perhaps on flip chart paper to refer to later. If there are any expectations that will not be met for some reason, make sure you explain why this is the case. Sometimes, learners have a pre-conceived idea of things they expect to do during the lessons. Giving them the opportunity to mention this will enable you to say if they can or can't be met. Otherwise, learners might complain that the course wasn't what they expected, so it's best to make things clear from the start. Keeping a record would be useful for you to refer to at the end of the course. This way, you can confirm that your learners have had their expectations met as they might have forgotten.

Ground rules

Ground rules, also known as *group rules, class rules,* a *group contract* or a *learning agreement*, are boundaries and rules to help create suitable conditions within which learners (and yourself) can safely work and learn. They can help underpin appropriate behaviour and respect for everyone in the group. They can also help establish the group norms and ensure that lessons run smoothly. If rules are not set, problems might occur which could disrupt the lesson and lead to misunderstandings or behaviour problems. You may find that your learners welcome a set of ground rules as it can give them a sense of order and safety.

It is best to agree the ground rules during the first lesson with your learners, perhaps after the icebreaker once everyone is feeling more relaxed. Ground rules should always be introduced and discussed with learners. Some ground rules can be negotiated so that learners don't feel as though they have been forced upon them. Involving your learners in the decision-making process will help give them ownership of what has been agreed. Some ground rules might be renegotiated or added to throughout the course, such as changing the break times. Others might be non-negotiable such as health and safety requirements. These might already be stated in a learner handbook, agreement, or learner contract, or be accessible via the organisation's intranet. You would need to make sure all learners have a copy, and know that they are in addition to any other rules agreed as a group. The types of ground rules you agree with your learners might depend upon their age and maturity. For example, mature learners might arrive early with the expectation of starting on time, younger learners might expect to use their mobile devices during the lesson.

When establishing ground rules, you will need to have an idea of what will be non-negotiable i.e. because of organisational requirements, and what can be negotiable.

Example

Non-negotiable ground rules (teacher-led):

* *be respectful towards others and the environment*
* *follow health and safety guidelines*
* *arrive on time*

Negotiable ground rules (learner-led):

* *eating is not allowed during lessons, soft drinks are*
* *mobile phones and electronic devices must be switched off*
* *15 minutes for break times.*

Having a few ideas in mind before agreeing the ground rules with your learners can help you to lead a discussion. Having clear rules which everyone understands will help your learners to feel comfortable and able to participate. If you have too many rules, learners might become over-cautious of what they can and can't do, and this could affect the learning process.

Ways to establish ground rules

One way to establish ground rules is by a process of discussion and negotiation, perhaps in small groups at first. A discussion will enable your learners to recognise what is and is not acceptable, giving them a sense of ownership and responsibility when they have an idea for a rule. It also enables learners to begin working together as a group and encourages aspects such as listening, compromise, and respect for others.

Alternatively, your learners could write down the rules individually, then discuss them in pairs and join into fours to create a poster or a list. One person from each group could present their ideas to the full group and agreement can then take place. Once agreed, a copy could be given to each learner or be made accessible electronically.

Ways to maintain ground rules

Keeping the ground rules visible throughout the lessons can act as a reminder of what is and is not acceptable. It can also enable them to be amended or added to as necessary. Any learners who have commenced the course late will be able to see them. It's useful to refer to the rules at the beginning of the lesson and when a rule is broken. For example, if a learner is late, they must be reminded that it is a requirement that all lessons start promptly; otherwise they might not make the effort to arrive on time for subsequent lessons. If other learners see that you don't say or do anything, they will feel the ground rules have no value. You therefore need to be consistent with everyone. It is also good practice to familiarise yourself with the rules in your college or organisation. Most will have a behaviour policy in place. You will need to ensure you know what is included in this, and that you follow the steps outlined within it.

Theory into practice

Research various icebreakers which you could use with your learners. If the time is right, try some out and then evaluate how effective they were. What strategies could you use to implement and manage the agreement of learner-led ground rules? What will you do if a learner breaks a ground rule?

Barriers and challenges to learning

A barrier to learning is something which might prevent or have an impact upon a learner's progress, achievement, and progression into employment. Some learners face particular barriers which might not be their fault, for example, a lack of public transport to get them to the venue. Others might have a barrier where you are able to help, or, if not, you could signpost them to a suitable person or agency.

The challenges learners encounter can also affect their learning and shape their expectations. If a learner faces significant difficulties in grasping a concept or mastering a skill, they may adjust their expectations accordingly. For instance, repeated failure in a particular subject might lead a learner to lower their expectations of what they can achieve, or seek additional support.

The following list includes some of the barriers and challenges your learners may experience, or be impacted by (in alphabetical order):

- a lack of motivation or interest

- absenteeism

- age: much younger or older than others in the group

- behaviour problems

- caring for others which might impinge upon the time available for study

- cultural differences

- disability: physical or mental

- family problems or commitments

- financial issues

- inequality e.g. stereotyped gender roles

- knowledge of or lack of using technology

- lack of concentration

- lack of study skills

- language concerns

- late arrival

- limited access to the learning environment

- limited mobility

- medical reasons, an illness or condition which might prevent full attendance

- over-enthusiasm

- physical/emotional or learning difficulties

- poor past experiences of teaching and learning

- pre-conceived negative feelings/ideas

- shift work inhibiting regular attendance

- shyness, or a lack of confidence or self-esteem

- specific needs or requirements not catered for

- transport difficulties.

These barriers and challenges could have a real impact upon whether a particular learner can attend a course, stay for the duration, or even achieve their aim. Having some knowledge of these could help you to plan ways of helping and supporting your learners when the need arises. You might have colleagues who have experienced the same issues and you may find it useful to talk to them. You could find out what support or specialist staff are available within your organisation. Never think you are on your own. If you are experiencing a learner barrier or challenge, it's highly likely someone else has too.

Learners' needs

Some learners will have particular needs which may affect their attendance, behaviour, learning, progress and/or achievement. If you can ascertain these prior to them commencing a course, you will have the knowledge to be able to support them when needed. This is providing it's within the remit of your role. If not, you could refer them to an appropriate person or agency, or ask them to find out for themselves (in Chapter 2).

The potential needs of learners which you might encounter could be quite diverse, such as a learner requiring privacy to take insulin for diabetes, the need to improve English, or just the need to talk to someone about a concern. Try not to assume that because a disability or a need is not visible, that it doesn't exist. For example, if a learner is in a wheelchair, you can see they have a disability. However, if a learner has diabetes, you cannot see this. This is known as a *hidden* or *unseen disability*.

Sometimes, learners might have a Statement of Special Educational Needs (SEN), now called an Education, Health and Care Plan (EHC Plan or EHCP). These are the official documents in England which record special needs, with supporting notes. These will include the reasonable adjustments teachers need to make, along with what extra support or therapy the learner might be entitled to. You will need to be aware if a learner has one, to enable you to support them, and to differentiate for their needs during lessons.

Some learners may experience certain challenges to learning and assessment which you could support in the following ways, providing that you are aware of them. For example (in alphabetical order):

- Autism Spectrum Disorder (ASD) – provide clear and consistent instructions using visual aids such as pictures, diagrams, or written instructions alongside verbal explanations. Break tasks into smaller steps and use visual schedules or checklists to help the learner understand expectations and manage transitions. Offer a quiet and organised learning environment with minimal distractions to reduce sensory overload.

- Dyscalculia – allow additional time if necessary and use calculators or other equipment for learners who have difficulty with calculations or maths.

- Dysgraphia – allow the use of a computer or other suitable media for learners who have difficulty with handwriting.

- Dyslexia – allow additional time or resources if necessary for learners who have difficulty processing language. Give written questions in a simplified format, for example, bullet points. Ask questions verbally and make an audio or visual recording of your learner's responses; allow the use of a computer for keying in responses rather than expecting handwritten responses.

- Dyspraxia – allow additional time and space if necessary for learners who have poor motor coordination.

- English as a second or other language (ESOL) – if allowed, try to arrange assessments in your learner's first language. Many awarding organisations can translate assessment materials if requested. There are also translation programs, apps and software which could be used. Bilingual assessments could be offered if required.

- Hearing impairment – use an induction loop or a sign language interpreter if available. Instructions and questions could be conveyed using sign language. Specialist computer software could be used.

- Mental or physical disability – use a more comfortable environment where appropriate and available. Allow extra time to complete tasks. Explain where the learner can take medication privately. Dates for assessments could be rearranged to fit around doctor or hospital appointments.

- Oppositional Defiant Disorder (ODD) – establish clear and consistent expectations for behaviour and boundaries, and communicate them in a calm and respectful manner. Provide frequent reminders of rules and expectations and offer praise and positive reinforcement for following them. Use a structured and predictable routine to help the learner feel secure and to understand what to expect. Offer choices whenever possible to empower the learner and give them a sense of control. Use de-escalation techniques such as offering a brief break or allowing the learner to express their feelings in a safe way when they become frustrated or upset.

- Visual impairment – use large print or braille and/or use specialist computer software if available. Ask questions verbally and make an audio recording of your learner's responses rather than expecting them to write.

A term often used for some learner challenges is neurodiversity. This covers autism, ADHD, dyslexia, dyspraxia, and Tourettes, or a combination. Neurodivergent learners experience, interact with and interpret the world around them in unique ways. They might not be able to maintain concentration, can lose focus, or could greatly excel at something. This is different to neurotypical learners who have brains which function in a similar way to most other learners. However, some of your learners might not want to disclose this information to you, which might make it more difficult to support them. Encouraging them to talk to you in confidence might help them to discuss ways in which you could support them. You should always check what the policy is at your organisation for supporting learners.

Identifying learners' needs

Identifying your learners' needs can take place as part of the application process, during an interview prior to the course commencing, when they start, or as part of the initial or diagnostic assessment processes (covered next in this chapter). Information, advice and guidance (IAG) should be given to learners regarding their course choice, which should be clear, unambiguous and impartial to ensure it meets their needs and capability. The application process should ensure learners are on the right course at the right level.

It's difficult to help your learners if they don't tell you about any specific issues, needs or concerns they might have. You could ask if there is anything you could do to help make their learning experience a more positive one. However, anything you do would have to be reasonable and not seen as favouritism by other learners. Encouraging learners to tell you at an appropriate time, perhaps during a break, would save your learner any embarrassment they might feel when in front of their peers.

Some learners may be uncomfortable or not wish to divulge personal information on application forms or at an interview. You could therefore have an informal chat with them to find out if they have any needs or specific requirements.

Example

Bridget's application form and personal statement to join the course contained several errors which led her teacher, Isla, to think she might have dyslexia. Isla arranged to have a chat with her prior to the course starting. Bridget said she had often thought she was dyslexic and wondered if she could find out. Isla was able to arrange for her to have a test via www. dyslexia.uk.net. This confirmed that she was, and appropriate help and support was then arranged.

If you are ever unsure about how to help your learners, just talk to them. They are best placed to tell you how you can support them. Always try to focus on what they can do, rather than what they can't do.

Group profile

A group profile is a list of all your learners, along with some information about each, for example, their individual needs, any barriers, and how you can support them. It can be a manual record with various column headings; or your organisation might have an online record. The profile is also useful for noting any attendance, behaviour, and motivation concerns. If a regular pattern emerges, you can find out why it's happening and address it. For example, a learner might have a health condition which requires regular time out for hospital visits. Coursework could therefore be emailed to them along with information regarding what has been missed.

The group profile can also be used for noting the results of initial and diagnostic assessments. It's useful for keeping track of additional targets to stretch and challenge individual learners, and for statistical purposes if required.

It might be difficult to remember details about each of your learners and the specific needs they may have. Therefore maintaining a group profile could help make this easier for you. It can also be useful to a colleague who might cover one of your lessons, if you are absent for any reason.

Learning support and learner support

If you have a learner requiring support for any reason, there is a difference between *learning support* and *learner support*. *Learning* support relates to the *subject* i.e. help with English, maths and/or study skills. *Learner* support relates to the *person* i.e. help they might need with any personal issues, and/or general advice and guidance such as financial support, transport, childcare, safety, and welfare.

Ideally, prior to or when your learner commences, you could discuss any support requirements they may have. You may need to find out who within your organisation can help, as well as those external to the organisation you could refer your learner to. Your organisation might have support systems in place to meet the individual needs of learners. However, you should always refer your learners to an appropriate specialist or agency if you can't deal with their needs.

You will need to consider any particular needs or requirements of your learners to ensure they can all participate during lessons. You (or the organisation) may need to make reasonable adjustments to adapt resources, equipment, or the environment as stated in the Equality Act (2010) for England, Scotland, and Wales. If anything is adapted, make sure that both you and your learners are familiar with the changes prior to use. Some adaptations might need to be discussed with the awarding organisation if the learner is working towards an accredited qualification. This helps ensure fairness and validity. Awarding organisations will have policies and procedures in place for learners who require adaptations to assessments. Make sure that you are familiar with these and that you follow the awarding organisation's processes when applying for an adaptation to an assessment activity (in Chapter 7).

Reviewing learner progress

It's useful to regularly review the progress of your learners, to not only know how they are progressing and what they have achieved, but to discuss what they could do to improve. It also gives you the opportunity to encourage learners to be independent and to aim high, and to discuss any concerns or particular needs they may have. Reviews of progress, often called *tutorial reviews* or just *tutorials*, could also provide the opportunity to carry out formative assessments in an informal way. They give your learner the opportunity to ask questions or discuss issues they might have been self-conscious about asking in a group situation. Feedback gained via the review process can help inform the evaluation process (in Chapter 9) for the course and the teacher.

Reviews can be part of timetabled lessons or take place on a one-to-one basis as the need arises. Informal reviews and discussions can take place at any opportune time; however, formal reviews should always be documented and records maintained. Reviews could take place online rather than in person if appropriate systems are in place for this.

Reviewing progress enables you to ascertain information to help you differentiate effectively. This helps ensure that the needs of your learners are met and that they are being challenged to develop to their full potential. If learners are working towards a higher level qualification, you could give them more autonomy and independence during the review process. For example, ask them to review their progress before meeting you to discuss it. The review process also helps ascertain if learners are experiencing any difficulties, enabling you to arrange for any necessary support or further training.

Activity

What do you consider are the advantages of reviewing a learner's progress? Make a list and then compare it to the following bullet points.

Reviewing progress with learners enables you to (in alphabetical order):

- ascertain any issues, concerns, or challenges
- confirm progress and achievements
- discuss any confidential or sensitive issues
- give constructive and developmental feedback
- involve your learners' employers and workplace witnesses (if applicable, in advance of, or at the same time) to gain more information about their progress and achievements elsewhere
- keep a record of what was discussed and agreed
- motivate your learners
- plan areas for further training and development
- plan for differentiation
- plan future learning and assessments
- plan more challenging or creative assessment opportunities
- review your own contribution to the learning and assessment process
- revise your teaching and assessment materials and resources if necessary
- revise your teaching and learning approaches to meet any particular needs or requirements.
- talk to your learners formally on a one-to-one basis, or informally when possible.

If possible, at least one formal one-to-one review should take place at some point during every course (i.e. termly, quarterly, yearly). It can be a key aspect of communicating with your learners and making them feel valued as individuals.

If there is no set review procedure, or you are not required to review your learners' progress, it would still be a useful activity if you have the time. The review process should be ongoing until your learner has completed the course, even if it is carried out on an informal basis. Regular reviews can help to keep your learners motivated, make them feel less isolated, and appreciate how they are progressing.

Theory into practice

What learner needs, barriers, and challenges might you encounter for your subject? Make a list and identify how you could deal with them, or who you would refer them to.

Initial and diagnostic assessment

Initial and diagnostic assessments are the formal processes whereby you can ascertain your learners' prior knowledge, skills, and understanding. It's also an opportunity to identify any aspects which might otherwise go unnoticed, for example, if a learner has poor numerical, writing, or digital skills. Initial assessment is carried out at the beginning of something, for example, a course or a lesson. Diagnostic assessment can be carried out at any time, to diagnose any gaps in learning, or any particular learning or learner needs.

Initial and diagnostic assessments can be carried out in person, for example, during an interview, or via an online form. It might not be your responsibility to interview prospective learners or to carry out initial assessment activities. However, you will need to know the results to enable you to support your learners.

Helpful hint

Try not to make any assumptions about your learners or their past experiences, skills, and knowledge. You will need to meet them and talk to them to get to know them as a person, and therefore be able to support them appropriately as an individual.

Initial and diagnostic assessments can help you to find a starting point for your learners. The processes might be carried out separately or they might be combined. The results of initial and diagnostic assessments should help you negotiate appropriate targets with your learners, ensuring that they are on the right course at the right level, with the support they need to succeed.

Examples of initial and diagnostic assessment activities include:

- application/enrolment forms: completed online or as a hard copy, prior to a learner commencing

- interview/discussion: asking your learner why they are applying and ascertaining that they meet any particular entry requirements

- observations: it may be necessary to observe your learner performing a skill, perhaps if they are based in the workplace, before agreeing an appropriate course and level. Observation during initial assessment activities will give you a sense of how your learner performs, and what they know and can do already

- self-assessment: asking your learner to assess their own skills and knowledge towards the course requirements. This is often known as a *skills scan* and relies on the learner being honest about their achievements

- structured activities, for example role plays or simulations to see how a learner performs, or how they can effectively work with others

- tests: for example, in English, maths and digital skills.

It's all about being *proactive* before learning starts, and *active* when learning is taking place, rather than being *reactive* to a situation when it might be too late to do anything about it.

You will need to keep appropriate records of the results (perhaps as part of the group profile), and you might need to discuss these with others who have an involvement with your learners. For example, other teachers or support staff. However, some aspects might need to remain confidential. You will need to find out your organisation's requirements for record keeping and confidentiality of information.

Initial assessment

Initial assessment should be carried out *with* your learner, rather than *to* them. It should be a two-way process to find out about your learner as an individual. It should help you to identify why they want to take the course, and to make sure they are on the right course at the right level. The process should also help to identify any particular needs they may have, to enable the correct support mechanisms to be available.

Initial assessment is often referred to as assessment *for* learning (AfL), as the results help inform the learning process. Assessment *of* learning (AoL) is about making decisions regarding progress and achievement. Assessment is an integral part of the teaching and learning process, and should not be completed in isolation from it (in Chapter 7).

Initial assessment can:

- allow for differentiation when planning lesson activities

- ascertain why your learner wants to take the course, along with their capability to achieve

- ensure your learner is applying for the right type of course at the right level

- find out the expectations and motivations of your learner

- identify any information which needs to be shared with colleagues

- identify any specific additional support needs or any reasonable adjustments which may be required.

Initial assessment can also take place during a lesson, for example, when you change topics, or the first time you meet your learners for your subject. You could ask what they already know or can do, and then build on their experiences. Although you might have obtained some information prior to your learners starting, you might need more as you progress.

Activity

During the initial assessment process, what information could you find out about your learners? How could you use this to assist you with your lesson planning and your learners' progress and development?

Diagnostic assessment

Diagnostic assessments can be used to evaluate a learner's knowledge, skills, strengths and areas for development in a particular subject area, and identify any gaps. It could be that your learner feels they are capable of achieving at a higher level than the diagnostic assessments determine. The results will give a thorough indication of not only the level at which your learner needs to be placed for the subject, but also which specific aspects they need to improve on. Skills tests can be used for learners to demonstrate what they can physically do, knowledge tests can be used for learners to demonstrate what they know and understand. Your organisation might have specific tests they require you to use or you might wish to design your own.

It could be that your learner has already achieved some units of the qualification elsewhere, and might just need to provide proof of this. This is known as recognition of prior learning/achievements (RPL/A). If acceptable, this could mean they would not need any reassessment in the areas in which they have already achieved.

Example

Florence had recently started at ABC College and signed up to a Level 2 Certificate in Health and Social Care course. She completed a diagnostic assessment process which was designed to assess her skills and knowledge towards the units of the qualification. Florence had started the qualification at another college prior to moving. She was able to provide a certificate as proof of three units which she had successfully achieved. This meant that she did not need to be reassessed for them. However, she still attended the lessons to ensure that her knowledge was current.

Diagnostic assessment can:

- enable learners to demonstrate their current level of knowledge, skills, and understanding regarding the subject

- ensure learners can access appropriate support for the subject

- give your learner the confidence to set challenging goals and to take ownership of their learning

- identify an appropriate starting point and level

- identify gaps in knowledge, skills, and understanding to highlight areas to work on

- identify previous experience, knowledge, achievements, and transferable skills

- identify specific requirements: for example, to help improve English, maths and digital skills

- ascertain learning preferences e.g. visual, aural, read/write, and kinaesthetic (VARK), where appropriate (in Chapter 4). However, it's best to check your organisation's policy and procedures regarding learning preferences (also referred to as learning styles), as there has been recent research to suggest that they lack empirical evidence supporting the concept.

Theory into practice

Find out what initial and diagnostic assessments are available at your organisation. Will it be your responsibility to administer these or is there a specialist person to do this? How will you use the results? If you are not yet teaching, investigate suitable initial and diagnostic assessment activities which you could use with your learners in the future, perhaps by searching the internet.

Creating and maintaining a safe, supportive, and effective learning environment

Learners need to know they are safe when they are with you and not in any danger. Safe also relates to learners feeling safe to express their opinions without being ridiculed by others. You have a duty of care to ensure that learning takes place in a supportive and effective environment. This duty requires you to take reasonable steps to ensure the safety of your learners.

Helpful hint

All equipment and resources should not cause harm, tables and chairs should be in an appropriate layout for the subject, and all areas should be accessible. Make sure that you inform your learners how to correctly use all equipment and/or to wear relevant protective clothing when necessary.

The teaching and learning environment can be thought of as having three aspects: *physical*, *social*, and *learning* as in Figure 3.1. Each has an impact on the others, and all three aspects should be appropriate and relevant. Some aspects will interact and overlap to ensure teaching, learning, and assessment can be effective for everyone.

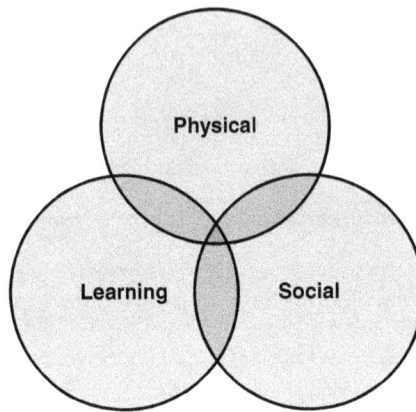

Figure 3.1 Physical, social, and learning aspects and how they interact and overlap

Physical

The physical environment is concerned with the surroundings and atmosphere. The temperature, lighting, and ventilation can all affect the learning process. While it is your responsibility to ensure the environment is safe and supportive, you might not be able to control some aspects such as external noise. However, what you can do is ensure that your lesson is interesting, meaningful, and engaging to your learners.

Social

The social environment is concerned with how you help put your learners at ease, establish a rapport with them, and help them to work and get along together. Using a suitable icebreaker will help learners get to know each other at the beginning of the first meeting. Creating a social and supportive learning environment will include agreeing ground rules. Helping learners to relax and feel comfortable should lead to effective two-way communication, and enable learning to take place. Learners should know that you, their peers, and others if necessary, will make their time meaningful, supportive, and productive.

Learning

The learning environment is concerned with giving your lesson a purpose by having a clear aim of what you want your learners to achieve, using suitable and varied teaching and learning approaches (in Chapter 4), and resources (in Chapter 5). How you plan to assess your subject (in Chapter 7) will be based upon the requirements of what your learner needs to achieve.

Example

A group of learners are attending a lesson about plant growth. Angie, the course tutor, ensures the following:

Physical aspect: the classroom environment is arranged to accommodate the plant experiment, with tables set up for small group work, and sufficient space for movement.

Social aspect: learners work in small groups, fostering collaboration, cooperation, and communication skills.

Learning aspect: the experiment is designed to teach learners about the life cycle of plants, the importance of sunlight and water, and how environmental factors affect growth.

Knowing your subject and teaching it in a meaningful way will help your learners to achieve their goals. You might need to adapt the learning environment to ensure all learners can access equipment and resources safely. This might involve carrying out a risk assessment to check that all equipment is safe to use. Your organisation will be able to explain how to go about this.

Safeguarding

Safeguarding is the term used to refer to the duties and responsibilities that those providing a health, social, or education service have to carry out or perform to protect individuals and vulnerable people from harm. You will have a responsibility to adhere to, and maintain, safeguarding measures as part of your role.

In 2006, the Department for Education and Skills (DfES) in the UK produced a document called *Safeguarding Children and Safer Recruitment in Education.* This guidance was aimed at local authorities, schools and further education colleges in England who are responsible for promoting the welfare of children and young people, up to the age of 18 (age 25 for those with learning difficulties and/or disabilities). The DfES has now been renamed the Department for Education (DfE).

Following this, the document *Safer Practice, Safer Learning* (NIACE, 2007) was produced to provide guidance in relation to adults in further education. It recommends that safeguarding duties extend to whole-organisation policies, values and ethos, and include all staff and learners. It is therefore everyone's duty to promote the concepts of the safe learner.

The Department of Health (2000) document (in England) *No Secrets* gives a definition of vulnerable adults. *A vulnerable adult is defined as a person 'who is or may be in need of community care services by reason of mental or other disability, age or illness and who is or may be unable to take care of him or herself, or unable to protect him or herself against significant harm or exploitation'* (Department of Health, 2000, page 8).

A vulnerable adult can be put at risk of harm through a variety of actions, inadequate policies and procedures, and failures of people to act. There are six types of abuse defined by the Department of Health:

- physical

- sexual

- psychological/emotional

- financial or material

- neglect and acts of omission

- discriminatory.

A young person or adult could potentially be the victim of any of the above. It is therefore your duty to ensure that you take proper steps to safeguard your learners. If a young person or vulnerable adult discloses any form of abuse to you, you must take the disclosure seriously and never dismiss any allegation. An allegation of abuse or neglect may lead to a criminal investigation. Asking leading questions or attempting to investigate the allegations may cause problems for any subsequent court proceedings. In this respect, don't make any promises regarding confidentiality, particularly if you discover something serious which will have to be reported to an authority as part of the law. Explain to your learner that you will need to report the disclosure and share the information with your organisation's Safeguarding Officer or the person responsible. They will, where possible, respect the wishes of the individual. However, information will need to be shared with external agencies where it is judged that a person is at risk of suffering significant harm.

Activity

Find out what the policies and procedures are regarding safeguarding at your organisation. What will your responsibilities be, and who can you go to should you have any concerns?

There might be situations where you will need to ensure that you are not placed in a vulnerable position. For example, by leaving the room door open if you are alone with a learner. You will also need to inform your learners if they overstep your boundaries, perhaps if an individual asks you to go for a drink with them after class, or asks you to join their social network. There could be circumstances where abuse, threatening behaviour, stealing, or bullying might occur. You might notice this, or a learner might tell you about it. If so, you will need to treat the matter seriously and follow it up. Your organisation might have a zero tolerance policy of this type of behaviour, and have a particular procedure which will need to be followed.

To help ensure that all people in the building are meant to be there, staff, learners, and visitors could wear an official name badge or carry identification. All visitors should be asked to sign in and out of the building, and will possibly need to be accompanied at all times. Anyone not wearing a badge should be challenged if it is safe to do so.

Your learners need to know that their safety and security is of paramount importance to you and your organisation, and that everyone has a responsibility for this. This information can be communicated to your learners in various ways i.e. through learner handbooks, marketing materials, induction procedures, learner contracts, tutorials, reviews of progress, online information, and learner discussion groups and activities.

The mental and physical health of both you and your learners is important to maintain a positive learning environment.

Theory into practice

What issues might learners encounter regarding their safety and security in the learning environment? How can you maintain a safe and supportive environment for your learners? What can you do if something occurs which is outside of your control?

Equality, diversity and inclusion

Equality is about the learner's right to have fair access to attend and participate in their chosen course. This should be regardless of age, ability, and/or circumstances. However, there could be certain entry requirements which might need to be met for some qualifications or courses, therefore restricting who could apply.

Diversity is about valuing and respecting the differences in learners. If you have two or more learners, you will experience diversity.

Inclusion is about ensuring all your learners have the opportunity to be involved, to contribute, and to be included in the learning process. It's also about recognising and treating all learners equally and fairly, without directly (by yourself) or indirectly (by someone else) excluding anyone.

Combined, equality, diversity and inclusion (EDI) will help embrace learners' experiences, cultures and differences during lessons. This should enable each individual's maximum potential to be achieved in a safe and positive learning environment. In a diverse and multicultural society, recognising and accepting individual differences is part of embracing equality and diversity.

Equality, diversity and inclusion (EDI) policy

Your organisation should have an equality, diversity and inclusion policy which both you and your learners should be aware of. There should be an action plan to ensure equality, diversity and inclusion are promoted and actioned within the organisation. The content of the policy should be understood and practised by all staff and learners.

Example

XYZ Training aims to ensure that equality, diversity and inclusion are promoted and actioned among all its staff and learners. Any unfair or unlawful discrimination, whether direct or indirect, will be abolished, to promote a climate of equality and respect. All staff and learners can expect to work in an environment free from harassment and bullying.

XYZ Training fully supports all principles of equality, diversity and inclusion, and opposes any unfair or unlawful discrimination on the grounds of ability, age, colour, culture, disability, domestic circumstances, employment status, ethnic origin, gender, gender reassignment, learning difficulties, marital status/civil partnership, pregnancy and maternity, nationality, political conviction, race, religion or belief, sexual orientation, and/or social background.

The policy could also include assurances to learners, for example, to:

- ensure that individuals are valued regarding their achievements, and progression opportunities are recognised

- ensure that reasonable adjustments can be made for learners' needs

- have a philosophy of equity as opposed to exclusivity

- place the learner at the centre of the learning process

- provide a curriculum and support which are relevant to each learner

- provide an inclusive learning environment i.e. by not excluding anyone for any legitimate reason.

Activity

Locate the equality, diversity and inclusion policy within your organisation. Does it include assurances similar to those in the previous bullet point list? Would you recommend any changes to the policy? If so, what and why? Make sure that your learners know where to access the policy and what to do if they have a problem or a concern.

If you had difficulty locating the policy, your learners might too. It could be that it's called something else, for example, an *Equal Opportunities Policy.* Having looked at it, would you know what to do if you or a learner had a problem or a complaint? This information should be accessible to all staff and learners. Usually, a policy will be accompanied by a procedure which may be located elsewhere. This will state the process that should be gone through, within specific timeframes, if there was a problem or a complaint, and what will be done about it.

The policy should be regularly monitored, for example, gathering information and data for statistical purposes such as recruitment and enrolment. Monitoring the implementation of the policy will also help to ensure that there is no unintentional discrimination. The policy should be reviewed regularly, for example, if there are any legislative or organisational changes. Having a policy often leads to a *reactive* situation where problems are dealt with afterwards. Policies should really be designed to prevent or respond to events or problems. However, it's best to be *proactive* and avoid problems occurring in the first place.

Helpful hint

Using handouts and presentations which reflect the local community and society could help your learners be more understanding and tolerant of each other. For example, you could use pictures which reflect people of different abilities, ages, cultures, genders and races.

When you are with your learners, try to make sure that you:

- are non-judgemental

- challenge any direct or indirect discrimination, stereotyping, prejudice, harassment, bullying and biased attitudes by yourself or others

- do not have favourite learners, or give some more attention than others

- do not indulge the minority at the expense of the majority

- ensure particular groups are not offended; for example, faith or religion

- ensure individual learners are not disadvantaged or overly advantaged

- reflect on your own attitudes, values and beliefs so that you are not imposing these upon your learners (consciously or subconsciously)

- treat all learners with respect and dignity

- use questions which are worded so as not to cause embarrassment to learners.

Valuing equality, diversity and inclusion

If you ever feel unsure as to whether you or other learners and colleagues are valuing equality, diversity and inclusion, just ask yourself the following:

- Is this fair?

- How would I feel in this situation?

- Would I want to be treated this way?

If your answer is 'no', then make sure you do something about it, perhaps by talking to your mentor. The changing and diverse nature of society can pose many challenges for individuals, groups, employers, and teachers.

Inclusive practice

Inclusive practice is about attitudes as well as behaviours, as learners can be affected by the words or actions of others. You are not teaching a group of learners who are all the same, but a group made up of individuals with different experiences, abilities and needs. These can be recognised, embraced, and respected during your lessons. When you are with your learners, try to promote a positive culture of equality of opportunity whereby all your learners can attend, participate, and feel safe and valued. If you can develop the conditions for learning that are based on respect and trust, and address the needs of individual learners, you will have created an effective teaching, learning, and assessment environment. However, you will need to be mindful of the culture of the organisation where you work. If there are aspects which you feel are negative, you might want to bring them to someone's attention. You should aim to be positive, proactive, and professional at all times.

The best way to ensure that you are effectively including all learners during your lessons, and treating them fairly, is to talk to them. If asked, learners will usually tell you if they have any particular needs, whether that is from a religious or cultural point of view, if they have a learning difficulty and/or disability, or an additional need. This will enable you to effectively support them, or refer them elsewhere.

Ways to promote inclusion

Ways to promote inclusion with your learners during a lesson can simply be by using their names when they arrive and when talking to them, using eye contact, speaking personally to them, and asking individual questions. Recognising each learner and not ignoring them in any way can help them feel at ease.

Access to resources can have an impact on whether learners are excluded from some activities. For example, if a learner can't afford the course text book, they could be at a disadvantage. Ideally, relevant books should be available from a library, or learners might be able to access an electronic version via the organisation. Some courses might require learners to purchase items, for example, cooking ingredients for a catering course. If a learner has financial problems and they are willing to talk to you about it, there might be the opportunity to obtain a grant or a loan to help them.

Ideally, you should consider how you can promote inclusion throughout all aspects of teaching, learning, and assessment.

Differentiation

Differentiation is about using a range of different approaches and resources to meet the needs of individual learners, a small group within the main group, or the full group. This should help to reduce barriers to learning, can stretch and challenge learners, and hopefully keep everyone interested and motivated. It is very rare that a teacher has a group of learners who are all at the same level of ability, with the same prior knowledge and experience and with the same needs. However, they might all be working towards the same outcomes or the same qualification. This will make your job more challenging but exciting and interesting.

You might feel that you want to pitch all your lessons at the same level, perhaps because you don't have time to prepare or to think how you can differentiate various activities. Although this might be easy for you, it won't help your learners. If you have a mixed ability group, you will have some learners who might be slower or quicker at learning than others. Learners who work quickly might soon get bored, and those who need more time might get left behind. You can achieve this by using different activities based around the same topic i.e. a gapped handout, crossword, or a complex puzzle to test knowledge at different levels (in Chapter 4).

Think of differentiation as a way of adding variety to your lessons, to ensure that learning is taking place by everyone. You don't have to differentiate everything you do, but you might like to differentiate what the learners do. This could alleviate boredom and aid motivation and interest.

Theory into practice

Think how you can use differentiation during a lesson with your learners. For example, by creating different activities based on the same topic. If you are currently teaching, create a differentiated activity, try it with your learners, and evaluate how effective it was. What would you do differently and why?

Communication with others

Your main communication will be with your learners; however, you will regularly communicate with colleagues, managers, stakeholders and others. Always make sure that what you are communicating is accurate, unambiguous and not biased in any way. You won't want to confuse anyone in case they misinterpret something, and you may need to adapt your style depending upon who you are communicating with at the time. Try and show your professionalism, not only in what you say, but in the way you say it. Professionalism can also be demonstrated with your behaviour, attitude, body language, and the way you dress and act. A confident and genuine smile, a positive attitude, self-assurance, and the use of eye contact and people's names should help put them, and you, at ease. The language you use when speaking and writing should reflect equality, diversity and inclusiveness, and not offend anyone in any way. You should never use racist, discriminative, or inappropriate words or actions.

When communicating, it needs to be in a way that the recipient (the person receiving it) can interpret and understand what you are wanting to convey. If you speak, you expect the recipient to listen. However, they might be thinking about something else and not really focus on what you are saying.

Communication is much more than spoken or written words. It includes how you portray yourself and the messages you give out, perhaps without realising. The person watching you might interpret things differently to the way you feel you are portraying them. For example, if your arms are folded, it could be perceived as a barrier. Try and be careful regarding how you write things, as the text could be interpreted differently when read. It's useful to read anything you have written, such as a handout, to try and understand it from the point of view of the person reading it.

You will need to use an appropriate communication method, depending upon the recipient and the situation. There are many methods of communication you can use, which might need to be adapted depending upon the situation and the person. These include:

- verbal: speaking i.e. face to face, telephone conversations, making digital recordings, video conferencing

- non-verbal: i.e. body language, appearance, dress, facial expressions, eye contact, gestures, posture, and the way you portray yourself

- written: i.e. letters, messages, reports, texts, progress reviews, worksheets, handouts

- visual: i.e. notice boards, adverts, posters, videos

- digital: i.e. emails, completing forms, online chats, social networking.

You will need to develop the skills which enable you to use relevant methods of communication which are appropriate at the time, and to decide which is the most suitable for a particular situation and person.

One of the skills of communicating effectively is projecting *confidence* when you are speaking. You may not feel confident when meeting a new group of learners for the first time; you might even feel quite nervous. You could imagine that you are an actor playing a character role to help you remain composed and focused. Your knowledge of, and passion for, your subject should help your confidence.

Transactional Analysis

Transactional Analysis is a method of analysing communications between people. Eric Berne, in the 1950s, identified three personality states within people: the parent (P), the adult (A), and the child (C) – called ego states. People behave and exist in a mixture of these states due to their past experiences and the situation they are in at the time.

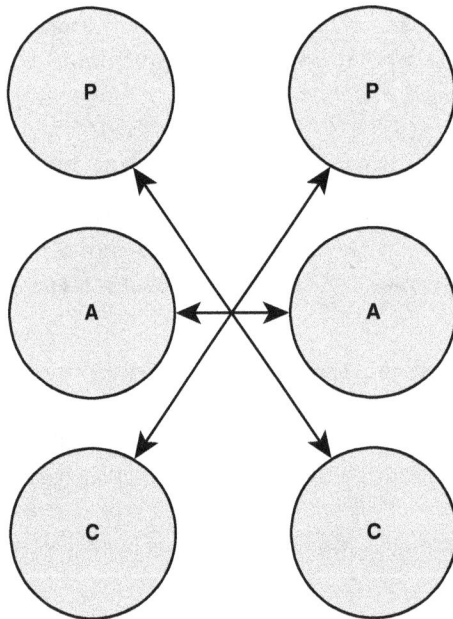

Figure 3.2 Adult to adult and crossed transactions

The best ego state is to be in the adult state, with another person being in the same state at the same time (adult to adult). As an adult, you feel good about yourself, respectful of the talents and lives of others, delighted with challenges, proud of accomplishments and expectant of success. These feelings can make you respond to others by appreciating and listening to them, using respectful language, and perceiving the facts.

If there are crossed transactions, where one person takes on a different ego state (parent to child, or child to parent as in Figure 3.2), the conversation may change its nature or come to an end.

If you ever feel like a child at work, it may be because your manager is operating in their parent ego state and you are responding in your child ego state. Your child can make you feel small, afraid, undervalued, demotivated, and rebellious; this may make you undermine, withdraw, procrastinate, or attempt to please in order to be rewarded. In this child ego state, you cannot become a successful professional.

You may find yourself acting like a parent with your learners. You might have learnt this from your parents' responses to you years ago. The parent ego state makes you feel superior, important, detached, and impatient. This can make you harden your tone, not listen, shout, and criticise more.

Transactional Analysis assumes all past events, feelings and experiences are stored within, and can be re-experienced in current situations. You may see this with colleagues who take on a different ego state, for example, acting like a child asking for help from you, yet acting differently with other colleagues. Understanding a little about the different ego states of the child, parent, and adult will help you to see how others might take on different roles (the ego states) in different situations with different people.

Activity

Research Transactional Analysis further, along with other communication theories such as: The Transmission Model, Cognitive Dissonance Theory, and/or Metacognitive questioning.

Communicating with learners

Communication is the key to encouraging learner motivation and respect, managing behaviour and disruption, and becoming a successful teacher. It should always be to the level of your learners, appropriate, and effective. For example, if you need to write on a board while speaking to your learners, don't do both at the same time. If you face the board, they may not hear you speak and you might miss something happening in the room. If you don't communicate effectively i.e. convey what you want your learners to hear in a way that they can interpret it, things may be misunderstood and learning might not take place.

Learning occurs best in an active rather than a passive environment where communication is a two-way process. Try and watch for signals from your learners to check that they are understanding what you are saying. Communication is an essential skill of a teacher, whether it's used verbally, non-verbally, or in written or electronic form. Used effectively, it will enable you to share your skills and knowledge, enabling learning to take place.

Helpful hint

You will need to plan what you want to communicate along with how and when you are going to do this. Your learners don't know what you know; that's why they want to learn. When communicating, try and keep things simple. There's no need to talk quickly and/or use a lot of jargon, as it takes time for your learners to assimilate new knowledge. Don't be afraid of repeating things, and try not to say 'I've told you that before' to your learners.

The Shannon and Weaver (1949) communication model

Embodying the principles of the Shannon and Weaver (1949) communication model as in Figure 3.3 can help to create an active learning environment which hinges on effective communication. In this model, which has been adapted over time to include other models, communication is not merely a one-way transmission of information, but a two-way exchange essential for facilitating learning. While originally developed for telecommunication systems, its key stages can be applied to various contexts, including communicating with learners.

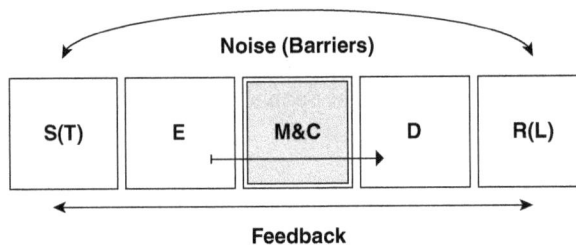

Figure 3.3 Shannon and Weaver (1949) communication model

Sender (Teacher): As the sender, the teacher initiates the communication process by: transmitting information; explaining; demonstrating; and/or using resources based on the knowledge required. Clear and concise messages are vital, ensuring learners understand what is expected of them.

Encoding: Encoding involves the teacher translating the message into a form that can be effectively transmitted to the learners. This involves choosing appropriate words, tone, and non-verbal signals to clearly convey the desired learning and understanding.

Message & Channel: The message encompasses the learning content communicated by the teacher. It should be crafted with clarity and relevance to engage learners and promote active participation. The channel refers to the medium through which the message is conveyed. For example, verbal communication, visual aids, written instructions, and non-verbal cues serve as the channels through which teachers transmit the information and interact with their learners.

Decoding: Decoding occurs as learners interpret and understand the message which has been conveyed by the teacher. It is crucial for teachers to monitor their learners' responses and comprehension, to ensure that the message is accurately decoded and understood.

Receiver (Learner): Learners serve as the receivers of the teacher's message. Active listening, engagement, and participation are essential as the learners receive and process the information, which contributes to the learning process.

Feedback: Feedback completes the communication, enabling teachers to assess their learners' understanding and adjust their approaches accordingly. Teachers should actively seek feedback from their learners, acknowledge their responses and address any misconceptions or concerns.

Noise (Barriers): A barrier to communication is anything that inhibits or prevents one person from receiving and understanding the message the other is trying to convey. It's not a physical barrier, but something that impedes the message getting through, for example, an individual learner's needs and the support required to ensure that learning takes place.

Example

Jodi considered potential communication barriers to be:

- *background noise*
- *seating positions too far away to hear and see her*
- *learners talking or whispering while she is speaking*
- *the way she explains a topic e.g. too complex*
- *learners who may have visual or hearing impairments*
- *learners with specific learning needs.*

By applying the principles of the Shannon and Weaver Model, you can create an interactive and engaging learning environment, where communication fosters understanding and active participation. By actively listening to your learners, monitoring their responses, and providing timely feedback, you can ensure that communication facilitates effective learning, and promotes a positive learning environment.

Theory into practice

Think of the last time you spoke to a learner where you felt that they didn't really listen to you or understand what you said. Why do you think this was, and what could you do differently? Do you use the Shannon and Weaver Model when communicating? Reflect on what (noise) barriers could have affected your learner or the learning environment.

Summary

This chapter has explored:

- Getting to know your learners
- Barriers and challenges to learning
- Initial and diagnostic assessment
- Creating and maintaining a safe, supportive, and effective learning environment
- Equality, diversity and inclusion
- Communication with others

4

Developing effective teaching and learning strategies

Putting theory into practice for teaching and learning

Introduction

Developing effective teaching and learning strategies, and knowing the differences between them, will help you to devise appropriate aims and objectives, schemes of work, and lesson plans for your subject.

It's useful to base your strategies on various learning theories, models and principles, which you will need to research further. Teaching is all about making sure that learning is taking place.

At the end of the chapter you will find a comprehensive table of teaching and learning approaches and activities, along with their strengths and limitations.

This chapter will introduce you to the following topics:

- Learning theories, models and principles
- Planning lessons
- Teaching and learning approaches and activities
- Promoting appropriate behaviour and respect
- Coaching and mentoring

Occupational Standards covered in Chapter 4

Duties	Knowledge	Skills	Behaviours
D1, D2, D3, D4, D6, D7, D9	K1, K2, K3, K5, K6, K7, K8, K10, K13, K16, K17, K19	S1, S2, S3, S4, S5, S9, S10, S12, S18, S19, S20, S23	B1, B2, B4

Learning theories, models and principles

There are many learning theories, models and principles which have been based on ideas, thoughts, experiences, and research. They are all aimed at helping you to understand the different teaching and learning approaches which you could use to teach your subject. Unfortunately, there isn't room in this book to explore them all; therefore you will need to research others for yourself. You could even create your own theory which suits you best, based on your experiences and/or after carrying out further research. However, ways of thinking change and develop over time and new theories emerge or are adapted. Whatever teaching methods you choose to use for your subject, they should lead to a change in behaviour, which demonstrates that learning has taken place.

Pedagogy and andragogy

Malcom Knowles (1975) brought the concept of *pedagogy* and *andragogy* to the fore in education. The *pedagogical approach* places the responsibility for making decisions about the learning process upon the teacher. Pedagogy therefore relates to the teaching and learning strategies which teachers use with their learners.

The *andragogical approach* places the emphasis on the learner to take responsibility for the learning process. They can then ensure they are learning in a way that suits them. This approach allows you to adapt your teaching approaches, activities, and materials to suit each learner's progress and development.

Domains of learning

Bloom (1956), an American educational psychologist, stated that learning often goes through five stages, which should lead to a change in behaviour. These stages are:

- attention
- perception
- understanding
- short-/long-term memory
- change in behaviour.

Starting with gaining your learners' attention and progressing through the stages should ensure that learning takes place, therefore leading to a change in behaviour. The stages relate to your learners' *thinking*, *emotions*, and *actions* which Bloom called *domains* of learning. These domains are known as *cognitive*, *affective*, and *psycho-motor*. Think of cognitive as thinking, affective as emotions, and psycho-motor as actions.

When planning to teach your subject, you will need to consider which domain you want to reach and how you can progress your learners through the five stages. It's useful to know this when planning your lessons. Bloom also advocated six levels of learning, covered later in this chapter.

EDIP

EDIP is an acronym for **E**xplain, **D**emonstrate, **I**mitate, and **P**ractise. Allen's (1919) four-step training method was originally devised for training shipyard workers in the United States, and is a useful method when teaching a practical subject.

- **E**xplain clearly to your learner in words that they can understand, all the main points of the task you are about to demonstrate and why. Keep the points brief and simple.

- **D**emonstrate the task slowly so that your learner can see exactly what you are doing.

- **I**mitate. Demonstrate the task again and this time ask your learner to mirror and copy what you do at the same time. Reiterate the main points as you progress.

- **P**ractise. Ask your learner to carry out the task on their own and correct any errors.

This method isn't very flexible as it was designed to get people performing a task quickly. It doesn't allow for a two-way conversation. However, if you wish to use this method you could include questioning to check understanding.

You could think of the process as *I do it, we do it, you do it*. EDIP is quite a formal method for demonstrating a task; however, you could adapt it to suit your circumstances. For example, you could add another stage so that the learner demonstrates the task to another learner. This gives the learner the opportunity to try out the task more than once. If the task will become part of their job role, they may need to try it out several times before they become fully competent.

Scaffolding is a term also used for this type of teaching model. For example, the teacher shares new information (I do it), then steps back and lets the learners find out more as a group (we do it), then the learners work individually (you do it). At the beginning of learning, the teacher is providing more support, which is gradually removed in stages as learning takes place.

An alternative method for more flexibility is PAR: **P**resent, **A**pply, and **R**eview by Petty (2009). This method enables the teacher to:

- **present** knowledge, skills and behaviours to facilitate the learner to be ready to learn. This can be by delivering new information, or scaffolding onto previous learning, for example, the teacher talks, or the learners watch a video clip or a demonstration.

- **apply** allows the learners to develop their learning by actively engaging with the subject or topic, for example, creating a leaflet, a group/paired discussion, or a research and presentation task.

- **review** involves both the teacher and learner summarising and clarifying the learning that has taken place, with significance placed on the aims and objectives. For example, questions, note taking, a quiz, or a test.

Although described as PAR, this method allows for the reordering of the stages: for example, Review, Present, Apply (RPA), and so on. Reviewing the learners at the beginning of a lesson enables the teacher to assess their knowledge, skills and behaviours of the current subject. Alternatively, while the learners are arriving to the lesson, the teacher could commence with Apply by asking them to complete a starter activity until everyone is in attendance.

Types and conditions of learning

Gagne (1985) identified five types of *learned capabilities* which he stated required a different type of instruction. These are:

- intellectual skills

- cognitive strategies

- verbal information

- attitudes

- motor skills.

Different internal and external conditions of learning are required for each. For example, for motor skills to be learnt, there must be the opportunity for the learner to practise new skills rather than just observe them. For attitudes, the learner must be able to explore them, perhaps by discussing or debating them.

Gagne believed all lessons should include a sequence of nine events. These should activate the processes needed for effective learning to take place. Each event has a corresponding cognitive process (in brackets).

1. Gaining attention (reception)

2. Informing learners of the objective (expectancy)

3. Stimulating recall of prior learning (retrieval)

4. Presenting the stimulus (selective perception)

5. Providing learning guidance (semantic encoding)

6. Eliciting performance (responding)

7. Providing feedback (reinforcement)

8. Assessing performance (retrieval)

9. Enhancing retention and transfer (generalisation).

It's useful to be aware of these events if you are following this model with your learners.

Retention of learning

Whatever teaching and learning approaches and activities you choose to use with your learners, you will want them to retain what they have learnt. There have been many studies regarding the retention of learning, which are usually expressed in percentages. One is Dale's (1969) Cone of Learning and Experience, as in Figure 4.1. This has been adapted over time to give a guide in percentages of how much people remember what they read, hear, see, and do. Dale said it was not to be used literally. The bands within the cone are not rigid but flexible, and the cone has been revised and argued against over the years. However, it can give you an idea of how learning occurs from being passive to active.

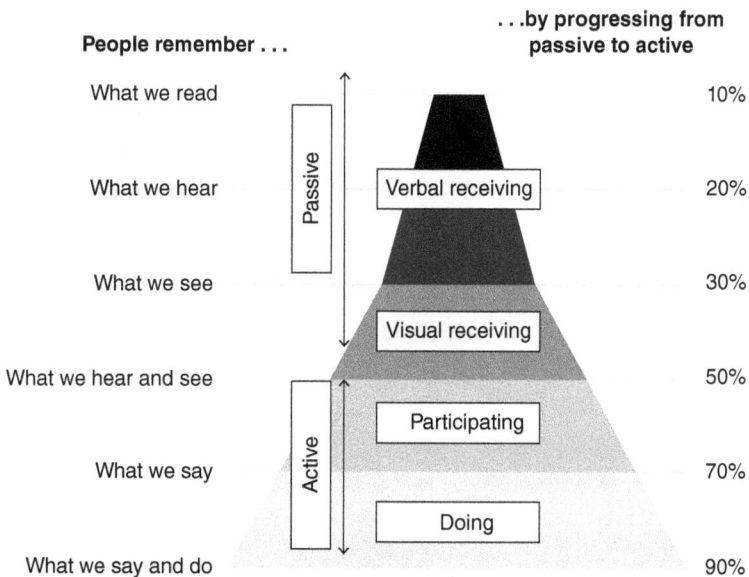

Figure 4.1 Dale's Cone of Learning and Experience (1969, page 108) adapted

Using activities from the top of the cone (passive) through to the bottom of the cone (active) might help your learners to realistically experience your subject. They should then remember more because they have *said and done* what they have *read and heard* i.e. they have put theory into practice.

If your learners can incorporate *reading, hearing, seeing, saying,* and *doing* during your lessons, their learning retention should increase. Once learners put theory into practice they should begin to understand what they have learnt. Some people learn by imitating or copying others. While they might then be able to perform the task, they might not know *why* they are doing it. Therefore, skills and knowledge are best learnt together to ensure understanding takes place.

Activity

Research 'retention of learning' and compare and contrast the various studies to Dale's Cone of Learning and Experience.

Other theories, models and principles (in alphabetical order)

Behaviourism is about people being conditioned to behave in a particular way. Learning is therefore measured by a change in behaviour, which is modified by external influences or _conditioning_. Behaviourist theorists include Pavlov (1927), Watson (1928), and Skinner (1974).

Cognitivism theory is about people constructing their own understanding and knowledge by experiencing something and reflecting on it. Learning is therefore an active process of personal interpretation. Cognitive theorists include Piaget (1959), Vygotsky (1962), and Bruner (1960).

Connectivism theory is about the importance of networks and connections in learning. Developed by Siemens and Downes (2005), it emerged in response to the digital age's increasing complexity, and the abundance of information available through technology. Learning occurs through the creation and navigation of networks of connections between people, resources, and information sources.

Humanism theory emphasises the value of human beings and places the onus of learning onto the learner to focus on their strengths. Learning is therefore based on a natural curiosity and the desire for personal growth and development. Humanism theorists include Rogers (1959) and Maslow (1987).

Neuroscience theory, often referred to as neuroeducation or educational neuroscience, is an interdisciplinary field that explores the relationship between neuroscience principles and educational practices. It seeks to understand how the brain learns and processes information to inform teaching methods and educational strategies. Neuroscience theorists include Fischer and Immordino-Yang (2008).

Pragmatist theory is about thought being a tool for problem solving and actions. It's about dealing with a problem in a sensible way, rather than following fixed ideas, and relating behaviour to experiences. Problems can be solved through the application of inquiry and experience, rather than being taught. Pragmatist theorists include Dewey (1938) and James (1907).

Social Learning theory is about the role of observation, imitation, and modelling in learning. It suggests that people learn not only through direct experience but also by observing others, and the consequences of their actions. This theory highlights the importance of social context, observation, and cognitive processes in learning and behaviour. Social Learning theorists include Bandura (1960).

Learning preferences

Most people learn in different ways and have a _preference_ or a _style_ to help them acquire new skills and knowledge, and to remember things. Some people prefer the term _preference_ to _styles_ so as not to categorise a learner. All people learn differently, perhaps influenced by experiences in their childhood, school, personal, or professional relationships. When you learn something new, you will probably adapt, change, or modify your behaviour as a result, and the same will apply with your learners.

There are critics of learning styles and not everyone agrees on their use with learners. In 2004, Professor Frank Coffield and three colleagues carried out a systematic and critical review of learning styles and pedagogy in post-16 learning. The report reviewed the literature on learning styles and examined in detail 13 of the most influential models. The implications for teaching and learning, he states, are serious and should be of concern. Coffield has since written widely on the subject and states... *it was not sufficient to pay attention to individual differences in learners, we must take account of the whole teaching-learning environment* (2008, page 31).

It's therefore important to consider other factors which influence learning. For example, the room where learning takes place (factors such as heating, lighting, and ventilation can impact upon learning).

VARK

In 1987, Fleming stated that people can be grouped into four styles of learning: visual, aural, read/write, and kinaesthetic, known by the acronym VARK. However, try not to be quick to place learners in one of the four styles, as they may be *multi-modal* i.e. a mixture of two or more styles, enabling their learning to take place more quickly.

In 1992, Fleming, along with Mills, published their findings in a journal. Other publications have since become available which have different views. Styles and preferences of learning can change over time depending upon many factors, such as lifestyles, the environment, personal circumstances and/or particular needs. It's best to use a mixture of each to ensure variety during your lessons.

Helpful hint

When planning your lessons (later in the chapter), try to balance the elements of VARK within your teaching and learning activities. This should enable your learners to experience a mixed learning approach and ensure that learning takes place.

Honey and Mumford (1992)

Honey and Mumford suggest learners are a mixture of four styles: activist, pragmatist, theorist and reflector. This could be interpreted as:

Activist

Activist learners like to deal with new challenges and experiences, often learning by trial and error. They like lots of practical activities to keep them busy and they enjoy a hands-on approach. They love challenges and are enthusiastic.

Pragmatist

Pragmatist learners like to apply what they have learnt to practical situations. They like logical reasons for doing something. They prefer someone to demonstrate a skill first before trying it for themselves.

Theorist

Theorist learners like time to take in information. They prefer to research and read lots of material first. They like things that have been tried and tested and prefer reassurance that something will work.

Reflector

Reflector learners think deeply about what they are learning and the activities they could do to apply this learning. They like to be told about things so that they can think it through. They will also try something, think about it, and then try it again.

Example

Archie has just bought a new mobile phone. He is an activist learner and therefore enjoyed learning to use it by tapping the icons and trying out the functions. If he was a pragmatist, he would have asked someone to show him how to use it. If he was a theorist, he would have read the instructions thoroughly first. If he was a reflector, he would have used the functions he was familiar with before thinking about different ways of using them, followed by using the phone's other functions.

It can be useful to ask your learners to complete a learning preference questionnaire. It can be fun and lead to an interesting discussion, as well as helping you to plan your approaches to reach all learning preferences. However, do check with your organisation if they advocate the use of this type of questionnaire or not.

Theory into practice

Choose four of the above theories or theorists and research them further. Compare and contrast them. How relevant do you think they are for your subject specialism? Do you agree or disagree with any, if so, why? You might like to discuss your responses with your mentor.

Planning lessons

It's extremely important to spend time planning your lessons i.e. what you will do and when. This will ensure that the teaching and learning approaches and activities you use will be innovative and purposeful. A way to help you with this is to use aims and objectives as a starting point for what you will do, and what you want your learners to do. These will then be used to help create your scheme of work (SoW) and lesson plans. You can also base what you will do on the theories you have just read about in the previous section.

Aims and objectives

These are educational terms used to express what you want your learners to achieve and how they will go about it. Using aims and objectives will help you to structure your lessons with relevant tasks and activities for the different topics related to your subject special-ism. Some courses or qualification specifications might already contain aims and objectives, which could be called something different, for example, learning outcomes, assessment/per-formance criteria, and competency statements. If aims and objectives or their alternatives are not provided for you, you will need to devise your own.

Aims

When writing an aim, you need to consider what it is you want your learners to be able to achieve. Your aim is a general statement, and will usually begin with words like: *to appreciate, to be able to, to raise an awareness of.*

For example: to <u>appreciate</u> the roles and responsibilities of a teaching assistant.

This aim is very broad and does not state *how* the roles and responsibilities will be appreci-ated. Therefore, objectives are needed.

Other terms which are sometimes used for aims, but are not really good practice to use, include *to know,* and *to understand.* Although these terms do state what you want your learn-ers to achieve, they do not tell you how to check that learning has taken place. This is where objectives will help you.

Objectives

Once you have your aim, you can plan what it is that you want your learners to do to meet it i.e. the objectives. Objectives are often referred to as *tasks* i.e. the activities which learners will carry out. When writing objectives or creating tasks, try not to use words similar to those in your aim.

Example

Objectives (by the end of the lesson, learners will be able to):

- *<u>Identify</u> and list the roles and responsibilities of a teaching assistant.*
- *<u>Discuss</u> these in small groups and agree the differences between them.*
- *<u>Design</u> a poster which shows the differences between the roles and the responsibilities.*

The key tasks which learners will carry out begin with *identify, discuss,* and *design.* They are all activities, which when achieved, show you that learning has taken place. There could be many more tasks for the above example, but this should give you an idea of the difference between an aim (what *you want* your learners to do) and the objectives (what your learners *will do*).

Objectives should always be SMART as in Figure 4.2, to enable you to teach and assess learning effectively.

Specific & stretching	S	Is the objective specific, clear, precise, and unambiguous? Is the objective stretching in some way (but still realistic and achievable)?
Measurable	M	Does the objective say what success will look like and how it will be measured, in terms of quantity or quality?
Achievable & agreed	A	Is the objective realistically achievable, taking into account the timeframe, resources and learning support required? Is it agreed?
Relevant & realistic	R	Is the objective relevant and realistic to what the learner needs to achieve? Will it maximise their achievement?
Time-bound	T	Has a specific date been agreed for when the objective should be completed? Is the target date related to the objective rather than simply coinciding with the end of the learning?

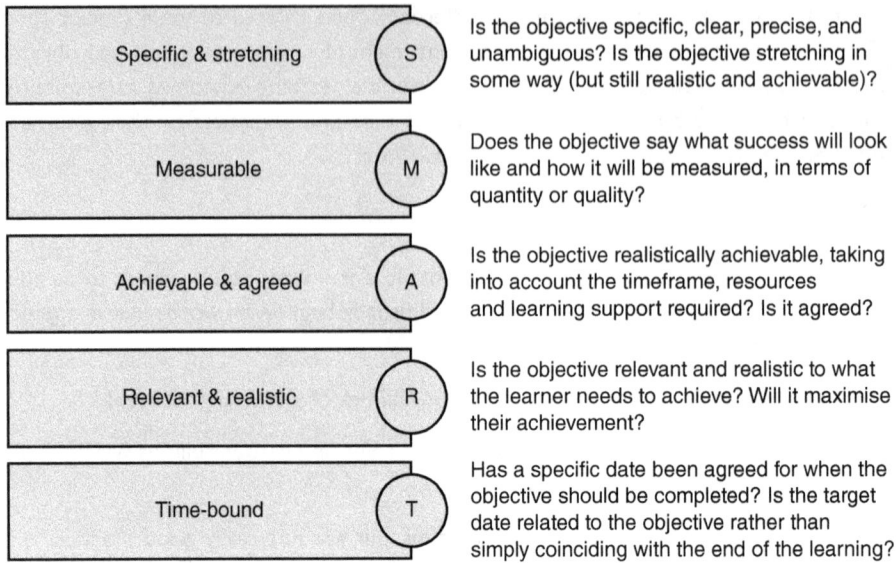

Figure 4.2 SMART objectives

Being SMART is all about being clear and precise with what you expect your learners to achieve. SMART objectives should always be at the right level for your learners; for example, to *list* is easier than to *evaluate*. Knowing your learners, and the level of the course or qualification they are working towards, will help you to plan which objectives (active verbs) to use. Active verbs are what the learner has *to do* to prove their knowledge, skills, understanding, and behaviours. They are tasks and activities which your learners will carry out, and which make it easier to assess that learning has taken place. They should be stretching and challenging enough to ensure learning is progressive, yet be inclusive to all learners to ensure they can achieve.

Having clear aims and objectives will help you to plan what will be covered during your lessons. They will also enable you to plan how much time is needed to carry out various tasks. You should inform your learners at the beginning of each lesson what the aims and objectives are, and how they relate to the overall course or qualification. This will help them appreciate what they are learning and why. You could keep them visible and refer back to them during a lesson. This can act as a motivator for learners, as they can actively see what they are achieving in a lesson. You could also ask your learners to self-assess themselves by asking them to write down or state how they have achieved the objectives when the lesson concludes.

Bloom's Taxonomy

Benjamin Bloom chaired a committee of educators in the early 1950s. As a result, in 1956, a framework was published which became known as Bloom's Taxonomy (a classification). It includes a hierarchy of six progressive levels of learning, ranging from simple to complex, as in Figure 4.3. Knowledge is first, with those following relating to skills and abilities. This is on the understanding that knowledge is necessary for the skills and abilities to be put into practice. However, this theory has been updated over time by other theorists, and some levels have since been renamed.

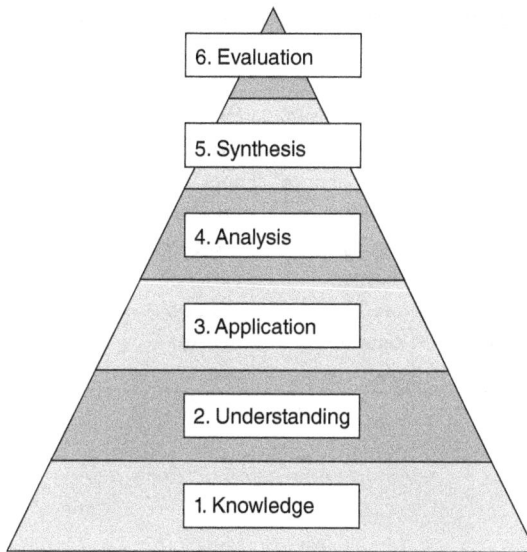

Figure 4.3 Bloom's (1956) six levels of learning

The six progressive levels have associated objectives (active verbs) to denote what learners will be able to know and/or do. They range from *actual* to *abstract* thinking and are:

1. knowledge: to remember and recall facts e.g. list, recall

2. understanding: to demonstrate knowledge e.g. describe, identify

3. application: to apply knowledge and understanding to real situations e.g. demonstrate, explain

4. analysis: to consider, explore, and work things out e.g. appraise, calculate

5. synthesis: to compile ideas and generate new ones e.g. compose, design

6. evaluation: to make and defend judgements e.g. critically evaluate, hypothesise.

Using Bloom's taxonomy will help you to differentiate the objectives and tasks you want your learners to achieve. Your learners might achieve at different levels throughout their time with you, perhaps if they are taking a long-term course. This might be by starting with an expression of their knowledge i.e. by recalling relevant facts, working up to critically evaluating something. You may even have individual learners who are at different levels within the same group. To help you differentiate for this during a lesson, you could ask them to complete the same task, but in a different way. For example, make a *list* (to demonstrate knowledge), *explain* (to demonstrate understanding) and *appraise* (to demonstrate analysis). All these tasks will enable you to check that learning is taking place.

Table 4.1 lists examples of objectives which could align with Bloom's taxonomy. The objectives in qualification specifications will differ depending upon the context in which they relate to, and the level of expected achievement. You may need to research the use of objectives further, to gain ideas of which to use for your subject.

Table 4.1 Examples of objectives which could align with Bloom's taxonomy

Objectives					
Knowledge	Understanding	Application	Analysis	Synthesis	Evaluation
define	describe	apply	analyse	arrange	argue
list	discuss	demonstrate	appraise	assemble	assess
name	estimate	devise	calculate	compose	choose
match	identify	explain	categorise	construct	critically-
recall	locate	illustrate	compare	create	evaluate
recognise	order	modify	criticise	design	differentiate
repeat	paraphrase	operate	debate	invent	hypothesise
state	select	use	test	summarise	judge

Activity

Choose an objective from each of Bloom's levels and create a task for your learners to carry out which is based on your subject specialism. For example: learners will define... (knowledge), learners will describe... (understanding) and so on. This will help you to practise how you can create tasks for your subject, and how you can stretch and challenge your learners if they are capable of achieving more.

Schemes of work

A scheme of work (also known as a scheme of learning) is a document which you can use to structure a sequence of lessons. Having a scheme of work helps you to plan what you will do and when; it is an overall view of all the planned lessons for a course. It allows you to identify what you will teach and when. This is useful in case there are any bank or public holidays which might reduce the number of lessons available. It's also useful in case you want to book a guest speaker in advance, take your learners on an external visit, or need to use certain resources which must be prepared or booked in advance. The content should be flexible to allow for any changes i.e. a cancelled lesson, and detailed enough in case a colleague needs to cover for you. It should reflect the use of different teaching and learning approaches (see Table 4.2), resources (in Chapter 5) and assessment methods (in Chapter 7) throughout the duration of the course. It is a live working document which shows what you will do and what you want your learners to do. It should reflect learning in a progressive and logical way through the course requirements. You wouldn't want to start with something complicated if you haven't covered the basics first.

If you teach the same subject as your colleagues, you could all work together to produce a standardised scheme of work. The amount of detail you are expected to include will vary depending upon the context within which you teach. The requirements of your organisation and external inspectors might also have an impact on the detail you need to include. Usually, an organisation will supply their teachers with a standard pro-forma to use. However, if none is available, you could create your own.

The main headings for a scheme of work could include:

- Aim of the course (and qualification title if applicable)

- Group composition (e.g. how many learners, their prior knowledge/experience)

- Date and times (e.g. how many lessons, the dates and times of each)

- Teacher activities (e.g. explanations, demonstrations)

- Learner activities (e.g. discussions, paired activities, practical tasks which are related to the objectives)

- Resources required (e.g. handouts, electronic whiteboard)

- Assessment activities (e.g. questions, assignments)

- Remarks (good for noting aspects such as booking guest speakers, the resources needed for future lessons, or room changes).

Starting point for a scheme of work

As soon as you find out what you will be teaching and when, you can create your scheme of work. This is an overview of the full course, broken down into individual lessons. The starting point for this will usually be based on the content of a qualification specification from an awarding organisation, or a particular course syllabus. Alternatively, it could be from work tasks, a job specification, or a set of standards. These might be written in sections i.e. units or modules which relate to different subjects or topics. While these might be written in a certain order, you can usually decide the order in which you teach them. You could also group some aspects together which are from different units. This would save repetition, as there is often an aspect which is repeated in more than one unit. This enables a holistic approach to teaching and learning. For example, if your course is 3 hours per week over 20 weeks, you must plan what will take place in each lesson, and it must be logical.

If you are teaching a non-accredited course, there might not be a qualification specification for you to refer to. You might therefore need to devise your own content. This is where the use of aims and objectives will really help you to plan what to do. Some courses are nationalised i.e. they are the same no matter where a learner takes it. Schemes of work for these might be provided for you, and often, changes can't be made without approval.

Planning your scheme of work

A rationale such as using the *five Ws and one H* format of **who, what, when, where, why** and **how** will help you to plan your scheme of work. For example:

- who: the learners and information about them

- what: your aim and the objectives you want your learners to achieve

- when: the number of lessons and hours, dates and times

- where: venue or environment

- why: the course or qualification your learners will be working towards

- how: the teaching, learning, and assessment approaches you will use, along with relevant resources.

You may need to check some aspects, such as will you be in the same venue for all the lessons, and what facilities, equipment, and resources are available. It might be that you need to book some equipment or a guest speaker in advance. Knowing the dates will help with your planning.

It's also useful to know something about your learners in advance. This can enable you to differentiate your lessons were possible, perhaps based on their prior learning, previous knowledge, and/or experiences. You can also draw on the experiences of some learners to help those who are less experienced. Initial assessment (in Chapter 3) can help you to obtain this information, or just ask your learners at the beginning of a lesson.

You might like to put yourself in the place of your learners when planning what to do and when. This way you can see things from a beginner's perspective to ensure that you keep things simple during the earlier lessons. Start with the *known* and move onto the *unknown* or *unfamiliar*, checking the progress of your learners as you go. Try to break your subject down into manageable chunks, topics, or tasks which a learner who knows nothing about it can easily follow. It's useful to recap regularly, and to ask questions to check that learning is taking place. Don't move onto more complex topics until you know that your learners understand the current topic. Try not to plan to include too much for each lesson, in case you don't have time to achieve it, and you end up rushing.

Your scheme of work should show a variety of teaching, learning, and assessment activities to ensure differentiation, and to keep the subject interesting for them. The activities you choose to use will differ depending upon the *subject* you are teaching, the *context* and *environment* you are teaching in, as well as the *length* of each lesson. You might need to show how you will embed additional skills such as English, maths and digital skills (EMD) (later in this chapter) and aspects such as employability skills (in Chapter 2) and sustainability (in Chapter 1). It would be useful if you could plan time for individual tutorial reviews. This will give you an opportunity to discuss progress with each of your learners on a one-to-one basis at some point during the course.

The very first lesson could include an induction, icebreaker, and ground rules (in Chapter 3). All subsequent lessons should begin with a recap of the previous lesson, time for questions, and an introduction to the current lesson i.e. the aim and objectives. They should end with a recap of how the objectives have been met, and an explanation of the following lesson.

Depending on how long the course will last, it would be useful to include an evaluation activity (in Chapter 9) to obtain feedback part way through, as well as during the final lesson. At the end of the course you could give details of how your learners can progress further i.e. what steps they can take to continue their learning and development, and how they can progress into employment.

Once you have created your scheme of work, you may need to show it to your line manager for their approval. Once approved, you could give a copy to your learners, or make it available electronically. However, as it is a working document, you might make changes to it, or it could confuse your learners if there's too much information in it. You could therefore give your learners a list of the topics which will be covered and when, rather than the full SoW.

Sometimes, teachers might have *administrative time* allocated each week as part of their timetable. This can be used for planning lessons, creating resources and marking work. However, many teachers don't get this time allocated; therefore creating a scheme of work, which can be very time consuming, might need to be carried out during your own time. The more time you take to plan what will go into your scheme of work, the easier it will be to design your individual lesson plans.

Helpful hint

When planning what you will do, how, and when you will do it, consider your own past experiences of being a learner. For example, how you reacted to a really good teacher and how they made the lessons interesting and engaging.

Lesson plans

A lesson plan (also known as a teaching and learning plan) is a document which should be produced prior to each lesson you will teach. You don't need to create them all at the beginning of your course, as things could change. Your organisation will probably have a standard template for you to use, and you will need to check what this looks like. You might be required to complete it electronically or manually. Although the content in a lesson plan is very similar to that stated on a scheme of work, it is much more detailed and should be adapted to meet the individual needs of your learners (in Chapter 3). Think of the scheme of work as an overview of the full course, which is supported by detailed lesson plans for each date. It will help you to effectively manage the time that you have with your learners, what you will do, and what your learners will do. If you are only teaching one lesson rather than a series of lessons, one lesson plan could be used instead of a scheme of work. It might be that you are teaching a course which already has the lesson plans prepared for you. If this is the case, you will need to familiarise yourself with them, and find out whether you can make any changes or not.

Lesson plans should flow logically through the three stages of a lesson i.e. the introduction, development, and conclusion (beginning, middle, and ending). This helps to ensure a logical flow of content for learning to be effective.

The main headings are usually similar to a scheme of work, and could include:

- date, time, and venue

- aim of the lesson

- group profile (in Chapter 3) – differentiation details

- teacher activities and timings

- learner activities/tasks and timings

- resources required

- assessment activities and timings

- embedding English, maths, digital skills (EMD), employability, and sustainability skills..

Once you have a set of lesson plans, providing the course doesn't change, you can adapt them in the future for different groups of learners rather than starting again. However, don't think that because everything worked well the last time that it will be the same again this time, as you will have different learners with different abilities and needs.

Embedding English, maths and digital skills (EMD)

English, maths and digital skills (EMD) should be embedded into your lesson plans to show how your learners can apply them to the subject. Your learners need to know how these skills can be contextualised to aid transferability, for example into employment. However, you might need to update your own skills and knowledge in these areas beforehand. English includes other terms such as language and literacy, and maths includes the term numeracy.

You should have enough knowledge to make the skills relevant to your subject and learners. For example, English: reading, writing, talking, and listening; maths: planning a budget or working out the cost of a shopping list; digital skills: researching topics online, emailing, word-processing, or maintaining an electronic diary.

EMD are designed to help learners to:

- apply their knowledge and understanding to everyday life

- engage competently and confidently with others

- solve problems in both familiar and unfamiliar situations

- develop personally and professionally as positive citizens who can actively contribute to society.

Rather than treating the skills as separate subjects, try and embed them as part of your subject specialism. This will help your learners to engage with real situations in the context of the subject. Opportunities might arise naturally or you might need to be creative and imaginative. You could plan ways of using the following activities during your lessons:

- English language: speaking, listening, discussing, role play, interviews, and presentations

- English literacy: reading, writing, spelling, grammar, punctuation, and syntax

- maths: calculations, interpretations, evaluations, and measurements

- digital skills: using online applications, e-learning programs, word processors, spreadsheet packages, emails, podcasts, webcasts, videos, searching the internet, and using artificial intelligence.

You might also need to embed employability skills (Chapter 2) and sustainability (in Chapter 1) into your lessons. You will need to check if this is a requirement at your organisation, and if there are any other areas which also need to be embedded.

Theory into practice

Create a scheme of work for at least six lessons based on your subject specialism, and plan a lesson for at least one date from this. Make sure you have an appropriate aim and suitable objectives for the level of your learners. Think about the three stages (beginning, middle, and ending) regarding the content you need to cover. Consider the resources you will need, how you will differentiate the activities for your learners, and how you will check that learning has taken place.

Teaching and learning approaches and activities

Managing the learning process is a big part of your role. Using various teaching and learning approaches and activities will help to do this effectively. Think of them as the techniques which can enable your learners to be *actively engaged* during the lesson and not just *passively listening* to you talking. Some teaching approaches include lectures, demonstrations, instruction and presentations which are usually teacher-centred, also known as *passive learning*. Other approaches include discussions, group work, practical activities, and role plays, and are usually learner-centred, known as *active learning*. Whenever possible it's best to use a mixture of the two, and to vary the activities used and the time spent on each. This will ensure that all learners are included and can participate, and will enable you to assess that learning is taking place. A comprehensive table of teaching and learning approaches and activities, along with their strengths and limitations, is at the end of this chapter.

Activity

Does your subject mainly relate to skills (practice), knowledge (theory) or attitudes (behaviours)? If it's practical, how can you demonstrate skills to learners in a way that enables them to practise for themselves? If it's theoretical, how can you impart knowledge in a way that shows that your learners have understood? If it's to change behaviour, how can you have an impact upon your learners for this to take place?

To be a good teacher involves not only having the skills and knowledge of your subject, but the confidence, ability, and enthusiasm to communicate this to others. Teaching and learning should not be in isolation from the assessment process. You can check that learning is taking place each time you are with your learners. This can simply be by observing practice or asking questions. If your learners are working towards a qualification, there will be formal methods of assessment such as an examination, assignment, or an observation in the workplace. However, you can devise informal methods to use with your learners to check ongoing progress (in Chapter 7).

While you might be extremely knowledgeable and experienced regarding your subject, until you try and teach it to someone else, you won't really know if you are good at teaching or even if you will enjoy it. Varying what you do during your lessons will give your learners more chances to engage with the subject, and for learning to take place.

Cognitive Load Theory

When planning to teach your subject, you should always consider how to maximise the learning which will take place. Cognitive Load Theory (CLT) devised by Sweller (1988) suggests that a person's working memory can only handle a limited amount of information. When teaching, you should seek to minimise the burden on working memory to maximise learning.

Sweller advocates building upon prior knowledge by activating the long-term memory first through the use of discussions and activities. This will bring information into the working memory so that it can be dealt with more easily. Another method to minimise the burden on working memory is to combine both visual and verbal information when presenting new content to learners. This is a theory which you might like to research further and try out with your learners.

Routines

Having a routine lets your learners know how you operate and helps them to know what they will do and when. This could include the aspects which are carried out during the beginning, middle, and ending of a lesson. For example, you could commence with a starter activity and end with a closing activity.

Starter activities

A starter activity can help to gain attention and focus learning from the start of a lesson. It should grab your learners' attention and make them inspired to learn and to want to participate. It should set everyone into a learning mode, yet still be meaningful to the subject. A starter activity, sometimes referred to as a *welcome activity*, can also have another use if a learner arrives late. If it's a fun activity, any learners who arrive late will realise they have missed something good. It might encourage them to arrive on time in future. However, try not to let the starter activity take up too much time, or let digression and discussions take over. If they do, you might not be able to adjust your timings for the other activities you have planned to use.

Example

Starter activities can include the following:

* *a gapped handout, crossword, or a puzzle to test knowledge gained in the last lesson*

* *a discussion about a relevant news event*

- *a paired/small group/full group discussion to open up thinking about the current topic*

- *a quiz where the group is split into teams and you ask questions, perhaps in the form of multiple choice to ascertain knowledge about the topic to be taught*

- *asking learners in pairs or small groups to devise a question based on what they think will be covered during the lesson. They can then ask the question at the end of the lesson to another pair or small group (as a closing activity).*

You may need to carry out a quick debrief regarding the starter activity if it is not apparent why you used it.

Progressing through the lesson

When commencing a lesson, if you are unsure what to say to gather your learners' attention, start with *Welcome to the lesson, today we will...* in a louder than normal but assertive voice. This should gain your learners' attention and enable you to introduce the starter activity.

When progressing from the starter activity to the main body of the lesson, make sure that you have recapped any previous lesson topics, and then inform your learners what it is that will be covered during this lesson. It's useful to refer to your lesson plan to guide you, and to refer to the aim and objectives. Always check if your learners have any prior knowledge and/or experience of the current topic. This can simply be by asking questions; you can then draw upon this as you progress through the lesson. Never assume your learners know or don't know something, always check, and don't be afraid to repeat things.

Helpful hint

If you are a new teacher who is a bit nervous, breathe deeply and pause for a second or two; it might seem a long time to you but it won't to your learners. Focus your thoughts, relax, and enjoy what you are doing. Remember that you are in control of the lesson, so try and portray confidence and professionalism.

As you continue with your planned approaches and activities, allow time for questioning and for repeating and reinforcing important points. Only move on when you are sure your learners have understood the current topic. Incorporate the knowledge and experience of your learners and, if you can, give relevant anecdotes and use activities to bring the subject to life. Try and relate what you are teaching to how the learners will benefit from it.

Try and ensure your lesson flows progressively i.e. that the topics are taught in a logical order and that you can assess progress before moving on. When changing topics, try to link them together somehow or summarise one before moving on to the other. Break aspects down into smaller manageable chunks.

Show interest, passion, and enthusiasm for your subject and encourage your learners to take pride in their work. Use tone and inflection to emphasise key points and don't be afraid of silent pauses; they will give you time to refocus and give your learners time to consider what you have said. Use eye contact when you can, and use your learners' names as this shows you are interested in them as an individual. You might want to move around the room rather than stay in the same position at the front. This will give you a chance to check that your learners are focused, and shows them that you are in control of the lesson.

If you feel you are overrunning on your timings, don't be afraid to carry something over to the next lesson, cut it out altogether, or give it as homework or self-study material. Alternatively, you can adjust the timings of the other activities to reduce or increase them as necessary. Don't feel you must keep to the number of minutes you have written on your lesson plan for each activity. It's more important to ensure that learning is taking place than to keep to your timings. If your learners tend to ask lots of questions and you are running short of time, ask them to write them on a piece of paper or a sticky note. You can collect them in and address them at the end of the lesson, or at the beginning of the following lesson. If your learners have access to an online learning environment (in Chapter 6), you could post your responses on there.

When you summarise at the end of the lesson, try not to introduce anything new as this might confuse your learners. However, you should explain what will be covered in the next lesson (if applicable) and make clear what homework or self-study activities the learners need to do. You should allow some time for questions from your learners and then you can finish with a closing activity if you wish.

Try not to end a lesson with 'Does anyone have any questions?' as often only those who are keen or confident will ask. This doesn't tell you what has been learnt, and might exclude some learners who might be shy, or do not want to embarrass themselves in front of the group. If you want to ask questions, try the pose, pause, pick method (in Chapter 7). This will enable all learners to think of a suitable response before you nominate someone to answer.

Closing activities

Closing activities are useful if you find you have some spare time towards the end of your lesson, or if you want to establish it as part of your normal routine. They are short activities to enable learners to attach relevance to what they have learnt. If a learner has to leave a few minutes early for any reason, they might only miss the closing activity rather than any important points. Additionally, while your learners carry out the activity, it can be an opportunity for you to close down and pack away any equipment and items you have used during the lesson.

You could hold a quiz by placing your learners in small groups and letting them confer on the answers. You could prepare and ask a few short questions based on the topic just learnt. A point could be allocated to the winning team and points built up throughout the course. Some sort of reward could be given to the winning team at the end of the course, or they might just like the fact they have received the most points. This method could be a fun way of closing the lesson and is also a good way to informally assess that learning has taken place.

You could be adventurous and ask your learners to come up with an idea of their own for a closing activity. You will need to give them time to think about this, and you could even create a starter activity based on the learners devising a closing activity. If you did this, you would need to guide your learners with their ideas, which could then be used over several lessons.

Example

Closing activities can be similar to opening activities and include the following:

- *a gapped handout, crossword, or a puzzle to test knowledge gained during the lesson*

- *a question to each learner in turn to ask for one aspect from the lesson that has had the most impact upon their learning*

- *a question to each learner in turn to say one word that sums up the lesson for them. If there is time, you can ask them to explain why, or to use a sentence instead of a word*

- *a question to pairs or small groups to come up with one way of putting the new learning into practice*

- *a quiz where the group is split into teams and you ask questions, perhaps in the form of multiple choice to ascertain knowledge about the topic covered*

- *asking pairs or small groups to review what has been covered during the lesson and to decide on one question to ask another pair or group.*

Always be aware of your timings. If you have a large group, the closing activity might be quite time consuming.

Activities to support learning

Activities are the tasks which your learners can carry out as part of the approaches you use. However, some approaches could also be classed as activities depending upon what you are doing at the time – it's just terminology. Do consider that what works with some learners might not work with others. Therefore it might be trial and error at first, but don't be afraid to try something new or to make a mistake and learn from it.

If you just talk to your learners about your subject, how do you even know they are listening? Furthermore, if you just show them how to do something, how do you know that they can do it for themselves? Using different activities, and by involving your learners doing or saying something, will help learning to take place.

It's useful to create a bank of activities in advance which are based on your subject specialism. You could create a *toolbox* (or a *virtual box* if your learners all have access to digital devices) which contains various activities.

These could include:

- gapped handouts with missing words of increasing difficulty

- multiple-choice questions which start off easy and get harder

- open questions requiring an answer of a particular word count e.g. 150 words

- past test paper questions for learners to attempt in a certain time

- pictures or statements to identify which is the odd one out (at different levels of learning)

- tasks which use objectives of gradually increasing active verbs e.g. list, describe, explain, analyse

- topics to compare and contrast which increase in difficulty

- worksheets which introduce new topics and include questions to check understanding.

The activities you use with your learners must relate to the topics being covered, which in turn relate to the course, qualification, job specification, or set of standards which the learner is working towards. It takes time to plan, prepare, and use them, but they will enable your learners to explore the topics in a far more interesting and inspirational way. This can be more engaging than just listening to you talking or watching you demonstrate something. Whatever activities you choose to use, it might be an idea to work through them first, looking at them from a learner's perspective. You will need to decide if the activity will be carried out individually, in pairs, or small groups. You will also need to give clear instructions and set a time limit for completion. Make sure you debrief the activity afterwards and state how it relates to the subject and the objectives.

Examples of activities

A/B/C/D responses

Learners write the letters A, B, C, and D on separate pieces of paper. You can ask a question and give four possible answers, one for each of A, B, C, and D. Learners then hold up the letter to denote the response they think is correct. You may need to repeat the question and responses, or reduce them to three instead of four if learners can't remember them all. Alternatively, you could have the questions and responses on display as part of a presentation. If you have the opportunity, you could create and laminate a set of A, B, C, and D cards and reuse them as and when required. Discussions could take place regarding the responses if any were wrongly answered.

Creating leaflets and posters

In small groups, learners could create a leaflet or a poster, in hard copy or online, to summarise the current topic. Alternatively, each member of the small group could research a different topic prior to discussing it within their group, and then create a poster together. A discussion can take place regarding how all the groups approached the activity and what they learnt from it.

Identifying similarities and differences

Give pairs of learners two or three relevant topics and ask them to identify the similarities and differences between them. Each pair can then join another pair and discuss their responses. This is known as *snowballing* as the pairs can keep increasing. A full group discussion and debate can then take place.

Open activities

These are activities in which you pose a question, but leave it open to your learners how they answer it. For example, posing a topical and relevant question and letting your learners (as individuals, pairs, or small groups) decide how they will answer it. They might choose to discuss it among each other, research text books, or the internet, create a poster or a display, a cartoon strip, or a drawing, write an article, poem, song, or a blog, act out a short play, or anything else which inspires them. A time limit must be set and you will need to check what has been achieved. You might need to guide your learners with some ideas if they are struggling to decide on their own. Feedback will need to be given as to whether or not the question was successfully answered.

Reading, researching, and presenting

Learners read and/or research the current topic or an upcoming topic (using text books, journals, newspapers, and the internet). They can then give a short (timed) presentation to the full group using appropriate resources. A discussion can take place regarding how the groups approached the activity and what they learnt. An alternative to a presentation could be to create a visual display either manually or electronically, or a video.

True/false questions

Learners write the words 'true' and 'false' on separate pieces of paper. You can ask a closed question and they hold up their response. You could plan questions which are based around difficult ideas or concepts and which can lead to a critical discussion if learners get the answer wrong. If you have the opportunity, you could create and laminate a set of true and false cards and reuse them as and when required.

Using sticky notes and mini whiteboards

You ask a question to the full group then each learner must write their response on a sticky note or a mini whiteboard (or a piece of paper). Learners then attach the sticky note on the wall or hold up the mini whiteboard for you to see. Learners (and you) can look at and discuss the different responses. Instead of asking a question, you could ask the learners to summarise the current topic in three bullet points or ten words, and then write them on the sticky note or mini whiteboard.

Alternatively, learners could do this activity in pairs and discuss the responses among each other. You will need to discuss their responses with them in case any are wrong.

Sticky notes can also be used throughout a lesson for learners to write questions on. This is useful if they don't want to interrupt or embarrass themselves in front of their peers, or there isn't time for you to keep answering questions. The sticky notes could be stuck on the wall and you could address the questions to the full group either at an appropriate time during the lesson or towards the end.

Theory into practice

Look at Table 4.2 at the end of this chapter, which contains many more activities. Choose four and devise an activity for each which you can carry out with your learners. If possible, use them during a lesson and evaluate how effective they were and why.

Promoting appropriate behaviour and respect

Behaviour is all about how you and your learners interact with each other, which should be in an appropriate way. Respect is about accepting others for what they are, not being rude to them, or lowering their confidence and self-esteem in any way. Depending upon the age range and maturity of your learners, the subject content, and the environment in which you will teach, you might encounter issues which you will need to deal with immediately. However, it's not just about being *reactive* to a situation. You need to be *proactive* and promote appropriate behaviour and respect whenever possible, to stop issues arising in the first place.

Your organisation will have a behaviour code of practice or a policy which you should read and implement. Having ground rules in place (in Chapter 3) could help avoid any issues. Ground rules, such as not speaking when someone else is speaking, can help to create suitable conditions within which learners (and yourself) can safely work and learn.

Being a role model for good behaviour might encourage the same from your learners. This can include being polite, showing respect, and saying *please* and *thank you*. Welcoming learners to your lesson when they arrive, with a smile on your face, can give a good impression. Some teachers like to stand at the door as their learners enter. This gives an air of authority, and shows the teacher is in control. Other teachers like to shake hands with each learner as they arrive, to say hello and state the learner's name. This is a little more informal, but still shows that the teacher is in control and that they know each learner's name. This might be better than being occupied inside the room and ignoring the learners as they arrive.

It would be wonderful if you could get through a lesson without any issues arising. However, behaviour issues often occur because a learner doesn't follow the ground rules, for example, their mobile phone rings, or they do something other than that which you have asked them to do. If this is the case, politely ask them to stop, remind them of the ground rules, and how they are also disrupting their peers' learning. Your learners need to know what is acceptable, what isn't, and why.

Behaviour issues could occur because learners:

- are bored
- are not being stretched or challenged enough

- are seeking attention

- don't understand what you are saying or doing

- have a learning difficulty and/or disability

- have an attention span which is different to other learners.

Behaviour patterns could highlight the need for additional support as disruption could be a way of asking for help. You may find it useful to maintain a record of the individual behaviour of your learners during your lessons. This could help you prepare for future incidents. For example, noting a particular learner who becomes disruptive after a certain time period has elapsed, or another who becomes annoyed when asked to carry out a particular task. This information can be useful when planning future lessons: for example, the timing of breaks, the use of energiser activities, or planning who will work with whom for a paired activity. The group profile is a useful document on which to note behaviour issues.

Attitudes affecting behaviour

If you can model good behaviour, and inform your learners that you expect good behaviour from them, this should lead to a positive learning environment. If you have a positive attitude, hopefully your learners will too. They will want to learn, and will not want their peers to affect that learning. Some learners might not have engaged with education in their past, perhaps had a bad learning experience or had a teacher who could not control the group. They will therefore have returned to education not wanting these experiences repeated.

It could be that your learners are not attending your course voluntarily, perhaps if they have been told to by their employer, or they may be there for social reasons rather than having an interest in achieving something. They may therefore not be as keen as you would like them to be, and you will need to keep them continuously interested and motivated. A way of overcoming this might be to try and relate the subject to their interests and/or their personal or working life.

Betari's Cycle of Conflict

Betari's Cycle of Conflict, as in Figure 4.4, also known as Betari's Box, is about how attitude affects behaviour. For example, *my attitude affects my behaviour, which affects your attitude which affects your behaviour, which in turn affects my attitude, and so on.* It's not clear where the name Betari came from or when it was created; however, attitudes, whether positive or negative are reflected in behaviour. Positive attitudes should encourage positive behaviour in yourself, as well as in others. This can be through words and actions, verbal and non-verbal messages, and body language. If an attitude is positive, it can help others be positive, and the same will apply if it's negative.

LEARNER
BEHAVIOUR

Ensure that your learners
don't become disruptive
and difficult to manage.

TEACHER
ATTITUDE

Your attitude can
either be positive or
negative.

LEARNER
ATTITUDE

Learners' attitude can
either be positive or
negative.

TEACHER
BEHAVIOUR

Recognise that your
behaviour has impact.

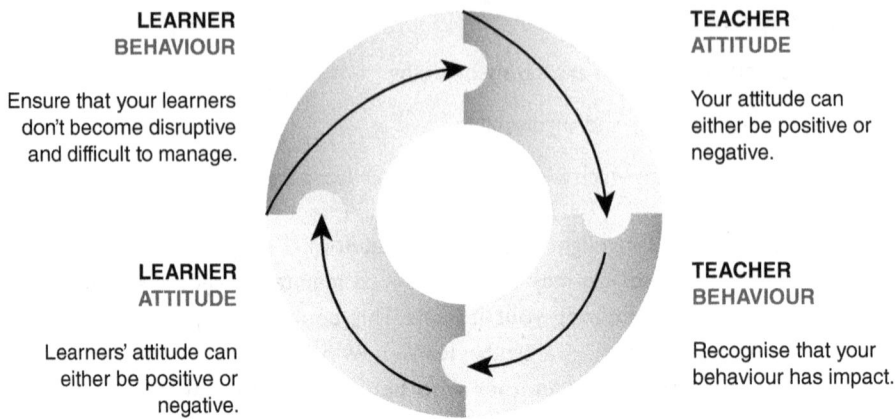

Figure 4.4 Betari's Cycle of Conflict

Example

Daisy, a learner attending a uniformed services course, really enjoys the subject. She likes being stretched and challenged and often tries new activities, makes mistakes and learns from them. Today, she has a different teacher, Robert, as her usual teacher is absent. Robert is quick to notice when Daisy is struggling and takes over what she is doing. This continues throughout the lesson. Therefore Daisy now stops when she is unsure of something and calls to Robert. This was due to Robert's attitude and behaviour towards Daisy's learning. Daisy has adapted her attitude and behaviour to fit in with Robert's.

To change the attitude and behaviour of others you may need to be aware of your own attitude and how it affects your own behaviour. You can then notice how your behaviour affects other people's attitudes and behaviour. You can break the cycle by noticing how the behaviour of others makes you do what you do, and refusing to let it affect you. You will need to recognise negative cycles and turn them into positive ones. This applies to yourself as well as to your learners.

The following are some strategies which you could use with your learners:

- allocate time at the beginning of the course, or each lesson, to find out what your learners' attitudes are to the subject i.e. have they had good or bad experiences in the past which might affect their learning?

- ensure all learners can participate and access the equipment and resources during the lesson

- hold group and individual tutorials with all learners to discuss progress and concerns

- use learners' names, use eye contact, and treat each learner as an individual

- make sure everyone is aware of relevant policies and procedures

- negotiate and agree appropriate ground rules

- schedule one-to-one discussions with learners who require additional support

- use a suitable and inclusive icebreaker, energiser, or starter activity.

There may be occasions during your lessons where behaviours exist that are offensive, directly discriminate, or are distressing to others. This behaviour may be obvious, but it can also be unintentional and subtle. It might involve a learner using nicknames, teasing, name-calling, or excluding someone. Although it might not have a malicious intent, it will still be upsetting. You will need to know what steps your organisation requires you to take, and deal with any inappropriate behaviour as it occurs. There are various ways of managing this depending on the circumstances, such as:

- challenging prejudice, discrimination, and stereotyping as it occurs

- creating an acceptable behaviour contract which learners sign up to, and revisit it regularly, perhaps as part of the ground rules

- embracing learner diversity within the group

- encouraging your learners to discuss, confidentially, their own behaviour concerns they have, for example, if they have an autism spectrum disorder

- ensuring all resources are inclusive through the use of positive images

- establishing at the start of the course what the unacceptable behaviours are.

There might also be instances where you do something inadvertently and not really think at the time how it could affect a learner. For example, by using a derogatory word or term that might have historically been acceptable, but no longer is.

Activity

Take a look at the previous bullet list. What other strategies could you use to promote positive behaviour and respect with your learners?

Motivation

Motivation is the incentive or reason why someone chooses to do something. It's useful to be aware of what motivates your learners, as their enthusiasm might affect their learning (in a positive or a negative way) and possibly their behaviour. A learner attending a lesson because they have been told to may not be as motivated as a learner who is there because they want to be. It's also useful to know what your learners are expecting from the course, as it might differ from what they will receive. Finding out the expectations of your learners and what motivates them should help you to teach the course in a way that will lead to successful learner achievement. Expectations could be ascertained during the first lesson simply by asking. If your learners' expectations don't match with what will take place, tell them why. Learners will want to know what's in it for them and why they should be there. They need to know the value of the course to them, either personally or professionally. It could be that they have been recommended to take a course or are on the wrong course and don't realise it. It's best to find this out at the beginning, rather than part way through.

Motivation is either intrinsic (from within), meaning the learner wants to learn for their own fulfilment, or extrinsic (from without), meaning there may be an external factor motivating them; for example, a promotion at work. If learners are keen and proactive towards learning, they should be self-motivated and want to learn. For example, obtaining the relevant resources and text books, asking for help when necessary, getting actively involved during lessons, and taking control of their studies. Conversely, if learners are passive, their motivation to learn will be less. For example, expecting the teacher to supply their resources, not asking for help when necessary, not participating during the lesson, and not wanting to take control of their studies. Passive learners might blame the teacher when they don't achieve something, whereas active learners might just blame themselves. If you can be positive and tell all your learners that you believe they can achieve, this will hopefully help to motivate them.

You could motivate your learners by using activities which are interactive rather than just speaking and listening. People are becoming accustomed to being more interactive due to social media. For example, some popular live television programmes encourage their audiences to get involved with online polls, and to get in touch via emails and social media. News and weather programmes also encourage interaction by asking viewers to upload pictures and videos. This way, people feel engaged, are involved, and are active rather than passive. Keeping your learners active and involved with various activities will hopefully keep them motivated.

Whatever level of motivation your learners have will be transformed, for better or worse, by what happens during their experience with you. You therefore need to promote a professional relationship that leads to individual trust and respect. Some learners may seem naturally enthusiastic about learning, but many need or expect you to inspire and engage them. It's hard to get someone to do something if they can't see a real benefit for themselves. You could try and relate the topic to something they are interested in, such as a hobby or a leisure activity. You could also relate the learning to how it will be applied in practice in the workplace. You might have stories you can tell your learners if you have worked in the subject area previously.

Helpful hint

If you can be enthusiastic and passionate about your subject, this might motivate and enthuse your learners. If not, they might wonder why they should bother attending, particularly if you are not showing interest in the subject, or are demonstrating that you are not enjoying your job.

Keeping yourself motivated might also be a challenge. There could be situations which occur which might make you feel like this isn't the job for you. It's hard work being a teacher; however, it's a very rewarding job, and you have the opportunity to help so many people. When times are hard, remember all the good you have done for your learners in the past, and will do in the future, such as helping them gain employment or becoming qualified. Make sure you have someone you can talk to, such as your mentor. Don't keep things to yourself as any problems or concerns you have might escalate in your own mind. It's probable that your mentor has also experienced what you are feeling, and can give you some useful advice. Things can and will go wrong, just learn from the experiences, be honest with yourself and remember why you wanted to be a teacher.

Maslow's (1987) Hierarchy of Needs

Maslow (1987) introduced a *Hierarchy of Needs* in 1954 which can relate to motivation and the ability to achieve something. He rejected the idea that human behaviour was determined by childhood events. He felt that obstacles should be removed that prevent a person from achieving their goals. He argued that there are five *needs* which represent different levels of motivation which must be met. The highest level was labelled *self-actualisation*, meaning people are fully functional, possess a healthy personality and take responsibility for themselves and their actions. They have achieved what they wanted to at a particular stage in their life. He also believed that people should be able to move through these needs to the highest level, provided they are given an education that promotes growth. Figure 4.5 shows the needs expressed as they might relate to learning, starting at the base of the pyramid.

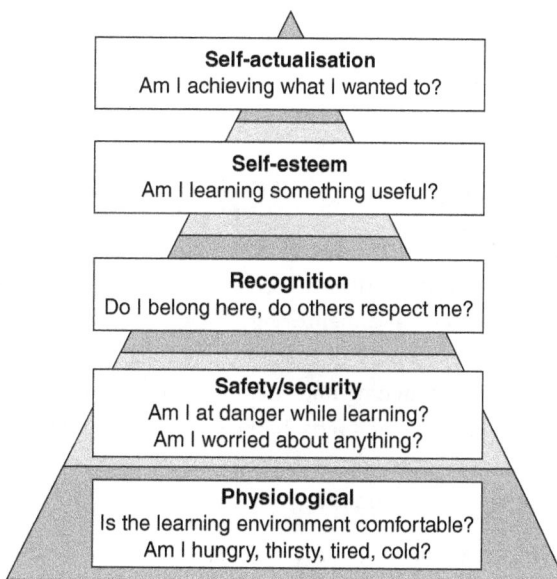

Self-actualisation
Am I achieving what I wanted to?

Self-esteem
Am I learning something useful?

Recognition
Do I belong here, do others respect me?

Safety/security
Am I at danger while learning?
Am I worried about anything?

Physiological
Is the learning environment comfortable?
Am I hungry, thirsty, tired, cold?

Figure 4.5 Maslow's (1987) Hierarchy of Needs expressed in educational terms

When learners satisfy their needs at one level, they should be able to progress to the next level. Something may set them back a level, but they should want to keep striving upwards. It is these needs that stimulate learning to take place. However, some people may not want to progress through the levels and may be quite content where they are at that moment in their life. There might also be age or cultural factors which could impact upon progression through the levels. You could think of the needs as relevant to your role too. If you are hungry, thirsty, tired, or cold as in the first level, you might not perform well.

To help your learners' motivation, try and ensure that the environment you create meets your learners' first level needs. This will enable them to feel comfortable and secure enough to learn and progress to the higher levels. You will need to appreciate that some learners may not have these lower needs met in their home lives, making it difficult for them to move on to the higher levels.

While you may be very good at teaching your subject, you might have no control over the environment, and will need to create a suitable learning climate if you can. However, your enthusiasm and passion for your subject should help engage your learners. If you can also make your lesson interesting, active, and varied, your learners will enjoy the experience and remember more about the subject and your teaching skills, rather than the environment or a lack of facilities.

Theory into practice

How can you engage and motivate your learners to progress through each level of Maslow's Hierarchy of Needs? What internal and external factors might affect a learner's motivation? How do you think these factors can be overcome?

Coaching and mentoring

Coaching and mentoring might form part of your job role, but how do these roles differ from being a teacher? You could think of coaching as providing a safe environment to explore and practise the subject, and mentoring about giving advice and support. Both of these roles could be considered part of teaching depending upon the context in which you work. Opportunities for coaching and mentoring might occur naturally. For example, demonstrating a task to a learner (coaching) or guiding a learner how to search for employment opportunities (mentoring). Both roles should be about helping the learner to become as independent and autonomous as possible.

Coaching could occur with more than one learner at the same time, whereas mentoring is usually carried out on a one-to-one basis. Both relate to knowledge, skills and behaviours.

Coaches and mentors employ similar techniques, with coaches focusing on asking, while mentors focus on advising. These are interlinked in their approaches, as in Figure 4.6, and these roles remain distinct in their methods of assisting learners. Coaching is beneficial when solutions aren't readily available, aiding learners in developing their problem-solving skills, especially if they possess extensive experience in the subject matter. Conversely, mentoring is advantageous when the learner requires access to opportunities they might not normally have, and which can be facilitated by the mentor's expertise and contacts. Additionally, mentoring is particularly effective when the mentee excels in adapting concepts to suit their unique circumstances, rather than merely replicating the learning objectives.

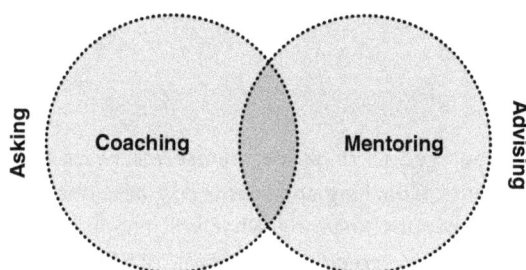

Figure 4.6 Coaching and mentoring interlinked

Helpful hint

A blend of coaching and mentoring can be beneficial to your learners. It can enable you to adapt your teaching and learning approaches based on their specific requirements for your subject specialism.

It's useful to treat the coaching and mentoring roles in a similar way to the teaching role; however, it might often take place on a one-to-one basis. It's a good idea to carry out an induction and initial assessment and to agree a few ground rules. This could include aims, objectives, targets, and timescales, and be updated as the learner progresses. Coaching and mentoring could occur spontaneously as the need arises, or be planned for certain dates and times. Both roles require patience and good communication skills.

There are three distinct areas where coaching and mentoring can be used within an educational environment.

- **Learner mentor** to support learners, in particular those with barriers to learning, supporting learners on a one-to-one basis.

- **Classroom coach** to enhance communication, support SMART objectives, engage and motivate learners to take an autonomous approach to their learning, supporting learners both individually and within a group.

- **Teacher coach** to enable experienced teachers to confidently support recently qualified teachers (RQT), newly qualified early career teachers (ECT) and returning experienced teaching practitioners.

Example

Kacie, who is Gabe's learner mentor, is due to meet him for the first time next week. They are aware of each other but they do not know each other well. They have agreed to meet for an hour to discuss what support Gabe would like from the learner mentoring process. This will help Kacie recognise the areas she can help and guide Gabe with. Future meetings will then follow a plan.

Learners should be encouraged to think for themselves, reach their own decisions and set their own action points. Coaching and mentoring sessions should always end on a positive note, with both parties knowing what will happen next. If at any stage the relationship breaks down to an irrecoverable point, the learner should be referred to someone else.

There will come a point when the learner is totally independent and no longer needs the coach or mentor. This is good, and means the learner is now confident and knowledgeable to carry out their role on their own.

Activity

What do you consider to be the differences between coaching and mentoring? Research definitions online and in text books to find out about different models and theories. You could also discuss them with your mentor to see what they think.

Advantages and disadvantages to the roles

Both roles can have similar advantages and disadvantages.

Advantages

- A professional working relationship can be built up over time.

- It can be formal or informal and occur as and when needed.

- The learner has someone to go to if they have any concerns, problems, or just need someone to talk to.

- The learner might progress more quickly with the right coaching/mentoring.

- The coach/mentor can act as a source of expertise, be an impartial listener, provide advice and guidance, and help the learner to explore issues for themselves.

- The coach/mentor can facilitate access to different experiences, activities, and people.

- The pace and approach of learning can be geared to the needs of the learner.

- The process can improve the confidence of the learner.

Disadvantages

- If unsupervised, the learner might make mistakes which could be dangerous.

- It can be time consuming.

- Resources and equipment may need to be prepared in advance.

- The learner may become dependent or reliant on the coach/mentor and not think things through for themselves.

- The learner might need support when the coach/mentor is not available.

- The learner might not feel that they can question or disagree with the coach/mentor.

- The learner might not feel that they want to do what the coach/mentor has advised.

- The coach/mentor might be frustrated if the learner does not take their advice.

- The learner might not find out different ways of performing the task, having only ever been shown one way to do it.

- The coach/mentor and the learner might not get on.

- The coach/mentor might have been assigned to the learner rather than being the right person for the role; therefore they do not take it seriously.

- The coach/mentor might resent the learner for the amount of time they take up.

Theory into practice

Imagine you are an experienced teacher who has been in the role for five years. A new teacher has just commenced at your organisation and you have been allocated to them as their mentor (or coach if you wish). What would you do first and why? How could you encourage the new teacher to become confident, knowledgeable and independent over time?

Table 4.2 Examples of teaching and learning approaches and activities

(See Table 7.1 in Chapter 7, as some assessment activities can also be used for teaching and learning)

Approach/activity	Description	Strengths	Limitations
Activities – group or individual	Different tasks related to the subject, often practical	Can be individual, paired, or group tasks to actively involve all learners Can be contextualised to be relevant and interesting for learners	Can be time consuming to devise and manage
Blended learning	Using more than one method of teaching which often includes the use of technology	Combines traditional and technological learning Formal teaching can be supported with informal learning	Not all learners may have access to the technology Some learners might prefer traditional face-to-face lessons
Buzz groups	Short topics to be discussed in small groups	Can break up a more formal lesson Enables learners to work together and focus their ideas Checks knowledge and understanding Doesn't require formal feedback Can be impromptu, or a time filler activity Once learners have spoken in a small buzz group they might have the confidence to speak in front of the full group	Learners may digress Specific points could be lost Checking individual learning may be difficult Time limits must be set Feedback should be taken from each group; otherwise they may think the activity was meaningless
Collaborative working	Involves pairs or groups of learners working together to solve problems, to create a product or to complete a task	Enables learners to work together and learn from each other Can involve the use of technology	Not all learners might want to take part Needs careful planning
Copying	Learners copy written text or what the teacher has demonstrated	A teacher-centred method which might suit some learners	It shows the learner is capable of copying something, but they might not understand what they are doing

Approach/activity	Description	Strengths	Limitations
Critical incident analysis	Learners explore something critical (which has occurred or which might occur) to understand it, and to find alternative ways of reacting and responding to it A critical incident is one which has a positive or negative effect on something or someone	Useful to help learners anticipate a situation and discuss how they would react Can challenge assumptions Gains different points of view which can be explored e.g. why learners made their decisions or arrived at certain conclusions If the analysis is based on a real incident, learners could benefit from the experience of those involved	Learners might recall aspects in a different manner to which they actually occurred The teacher needs to guide the learners to a successful conclusion
Debates	Learners or guest speakers present a case to learners, with subsequent arguments, questions and discussions	Learner-centred Allows freedom of viewpoints and can demonstrate understanding	Some learners may not get involved, others may dominate The teacher needs to manage the debate carefully and keep track of time Learners may need to research a topic in advance Can generate inappropriate behaviour
Demonstration	A practical way of showing learners how something works	Can set a good example of how to do something Can inspire learners to try it out for themselves Learners could demonstrate to each other, to show understanding Can be supported with handouts and practical activities i.e. getting the learners to do it for themselves	Equipment might not be available or in working order Learners in larger groups might not be able to see what is going on The teacher might go too fast and/or learners might miss something The demonstration can be overdone or overcomplicated if not broken down into smaller stages There might not be enough resources for all learners to have a go Some learners might be quicker or take longer than others to do it

(Continued)

Table 4.2 (Continued)

Approach/activity	Description	Strengths	Limitations
			Some learners may not pay attention or get bored watching a long demonstration
			Can be time consuming to set up
			Questions must be asked to check knowledge and understanding
			Should be supported with a handout of detailed instructions on how to use
Discovery learning	Learners try out a skill or carry out a task before being taught about it	Learners can experiment and discover aspects for themselves (providing it's safe to do so)	Careful planning is required
		A discussion can take place about what they have experienced, followed by having another go if necessary	Learners need to be gently directed and encouraged
			A clear purpose is needed
Discussion	Learners explore a topic, or the teacher can introduce a topic for the learners to discuss	All learners can participate and share knowledge and experiences	Some learners may be shy or not want to be involved
		Smaller groups could discuss different topics and then pass on their findings to the other groups for further discussion	Some learners might dominate others
		Learners might feel more comfortable talking rather than writing	Teacher needs to make sure all learners can contribute
			Teacher needs to keep the group focused
			Easy to digress
			A time limit must be set
Distance learning or open learning	Learning which takes place away from the organisation offering the course	Learning can occur at a time and place to suit the learner	Could be a long gap between submitting work for assessment and receiving feedback
	Work can be issued to learners via post, email, or a web-based application	Can be combined with other learning methods e.g. blended learning	Self-discipline is needed
			Targets must be clearly agreed
			Learner may never meet the teacher

Approach/activity	Description	Strengths	Limitations
Drawing	Illustrations to show how something works (by the teacher and/or learner)	Several drawings can be used to show how something works in a simple way Learners could draw their own version	Needs explaining carefully Some learners might not be good at drawing
e-learning/online learning	Learning which is supported or enhanced using information and communication technology (ICT) Learning which takes place in a virtual learning environment (VLE) via a device connected to an intranet or the internet	Learning can take place anywhere a digital device is available Learning can be flexible Ongoing support can be given	Learners need access to a digital device and need the skills to use it A reliable internet connection may be required Self-discipline is needed, along with clear target dates for achievement Authenticity of learner's work may need validating Technical support may be required
Experiential/experimental	Practical tasks enabling learners to act out, experience, or experiment with a particular topic	Learners can put theory into practice Learners can be in control, find out things for themselves and learn from their mistakes (if it's safe to do so) Can be exciting and engaging	Not all learners may want to participate Some learners may lack confidence or not want to embarrass themselves in front of their peers Can be time consuming
Extension activity	An additional task which can be used to stretch and challenge learners' potential further	Can be used when learners finish a task earlier than others during a lesson Ideal for differentiation Can be used to extend a learner's thinking about a topic	Some learners might feel pressured to complete them when they are not able to i.e. peer pressure Can be demeaning if some learners see others completing them; they may feel left behind, or unable to achieve
Flexible learning	Learning that can take place at a time and place to suit the learner and/or using different teaching approaches within a lesson to meet particular challenges	Suits learners who cannot attend formal lessons Ideal for varying the pace of a lesson	Ongoing support and monitoring of achievement is required Not all learners are motivated to this style of learning

(Continued)

Table 4.2 (Continued)

Approach/activity	Description	Strengths	Limitations
Flipped learning	The work normally carried out during an attended lesson is flipped with what would be carried out elsewhere e.g. swapping classwork and homework	Enables discussions to take place during the lesson based on what has been learnt outside of the lesson	Requires learners to carry out what is required before attending the lesson Some learners might not feel comfortable studying outside of the lesson, or lack motivation to do so Takes time for the teacher to plan what the learners will do as homework, and to manage the activities during the class lesson
Games/gaming	A fun way of learning to enable problem solving and decision making to take place	Board or card games can be designed to make learning enjoyable Physical games put theory into practice Online games can develop digital skills Can be used to open or close a lesson Encourages interaction and healthy competition	Needs to be well planned in advance Learners need to remain focused and all should be given a chance to take part Objectives need to be clear Careful supervision is needed Game rules should be followed
Gapped handout	Blank spaces within a handout for learners to fill in the missing words from sentences	Different versions for different levels of learners could be devised Useful to fill in time during a lesson	Some learners might find it too easy Learners who complete them slowly might get left behind
Group work	Enables learners to carry out a specific activity by working with others	Allows interaction between learners Learners learn from each other's experiences and knowledge Encourages participation and variety Rotating group members over time enables all learners to work with each other Can be practical or theoretical	Careful management by the teacher is required regarding who is in the groups All group members need to be clear regarding the requirements Potential for personality clashes One person may dominate Time limits must be set Learners might get left out or be too shy to contribute

Approach/activity	Description	Strengths	Limitations
			Ground rules might be needed to keep the group on track
			Time is needed for a thorough debrief and feedback
Guest speakers	An expert in the subject area speaks to the learners	Can add variety and expertise to a topic from someone with a different perspective to the teacher	Must be arranged well in advance
		A discussion can take place beforehand regarding what questions the learners want to ask the speaker	Some speakers may charge a fee or cancel beforehand
			Time should be allowed for questions and discussions
			Some learners might ask inappropriate questions
Guided learning	Creates a bridge between whole group learning and independent learning with guidance from the teacher	Enables learning to take place in a group context, followed by individual independent learning	Not all learners like this method
			Needs careful planning and timing
Handouts	Written and/or visual information/ drawings/text/pictures to promote and support learning	Useful for learners to refer to after a lesson	Should be used in conjunction with other activities
		Can incorporate questions for learners to answer as a homework or self-study activity	Need to be adapted for any special learner requirements e.g. a visual impairment
		Can be differentiated	Should be produced well in advance
		More information could be covered in handouts which is not covered during the lesson	Spelling, grammar, punctuation, and syntax must be accurate
			Relies on the learner reading and understanding the content
Homework	Activities carried out between lessons e.g. further reading and research	Learners can complete at a time and place that suits them	Target dates must be set
	Learning doesn't have to stop just because the lesson has ended	Maintains interest between lessons	Learners might not do it
		Encourages learners to stretch and challenge themselves further	Must be discussed, or marked/assessed and individual feedback given; otherwise learners might feel it's meaningless

(Continued)

Table 4.2 (Continued)

Approach/activity	Description	Strengths	Limitations
Interactive whiteboard	Teachers and/or learners use a board with various technological functions including linking to the internet	Ideal for group work and presentations	Not all learners can use it at the same time, or might not know how to use it Not all learners might be able to see what is taking place
Journal or diary	Learners keep a record of their progress, their reflections, and thoughts	Develops self-assessment skills Relates theory to practice (if learners are undertaking work experience) Helps assess English skills	Should be specific to the learning taking place and be analytical rather than descriptive Learners need to be guided as to how to write in a particular way to meet the criteria Content needs to remain confidential between the teacher and learner Can be time consuming to read
Lecture	Traditional *teacher-centred* technique of imparting information	Ideal for imparting knowledge to large groups Useful for teaching theoretical subjects Key points can be prepared in advance, perhaps on small cards as prompts to read Can be supported with videos, images, text, and sounds Useful if learners need to know a lot about a topic in a short time	Learners are passive, they might not listen, and may lose concentration Learners may not feel they can interrupt or ask questions to clarify points Learners need good listening and note-taking skills Good voice projection and clarity of speech is required by the teacher Learners need to work at the pace of the teacher Difficult to know if learning has taken place
Micro-teaching	A short teaching and learning lesson Usually a simulated lesson taught by a trainee teacher in front of their peer group	Enables learners to practise in a safe environment Can be recorded to aid self-evaluation Peer feedback can be given	Not all learners enjoy the experience Recording equipment, if used, can be difficult to manage while observing learners Some peers might not give constructive feedback, or know how to

Approach/activity	Description	Strengths	Limitations
Mind maps/ spider grams	A visual way of organising information and making plans, learners can draw a circle with a key point in the middle of a page. They then branch from this with subheadings to explore and develop aspects further	Learners are active Topics can be explored in a fun and meaningful way Links between ideas are easy to see New information can easily be added Can be created by using technology	Not all learners may want to contribute or understand what to do One learner may dominate Needs careful supervision Large-sized paper, a board, and marker pens or electronic devices are required
Models	Useful where the real object cannot be seen Life models can be used e.g. in art classes, or machinery models in engineering	Learners have a chance to see how something looks and/or works, and to ask questions	Must be clearly explained and demonstrated May require funding to purchase Needs careful planning and preparation
Paired work	Enables learners to carry out a specific activity with a peer e.g. problem solving or checking each other's work Can be practical or theoretical	Allows interaction between learners Learners learn from each other Encourages participation and variety Pairs can link up as fours and so on to share their experiences and knowledge (known as snowballing) Tasks could be differentiated to stretch and challenge particular learners	Careful management by the teacher is required regarding time limits Each pair must be clear about the requirements Learners need to get along with each other The teacher could nominate who will work together, perhaps placing one knowledgeable learner with one less so Difficult to assess individual contributions Time is needed for feedback from each pair and to check what they have achieved
Peer learning/tasks	Learners gaining skills and/or knowledge from their peers Learners setting tasks for their peers to carry out	Helps learners to engage with the subject Enables learners to work together in an informal way to learn from each other's experiences and knowledge	There may be personality clashes between learners which prevent learning taking place Not all information given by learners may be correct

(Continued)

Table 4.2 (Continued)

Approach/activity	Description	Strengths	Limitations
		Learners can support each other throughout the lesson or course Learners can create tasks based upon the topic, and provide feedback to each other	If learners are creating tasks, they will need to fully understand the topic/subject If learners are providing feedback, they must understand how to do it effectively
Plenary	An opportunity to summarise the lesson, recap what has been learnt, and relate it to the aims and objectives	Could be combined with a closing activity to gain feedback from the learners Formally ends the lesson and links to the next lesson (if applicable)	Enough time has to be planned for it
Podcast	A digital audio file which can be uploaded to the internet, based on a particular topic	Can supplement learning for many topics Learners can listen at a time to suit them	Some learners might not be able to access them, or have the skills to
Pose, pause, pick questioning technique	Ask a question, then pause for a few seconds so that all learners are thinking about a response. Then pick a learner to answer the question by stating their name	Enables all learners to consider the answer if they think they might be asked	Chosen learner might not know the answer
Problem solving	Enabling learners to find things out for themselves	Helps learners to become more autonomous and take responsibility for their own learning Enables learners to communicate with others if working in pairs or groups	Needs careful planning of what is required Timings need to be specified and kept to
Presentations	Similar to a lecture with greater use of audio-visual aids	Interaction can take place between the teacher and learners Effective use of media can make presentations stimulating, motivating, and inspiring Learners could carry out research and present their findings to others, rather than the teacher doing it	Some learners may not pay attention or might get distracted Too many slides with too much detail can be daunting, learners often read the slides rather than listening to what is being said Needs to be interactive and to the pace of the learners; otherwise they might be left behind or get bored

Approach/activity	Description	Strengths	Limitations
Reading	Learners work from relevant texts/books/journals, and other suitable documents including online reading	Learners could choose what they wish to read providing it is relevant Learners can read to themselves or out loud to the group, however, the latter might demoralise some learners who lack confidence at speaking in front of others Learners can explain to the teacher and/or each other how they have understood a topic Learners could write a summary of the main points and identify any mistakes or misconceptions Encourages further learning	Reading and note-taking skills are required Learners can get bored or easily distracted May need to have differentiated texts to account for a range of levels within the group
Repetition, reciting or rote learning	Learners repeat aspects such as important figures, dates, or poems For example, the times tables: 1 x 6 is 6, 2 x 6 is 12 and so on	A good way of remembering useful figures, facts or poems	Does not test knowledge and understanding, only the ability to repeat, recite, or recall something
Reports	Learners produce a document to inform, recommend, and/or make suggestions based on a given topic	Useful for higher level learners Encourages the use of research techniques	Good writing skills and the use of referencing might be required Learners need to interpret and evaluate key points to demonstrate their understanding
Research	An in-depth way of finding out answers or obtaining more information regarding a topic	Learners can use the internet, read text books, access journals and other documents during class time or in their own time Learners could choose what they want to research providing it is relevant	Learners need to know how to research and what to do with their findings Learners might not know how to apply their research to real situations Time is needed to check what has been researched and to ensure it is relevant

(Continued)

Table 4.2 (Continued)

Approach/activity	Description	Strengths	Limitations
Rhyme, rap, and mnemonics	Reciting, recalling, and creating phrases or songs to aid memory For example, *30 days has September, April, June, and November* Mnemonics can be based on the first letter of words, for example, the colours of the rainbow could be: *ROY G BIV which stands for: red, orange, yellow, green, blue, indigo, violet*	Learners can create their own phrases or songs to help them remember points Can be fun	Can seem trivial to some learners Does not test knowledge and understanding, only the ability to recite, recall, or create something
Role play	A practical activity to demonstrate learning Can be used to act out a hypothetical situation or scenario to see how learners would respond	Can see how a learner reacts to certain situations Can help improve self-confidence Encourages participation in a safe environment Can be a fun method of learning Can lead to debates Links theory to practice Gives learners the opportunity to demonstrate communication skills Learners can observe and give peer feedback	Can be time consuming to plan and manage Clear roles must be defined Not all learners may want or be able to participate Time limit should be set Some learners may get too dramatic Time is needed for a thorough debrief Individual contributions must be assessed
Seminars	A presentation of ideas, followed by questions and a discussion	An informal teaching approach If a learner leads the seminar, it can help them to gain confidence at speaking to their peers Can lead to worthwhile discussions	Learners need specific topics or a paper/thesis to present Teachers need to agree topics well in advance, along with a running order of who will lead first A time limit needs to be set and kept to Some learners might not pay attention or want to participate

Approach/activity	Description	Strengths	Limitations
Simulation	An imitation activity carried out when the real activity would be too dangerous For example, the evacuation of a building when the fire alarm goes off: there's no need to set fire to the building for a simulated evacuation	Enables learners to demonstrate what they might do in a real situation Learners may realise things about themselves they were not aware of	Careful planning is needed Can be time consuming Specialist equipment may be needed Not all learners may be able to participate fully May not be taken seriously by some learners Thorough debrief needed
Starter/closing activity	A short activity at the beginning or end of a lesson It could be a quiz to test knowledge gained so far, a discussion to open up thinking about the current subject, or an energiser activity focusing upon the current lesson topic	If a learner arrives late or leaves early, they only miss the activity Can be used as extension activities	Some learners might feel it's trivial or wasting their time unless they can see how it relates to the subject
Surveys	Gaining information from others	The survey can be created by the teacher to gain feedback from learners either online, written, or verbally Surveys can be short or long term Learners can design and use a survey to find things out from others	Permission may be required depending on the type of survey used Ethics and confidentiality required Quality of question content is important Could be time consuming to analyse
Tasks	Practical or theoretical activities carried out by an individual, in pairs, or a group, which are relevant to the topic being taught	Learners are active Useful backup activity if spare time is available Can be individual, paired, or group-based Can develop group interaction, communication, and learner confidence Learners can relate the activities to real life situations Help and advice can be given as needed	Can be time consuming to plan and prepare Not all learners may want to participate Clear objectives should be set The task must be clearly explained Time limit required Time needed for feedback or a debrief

(Continued)

Table 4.2 (Continued)

Approach/activity	Description	Strengths	Limitations
Task analysis/skills analysis	The breakdown of a task or a job into its smaller component parts	Demonstrates or lists a logical progression, or an order of something Enables learners to follow a precise order	Time consuming to think about and break down Some aspects could be missed
Team-teaching (co-teaching or collaborative teaching)	Teaching a lesson with a colleague	Enables learners to see different teaching and learning approaches Teachers can bring their experiences to the learning process, as well as personal anecdotes Shares the responsibility of a lesson between teachers	Some learners might get confused with more than one teacher in the room Teachers need to carefully plan who will do what and when One teacher might dominate Teachers might not communicate well together
Technology-based learning (also see blended learning, and e-learning/online learning)	Using relevant equipment, media, and materials e.g. those which incorporate visual, audio and digital uses	Enables learners to be active, if finding things out themselves Can generate discussions and improve communication Gives learners responsibility for their own learning	Can be time consuming to plan and prepare Learners need to remain focused Learners may need to be supervised There could be a lack of equipment/devices A reliable internet connection might be needed
Tutorial reviews	A one-to-one or group discussion between the teacher and the learner/s with an agreed purpose e.g. discussing progress and achievements so far	A good way of informally assessing a learner's progress and/or providing feedback An opportunity for learners to discuss issues or for informal tuition to take place	Needs to be in a comfortable, safe, and quiet environment as confidential issues may be discussed Tutorial time may overrun Records should be maintained and action points followed up

Approach/activity	Description	Strengths	Limitations
Undoing	Learners can undo or take apart an object to learn how it was put together An example is taking a plug apart to see how it was originally wired	Good for developing practical skills Needs to be demonstrated by the teacher first Useful in practical lessons	Objects/resources need to be available for all learners Needs to be supported with further information and careful guidance Risk assessment may be needed
Viewing e.g. a video/TV/DVD/ webinar and online recordings	Watching a recording or a live programme via various media including the internet	Can be used to show good and bad practice to generate discussions Can show alternative ways of doing something if the teacher does not have the resources to do this Learners could make and then watch a recording of themselves performing a task, and identify what needs improving, or give peer feedback	Not interactive All learners need to be in a position to see the screen and hear the sound Doesn't demonstrate understanding, only the ability to watch Some learners might not pay attention Extra tasks should be set or questions asked to check knowledge and understanding
Virtual learning environment (VLE)	An online platform for teachers to upload learning materials to, and interact with learners	Enables learners to access materials outside the lessons Can be used for online learning instead of attending lessons Allows online interaction between learners and the teacher Assignments can be accessed by learners and uploaded once complete The teacher can provide feedback via the VLE and records are automatically maintained	Not all learners might be computer literate or have the skills to use it Not all learners have internet access

(Continued)

Table 4.2 (Continued)

Approach/activity	Description	Strengths	Limitations
Visits/field trips	Learners visit a venue relevant to the subject, such as a museum	Learners can be involved with fact finding and planning Can be active, interesting, and stimulating Makes the subject real Can put theory into practice Can be discussed in subsequent lessons Can link with projects and assignments Can be a welcome change to routine	Needs careful planning Organisational and health and safety procedures must be followed Needs finance e.g. for transport or entrance fees Learners need to be well briefed and prepared Ground rules must be agreed for how learners will behave Supervision usually required Debrief needed
Worksheets	Interactive documents which learners read, followed by responding to questions or carrying out practical activities	Informal activity which can be completed individually, in pairs, or groups Helps put theory into practice Useful for lower level learners or to set as homework or self-study material Can be created at different degrees of difficulty to address differentiation	Some learners may consider them inappropriate Too many worksheets can be boring to some learners Learners might not be stretched and challenged enough
Workshops	An opportunity to share practice, use activities, and develop knowledge and understanding in a real or simulated working environment	Enables learners to work at their own pace in a safe environment Learners can support each other and learn from each other's experiences	Individual support and supervision might be required Suitable worksheets/activities might need to be produced to enable learners to progress at their own pace

Summary

This chapter has explored:

- Learning theories, models and principles
- Planning lessons
- Teaching and learning approaches and activities
- Promoting appropriate behaviour and respect
- Coaching and mentoring

5

Fostering inclusive learning through resources

Putting theory into practice when using resources

Introduction

Resources are all the items which you can use to aid the effective teaching, learning, and assessment of your subject specialism. They should be used to foster inclusive learning, and to enable the acquisition of knowledge, skills, and understanding.

Resources should stimulate learning, reinforce points, add impact, and promote interest in your subject.

This chapter will introduce you to the following topics:

- The purpose of resources
- Creating, using, and adapting resources
- Assistive resources
- Evaluating resources

Occupational Standards covered in Chapter 5

Duties	Knowledge	Skills	Behaviours
D1, D2, D3, D4, D5, D6, D7, D8	K4, K6, K11	S2, S8, S12, S21, S22	B3

The purpose of resources

There should be a purpose to all the resources you use; they should not be used just for the sake of it. Their use should lead to increased knowledge, skills, and understanding. All resources should be safe, relevant, accessible, and inclusive, as well as being at the right level for your learners. Too often teaching is worksheet and handout driven. This might be easier for the teacher, but it could be boring for the learners.

Example

Tom is a new teacher and has been relying on visual presentations and handouts during his lessons. This is what his teachers used with him when he was at college, and he wasn't aware of what else could be used. After a meeting with his mentor, he realised that there are lots of other resources available to him. These should make his lessons much more interesting, engaging, and motivating for his learners.

Resources can be used to (in alphabetical order):

- add variety
- allow for differentiation, equality, diversity and inclusivity
- consolidate and identify gaps in learning
- create interest
- enable learners to try things out for themselves
- encourage and stimulate learner interest
- help with revision and aid memory
- increase knowledge, skills, and understanding
- inspire, engage, excite, and motivate learners
- provide relevant information
- reinforce key points

- stretch and challenge the capability of learners

- stimulate the senses e.g. sight, hearing, touch, smell, and taste

- support teaching, learning, and assessment.

Depending upon where you will teach i.e. a classroom or a workshop, there should be some resources already available for your use, such as an interactive whiteboard, a piece of equipment, or a flip chart stand and paper. There might be some external resources your learners could benefit from accessing which could give them valuable insights into your subject. For example, visiting a museum or exhibition (perhaps in their own time). Make sure you discuss the experience with your learners afterwards and/or ask them to write about it. This way, you can check what they have learnt and what impact it has had. You should also evaluate how successful the experience was for them.

You should always have a clear rationale to justify the resources you use. Using the: *who, what, when, where, why,* and *how* rationale is a good basis for determining how relevant, purposeful and effective your resource will be.

Activity

Think of a resource you would like to use with your learners for a particular topic. For example, a piece of equipment. What is its purpose? Write a rationale using: who, what, when, where, why, and how. This should help you to focus on its relevance to the topic.

If you will be demonstrating how to use a piece of equipment, keep what you say as simple as you can. You will be familiar with it, but it might be the first time your learner has seen it. After a learner has used it, you could ask them to demonstrate its use to another learner, if safe to do so. This would show you what they have learnt.

Helpful hint

After demonstrating how to use a piece of equipment, ask your learners to write a set of instructions on how to use it. This would reinforce their learning in their own words, and they could test it out on each other.

There are many types of resources which you could use, and several examples are listed in Table 5.1. (See Chapter 5 regarding using digital and online resources.)

Table 5.1 Examples of resources

Information and communication technology	Objects	External resources	People	Other
• 3D printers	• Animals	• Cinema/theatre/concert	• Internal e.g.	• Advertisements
• Audio, visual, and digital recorders	• Apparatus	• Conferences	colleagues, teachers,	• Binoculars
• Augmented reality	• Artefacts	• Events	trainers, managers,	• Books
• Blogs, vlogs, podcasts, forums, wikis	• Engines	• Exhibitions	mentors, technicians,	• Catalogues
• Calculators	• Games and	• Field trips	administrative staff,	• Card sort activities
• CDROMs/DVDs	board games	• Lectures	support staff	• Comics
• Computers/laptops/netbooks/	• Laminator	• Libraries	• External e.g.	• Drones
tablets/smartphones	• Machines	• Museums	employers, guest	• Epidiascope
• Digital cameras	• Models	• Specialist shops	speakers, supervisors,	• Food and cooking ingredients
• Gaming	• Plants	• Sports/leisure centres	work-based	• Gapped handouts
• Handheld devices	• Puppets		witnesses	• Handouts
• Interactive whiteboards	• Robotics	**Visual aids**	• Friends and relatives	• Headsets
• Internet/Intranet	• Robots	• Chalk board	• Information, advice	• Information leaflets
• Microscope	• Samples of	• Charts	and guidance, and	• Instruction, guidance, and training sheets
• Mobile phones and smartphones	products	• Display board	careers staff	• Instruction books
• Personal digital assistants	• Specimens	• Electronic boards	• Learners	• Journals
• Photocopier	• Sports	• Flannel/sticky/magnetic	• Manufacturers and	• Magazines
• Programs, software, and	equipment	boards	suppliers	• Manuals
applications	• Subject-specific	• Flip chart paper and	• Other professionals	• Newspapers
• Radio	resources	pens	such as agency staff,	• Original documents
• Scanners	• The *real thing*	• Learning wall	quality assurers,	• Periodicals
• Social networking sites	• Tools	• Maps	awarding organisation	• Photocopies of documents
• Television	• Toys	• Mini whiteboards	personnel, subject	• Promotional literature
• Video conferencing		• Overhead projectors	experts, language	• Publicity materials
• Virtual learning environment (VLE)		(OHPs)	interpreters	• Puzzles and quizzes
• Virtual/mixed reality goggles		• Posters	• Volunteers	• Reference books
• Visual presentations		• Projectors	• Yourself	• Reports
• Voting technology		• Photographs		• Stationery
• Wearable technology		• Presentation software		• Telescope
• Webcam		• Slides		• Text books
		• Videos		• Wordsearches/crosswords
		• Whiteboard		• Worksheets/workbooks

Theory into practice

Take a look at Table 5.1. Which resources are relevant for your subject and are available for you to use? If you are currently teaching, choose three and use them with your learners. Evaluate how effective they were and why.

Creating, using, and adapting resources

Creating, using, and adapting resources requires an in-depth knowledge of the subject you will be teaching. This is to ensure that they are relevant and fit for purpose. Once you know what resources are currently available, you will have a starting point. It might be that you are based in the same room for all your lessons, which has suitable equipment and resources within it. Some equipment might be out of date, but still useable. If there isn't enough funding to purchase the latest piece of equipment, it might be that there is a video available online which your learners could watch. Some equipment might be available in other areas of the building which you could take your learners to. Alternatively, you could contact local organisations to see if your learners could visit to see their equipment in operation, for example, the latest printing equipment at the local newspaper offices. You could also ask if they have any relevant equipment or resources which they no longer need. Often, organisations will be happy to donate to educational organisations.

If you use handouts and learning materials, the content should be appropriate in terms of level, quality, quantity, and be relevant to the subject and the learning which is expected. Text and pictures should portray all aspects of society i.e. people from different races and cultures, and who are able-bodied and disabled. You should always check the spelling, grammar, and punctuation of all content; otherwise you could come across as unprofessional. If you are unsure, ask a colleague to read it for you, as online spelling and grammar checkers are not always accurate.

You might have created or adapted your own or a colleague's resources in the past, either based on feedback, the success (or otherwise) of their use, or to meet an individual learner's needs. However, you will need to make sure that they are still fresh, professional-looking, and current i.e. reflecting the latest developments regarding your subject.

Resources, such as visual presentations, handouts, and worksheets, could be created by a team of staff who all teach the same subject or topic. There's no point you creating a handout if there is one available already. These could be held centrally, or saved remotely for electronic sharing and updating. Always make sure that you have a backup copy in case of any access issues. If you attend standardisation meetings (in Chapter 7) with colleagues, this would be a good time to find out what is available and what can be created, shared, or updated.

Before you create any of your own resources, such as handouts, take a look online for any which relate to your subject. There are lots of resources and learning materials freely available. Resources can also be created using artificial intelligence (AI – in Chapter 6).

You will probably need to purchase some resources to assist your job role, unless there is funding available, or the items are freely given to staff. These could include a small clock, memory stick, pens, plastic wallets, scissors, stapler, sticky notes, and whiteboard markers. It's always useful to have spare pens in case a learner forgets to bring their own.

People as resources

Other teachers, your colleagues, and guest speakers can be effective resources as they can provide interesting information to aid learning. For example, a guest speaker from a local organisation could talk to your learners about their current experiences of working in the subject area.

Example

Rosie teaches motor vehicle studies and has invited a friend of hers, George, who works in a local garage, to talk to her learners. The topic was customer service. George talked about what it's like to deal with members of the public who bring their vehicles in for repair. Rosie's learners asked lots of questions and enjoyed the anecdotes George told them. Feedback to Rosie from her learners was that they enjoyed listening to someone different, who was working in the industry they wish to be employed in.

Learners can also be considered as a valuable resource. Those who have completed their course could be asked to return to give a talk to your current learners. Learners could ask questions about how the course helped them personally and professionally, how to apply for jobs, and what it's like working in the industry.

Meeting individual needs through the use of resources

Some learners might have individual needs which you will need to take into account when using resources. This information should ideally have been ascertained via initial assessment (in Chapter 3). For example, you might have learners with different levels of knowledge and experience within the same group. You could create an activity for everyone to carry out, but which is slightly different. For example, a gapped handout for lower level learners to fill in the missing words, a wordsearch for intermediate level learners, and a complex cross-word for higher level learners.

You will also need to consider the fact that some learners might not have access to certain resources away from your lessons, such as the internet or relevant text books. If some learners can't afford to purchase any resources which are a requirement of the course, you could ask at your organisation if there is any funding available to help them.

Depending upon your learners' needs, you might need to differentiate some of the resources you use. For example, a learner who has dyslexia or visual stress might prefer a handout in a larger-sized font which is printed on pastel-coloured paper. Rather than do this for one learner, you could do it for all your learners. This way, no one is singled out. You could also check whether left justified text is easier for them to read, rather than fully justified text.

You might need to consider how adaptable your resources can be to stretch and challenge your learners, and how they could be used in other contexts. A handout you use with your current group might or might not be suitable for use with another group, even if it's for the same subject. Therefore, resources may need to be adapted to suit any changes or develop-ments which may occur in the future regarding your subject.

Activity

How can you ensure that the resources you use will be relevant and appropriate to support the individual needs of your learners?

Intellectual property protection

If you create resources as part of your job role (even if it's during your own time), you might find that your work contract entitles your organisation to have the rights over them. Copyright, designs, patents, and trademarks are all types of intellectual property protection. Some types of protection can apply automatically, for example, writing the word *copyright* along with your name and the date, on any original work you produce. This could be useful to protect blogs or magazine articles you write, and handouts which you create.

If you are using, adapting, or copying the work of others, you will need to check that you are not in breach of any copyright legislation. The Copyright, Designs and Patent Act (1998) in the UK covers the copying, adapting, and distributing of materials, including applications and materials found via the internet. It may be that you will have to ask the author's permission to use their materials, and they may need to be acknowledged on your resource. You will need to be very careful if you are copying anything via the internet or a chat generator (in Chapter 6). The source might not be reliable, or you could accidentally plagiarise the work of others.

Organisations can apply for a licence to photocopy a small amount of books or periodicals for use with learners. You will need to find out if this applies where you work, in case you are planning to photocopy extracts.

Create a visual presentation, handout, worksheet, or instruction sheet for a topic you will teach. Alternatively, create a handout but differentiate its complexity for different levels of learning. If you are currently teaching, use the resource with your learners and ask for their feedback to evaluate its appropriateness.

Assistive resources

Assistive resources can include anything that will assist your learner and the learning process. For example, a desk that can be raised higher to accommodate a wheelchair, or a handout printed in a large font for easier reading.

Example

Sam noticed that one of his learners, Geoff, was often quiet when group discussions took place. He asked Geoff during the break if anything was worrying him. Geoff felt embarrassed but said that he had a hearing problem. Sam spoke to the learner support department, who arranged for the lessons to take place in another room. This room was fitted with a hearing loop which was compatible with Geoff's hearing aid.

Whenever possible, you will need to find out what you can about your learners to be able to effectively support them. Initial and diagnostic assessment will help with this (in Chapter 3), as will the interview process before they commence the course, and ongoing reviews of progress. For example, a learner may wish to bring their own assistance resources and/or assistance dog, or an interpreter.

Activity

Look at the following bullet points. If you are not familiar with any, ask a colleague or carry out some research as to how you could use them to assist your learners.

Assistive resources include (in alphabetical order):

- adjustable seating
- audio books
- braille smart watches
- communication boards e.g. using images and diagrams instead of text
- computers with special screens, keyboards, and pointing devices
- desks on risers to accommodate a wheelchair
- digital voice and video recorders

- grab tools to reach for small items

- hearing loops and hearing aids

- items for left-handed use

- laser readers/pens to convert text to sounds i.e. to help with the pronunciation of words and to read text out loud

- mobility devices to help a learner move around

- motion input software such as those activated by eye movement

- positioning/attaching devices for keeping things securely in place

- screen overlays and magnifiers

- smartphone applications such as those which translate speech to sign language, or English to other languages (and vice versa)

- talking clocks

- technology and speciality software e.g. voice recognition, text to speech, speech to text, braille translation

- tinted glasses/screens/overlays for learners who have dyslexia, visual stress, or Irlen Syndrome.

Helpful hint

Your learners will be best placed to know what works for them, so never be afraid to ask them. However, always consider what they can do, not what they can't do. It could be that they have a particular need, a learning difficulty and/or a disability that can be supported by using various assistive resources.

Other items which can help in the learning environment include: ramps, lifts, grab bars, automatic door openers, hoists, remote switches, senses, and remote controls. It might be possible to borrow, hire, or lease some specialist equipment if this option is available to you.

Theory into practice

If you are currently teaching, find out what assistive resources are available for you and your learners to use. You may need some training to use a particular item. Never be afraid to admit if you don't know how to use something.

Evaluating resources

It's useful to evaluate (in Chapter 9) the resources you have used in order to improve or amend them. For example, it could be that a handout you used was not read thoroughly by your learners because there was too much text, or the language used was too complex.

Alternatively, it could be that you used a working model to demonstrate something but it didn't function on the day.

Helpful hint

Ask your learners how useful a particular resource was for their learning. You might have thought it was effective, but your learners didn't.

It's best to practise with your resources in advance of using them with your learners, just in case anything could go wrong. Always have a contingency plan if this happens.

Example

Agata designed a card activity to use with her political history learners. She printed two sets of cards, one with key dates on, and the other with the events which occurred on each date. She created four sets of each, for use with four small groups of learners. She had planned for her learners to match each date card with the relevant event card. However, when the groups were struggling, she realised she had given two groups all the date cards, and the other two groups all the event cards. This caused confusion and wasted time.

This example shows that had Agata checked all the cards were grouped accurately, this would not have happened.

Activity

At your next meeting with your mentor, ask them how they evaluate the resources they use for their particular subject. What can you learn from your discussion to help you evaluate the use of resources for your subject?

After evaluating how effective a resource was, you can make any necessary changes before using it again. You might find the following checklist useful.

Checklist for evaluating resources

- ☐ What was the purpose of the resource and was this achieved?
- ☐ Did the resource do what I expected? If not, why not?
- ☐ How did it support and reinforce learning?
- ☐ Were all learners able to access and use it correctly? If not why not?

☐   Was there enough of everything for everyone? If not, why not?

☐   Did it motivate the learners to want to achieve more? If not, why not?

☐   Was it up to date and relevant to the subject? If not, why not?

☐   Was it active or passive? Do my learners prefer to be actively engaged when using resources, such as a working model, rather than passively reading a handout?

☐   Was it easy for me to create? If not, why not?

☐   Can I update/adapt it easily? If not, why not?

☐   If it was a document/visual presentation, did I (or the learners) notice any mistakes? How can I ensure there are no errors?

☐   Can I share it with others? If so, who and why?

☐   Did I encounter any problems setting it up and using it? If yes, how can I ensure this doesn't happen again?

☐   Was it too time consuming or cumbersome to use?

☐   Was it of a high quality and did it look professional?

☐   Did it cause any confusion or was anything ambiguous?

☐   What were the overall strengths and limitations?

Theory into practice

If you are currently teaching, use a resource with your learners (perhaps one that you have never used before to challenge yourself). Make sure that you have a contingency plan. Use it with your learners and then evaluate it by using the previous checklist. What would you change and why?

Summary

This chapter has explored:

- The purpose of resources
- Creating, using, and adapting resources
- Assistive resources
- Evaluating resources

6

Embracing digital and online technologies

Putting theory into practice when using digital and online pedagogies

---

Introduction

Embracing and using digital and online technologies for your teaching role can help you to organise and simplify various tasks, and make the learning process more interesting.

Technology is rapidly developing and improving, and both you and your learners will need to embrace and use it in a relevant and safe way.

This chapter will introduce you to the following topics:

- The role of digital and online technology in education
- Pedagogical skills and knowledge
- Artificial intelligence
- Social networking, social media, and online safety

Duties	Knowledge	Skills	Behaviours
D1, D3, D4, D5, D8	K10, K14, K20	S7, S8, S9, S21, S25	B1

The role of digital and online technology in education

Digital technology should be used whenever possible to engage, inspire, and stimulate your learners to help improve their knowledge, skills and behaviours. It can also be really useful to support your role as a teacher, and to assess that learning has taken place. However, its use should have a purpose, and not be relied on as a means to entertain learners or used to unnecessarily fill in time.

Learners today live in a world of easy access to the internet and often use devices and/or smartphones as part of their everyday activities. Therefore you will need to consider how you can incorporate their relevant use into your lessons. However, don't be too keen to overload your learners by using too much too soon. It's important to get the balance right by using other resources and activities to complement its use.

You might have some learners who know more than others, or know more than you. This is nothing to be concerned about and can be used to your advantage. For example, you could ask an experienced learner to demonstrate an activity to other learners. This could generate a discussion and enable you to benefit as well as your learners. Don't be embarrassed to tell your learners that you don't know how to use something. It's best to be honest than to bluff your way through. Your learners will respect you for being truthful and will often be happy to share their knowledge. It could be that your subject doesn't lend itself to using technology. If this is the case, you could ask your learners to carry out some research via the internet regarding a particular topic. They might find some interesting facts or videos to help them.

Example

Matt is a music teacher who usually sits with his learners to demonstrate how to play various instruments. He wondered how he could embrace the use of technology to make his lessons more interesting. He decided to ask his learners to research four online videos as a homework activity. He asked them to choose an instrument of their choice to see how others demonstrate its use, and to report back on how effective the videos were. The activity worked well, and Matt now regularly uses online videos during his lessons, as well as setting research activities as homework.

Digital technology can make a huge difference to the teaching, learning, and assessment process. It can make things easier, for example, uploading course materials to an online platform for learners to access during the lesson, rather than using paper copies. Many aspects of your role could be carried out digitally, such as completing the attendance register, marking work, providing feedback, and messaging colleagues. There are limitations as well as strengths regarding using digital and online technology, as in Table 6.1.

Table 6.1 Examples of strengths and limitations of using digital and online technology (in alphabetical order)

Strengths	Limitations
• ability to create, copy, and paste text, data and images • accessible and inclusive • addresses sustainability i.e. no need for paper copies • an efficient use of time • assessment activities can be automated • auditable and trackable, can be timestamped • available and flexible i.e. resources and materials can be accessed at a time and place to suit teachers and learners • cost-effective i.e. available to many learners in large online classes, and can save on the purchase of printed copies of text books or the printing of handouts and resources • documents can be saved and shared in the cloud i.e. they are stored remotely and can be accessed anywhere at any time via an internet-enabled device • flexible teaching and learning programmes can be created • gives immediate results from online tests and polls • learners can *bring your own device* (BYOD) to use during lessons (if allowed) • on demand i.e. tests can be taken when a learner is ready, and results can be immediate	• an internet connection is often required to access certain websites • artificial intelligence (AI) might be used by learners to answer questions • finance is required to purchase or upgrade equipment, some software/applications might be expensive • it could lead to plagiarism, copying or cheating by learners • it is time consuming to initially set up • it might create barriers if a learner cannot access it, is not confident to use it, or has health issues which prevent using it • learners might feel isolated, or might not follow online protocols • learners might misuse it • learners/teachers/assessors accessing the internet via their own devices might run out of credit if paying for wifi, or accidentally download a virus • power cuts/low broadband speeds/limited wifi networks can affect connections and access • security of data could be compromised • some organisations block access to certain sites • some people might be afraid of using technology or certain devices • the identity of the learner and the authenticity of their work must be verified • there might not be enough resources available for all learners to use at the same time

Activity

Look at Table 6.1 and list the strengths and limitations which are applicable to your subject. Are there any personal barriers which might prevent you from using anything? If so, how can you overcome them? Are there any more strengths and limitations you can think of?

ICT resources

Information communication technology (ICT) includes all the tools and resources which you can use to support the teaching and administration of your subject. You will prob- ably already be using many resources such as computers, electronic whiteboards, cloud computing applications (apps), video conferencing, and virtual learning environments (VLEs). However, there are probably many more resources you could use which might make the learning process more interesting. For example, online voting and quizzes during lessons. You will need to find out what is available and approved for use at your organisation. You will also need to know what technical support is available if you experience a problem, and who to ask if you need any training.

There might be a learning resource centre (LRC) or a library within your organisation, or a public library which is accessible locally. They are no longer places which just contain books; many have computers and devices which are permanently connected to the internet, offer photocopying and printing facilities, and resources such as journals, magazines, newspapers and periodicals (hard copy and electronic). If there is an LRC or library at your organisation, you could arrange for a member of their staff to give your learners a tour of the facilities. Often, the LRC will have a licence to enable learners to access and read texts and journals online from their own devices.

Some organisations have a set of devices such as tablets or laptops which the teacher can reserve for use with their learners. If this is the case where you work, you will need to find out how you go about reserving them, and whether you need to collect and return them, or if someone else will. Devices are often stored in a lockable trolley which can be wheeled to and from the learning environment. Ideally, you will need to track their issue and return, to make sure none go missing.

Helpful hint

If you are using your organisation's portable devices, check beforehand that they are fully charged up, or that there is access to power sockets in your room. If any device develops a fault, make a note and report it to technical support; otherwise the next group who use them will experience problems.

Supporting learners

Never assume that your learners are capable or confident at using technology. Always carry out an initial assessment to ascertain their prior knowledge, skills, and understanding. The use of technology can also assist when differentiating activities to meet a particular learner's requirements. For example, using a screen reader or text enlargement software for a learner who is partially sighted. *Assistive resources* (in Chapter 5) or *adaptive technology* are the terms used to denote devices and their use for people with disabilities or difficul- ties. Their use can lead to greater learner independence by providing enhancements to or changing the methods of use. This should enable learners to accomplish tasks they might not have been able to do without it. Using them also helps create an inclusive learning environment for all learners. It's always best to check if your learners have any anxieties about using technology, including any health-related concerns, or physical conditions which could affect their access and use. Technological advances have made an enormous difference to learners who have particular needs, enabling them to access suitable learning opportunities. Technology can provide a means of access to learning for those who:

- are hearing impaired

- are visually impaired

- have a degenerative condition which is physically tiring

- have a first language which is not the one used during the course

- have difficulty in speaking

- have difficulty with manipulation and fine motor control.

Digital and online technologies

Digital technologies relate to devices which can create, store, transmit, share, and/or exchange information. Online technologies relate to the ways in which you can access information and communicate via the internet.

Examples of using digital and online technologies can include (in alphabetical order):

- accessing blogs, vlogs, chat forums, social networking sites, social media, and discussion forums to help learners communicate and collaborate with each other

- accessing cloud storage facilities which teachers and learners can use to upload, share, collaborate on, and access from various online devices at a time to suit

- accessing digital media for visual/audio recording and playback

- annotating text, images, and videos

- checking learners' assignments for plagiarism with specialist software

- creating a private social media video-sharing channel and empowering learners to make and add videos for their peers to review and comment on

- creating a wiki for learners to collaborate on with their peers. They can contribute to a discussion with a trackable history of changes

- creating an online glossary for the subject, either in a VLE or as a document saved to the cloud. Learners can add new words, acronyms, jargon, and phrases with meanings. A completed list can be downloaded by each learner at the end of the course

- creating electronic portfolios for learners to save and access their work, and for teachers to assess it

- creating and using online and on-demand tests and polls which can give instant results

- creating online discussion and chat forums which allow asynchronous (taking place at different times) and synchronous (taking place at the same time) discussions

- enabling BYOD (bring your own device) where learners use their own devices for learning and assessment

- enabling internet access for research to support assignments and presentations

- encouraging learners to keep an online diary, blog, vlog, or reflective learning journal

- setting a task for learners to carry out by asking them to come up with digital approaches to complete it

- synchronising online calendars with members of staff for meetings, or with learners for attending online or onsite lessons

- using drones for subjects such as land-based industries

- using software for learners to complete multiple-choice tests and assignments, to save and back up their work

- using educational gaming software, augmented reality, and virtual reality to complement the subject

- using email for electronic submission of assessments, communication, and informal teacher feedback regarding learner progress

- using interactive whiteboards for teachers and learners to use during lessons

- using live webinars for learners to view if they can't attend a lesson, or recording the lesson and uploading it to a VLE or video-sharing site for later access

- using mobile phones and tablets for taking images, creating video and audio clips, and communicating with others

- using an organisation's networked system to allow access to software and documents from any computer linked to the system (an *intranet*)

- using artificial intelligence to create course materials

- using online voting, surveys, and questionnaire apps to use during or after a lesson

- using puzzle software for creating fun activities, for example, crosswords, quizzes, flash cards, and domino type games

- using scanners for copying and transferring documents to a computer

- using virtual worlds with virtual reality headsets to demonstrate and recreate activities where it's difficult to do in real life, such as medical procedures.

Theory into practice

Find out what digital and online resources are available for you to use with your learners, or which you can access for your teaching role. Do you need to request to use anything in advance or is it always accessible? Is there a permanent internet connection or wifi access for staff and learners, and do you and your learners need passwords? Being prepared with this information will help when planning to use technology.

Pedagogical skills and knowledge

You will already have pedagogical skills and knowledge regarding your subject specialism; therefore you just need to adapt these to the use of technology. Digital pedagogy is the term used to denote teaching using technology. However, you do need to know your own strengths and limitations, and you may need to partake in some further training. There are lots of free online courses you could search for and carry out, or your organisation might offer certain training.

Helpful hint

You could invite a colleague who is familiar with using digital and online technology, to deliver an awareness lesson to your learners. This would also help to increase your own skills and knowledge.

When planning to incorporate technology during your lessons, you could ask yourself the following questions:

☐ Do I feel confident at using it? If not, who can help me?

☐ If the learners will use it, do they already know how to? If not, how can I show them, or how can they learn for themselves?

☐ Will I need any technical support? If so, how can I access it?

☐ Are the devices and/or software/apps accessible? If not, what do I need to do? Will the devices need charging up beforehand?

☐ Do I need an internet or wifi connection? If yes, how can I make sure it is safe and reliable?

☐ Do I need to download any particular software or apps? Am I allowed to do this at my organisation or must I go through technical support?

☐ Do I need separate passwords for work than I use at home? The same will apply for learners.

☐ How much time will I need to plan and prepare for its use?

☐ How can I make sure the resources are presented well and are accessible?

☐ What will I do if something goes wrong?

☐ Will it enhance what the learners are doing and increase their understanding of the subject?

Technology is only as good as the person using it; therefore both you and your learners need to know how to use it effectively. It should always be used in a way that educates and informs. For example, to illustrate a point, to promote a discussion, and to further knowledge, skills, and understanding. As you begin to use it, you will soon find out what works and what doesn't. It's a learning process for you as well as your learners. For example, you could give small groups the responsibility for researching a topic during the lesson, then collaborate between lessons to produce a presentation of their findings for the next lesson. Their peers could provide feedback via an online survey or questionnaire that has been devised by them beforehand. This will help build on and improve your learners' digital literacy skills i.e. the skills they need to live and work in a society where communication and access to information is increasing.

You could allow your learners to bring their own devices to use during lessons, if this is allowed by your organisation. However, some organisations might require that personal devices are PAT tested (portable appliance testing). This could be for internet research, reading downloaded text books, and/or for writing notes rather than using physical text books, pen, and paper. However, you will need to ensure that all learners have a suitable device; it wouldn't be fair if some don't. If this is the case, your organisation might have spare tablets or laptops which could be used.

Example

Jacqui wanted to use digital technology with her beauty therapy learners. As all her learners had their own mobile devices she felt she could incorporate their use somehow. She created an online quiz based on the current topic. Her learners were able to access the quiz during the lesson via an app on their devices. They completed the quiz individually and then compared their results in pairs. The activity went well, and Jacqui now uses other apps with her learners, such as voting tools and surveys.

Blended learning

When technology is combined with traditional in-person methods of teaching and assessment, it is known as *blended learning*. For example, learners could use the internet to research a topic further at home, which a teacher has just explained during a lesson. It's about making best use of what's available at the time to support teaching and learning, and to add variety. A blended approach is ideal if learners cannot always attend lessons. They could partake live online, or watch a recording later.

Flipped learning

The term *flipped* learning relates to flipping the work normally carried out *during* a lesson, to that which is carried out *away* from the lesson. It puts the emphasis on learners to carry out research outside of the lesson so that they can apply their knowledge and skills during the lesson, by interacting and collaborating with others. Examples include learners using multimedia i.e. watching videos, listening to podcasts, and collaborating with their peers while away from the in-person lesson. They will then discuss this during the next lesson and contextualise it to the subject. This gives the teacher the opportunity to give a more personalised approach when with their learners. The teacher becomes more of a facilitator of learning, guiding, and supporting learners to find things out for themselves.

E-learning technologies

E-learning, short for *electronic learning* is about using electronic learning technologies, devices, tools, and systems with learners. For example, e-portfolios, interactive white-boards, online polls, and virtual learning environments (VLEs). They don't always have to include the use of the internet.

Electronic books (e-books) and journals can also be classed as using e-learning. Learners with any particular disabilities might find they can view the texts in a range of formats with an e-reader program. Many e-books will also play audio, read the text out loud, or contain links to relevant websites where the reader can find out more. You could encourage your learners to access chapters of relevant e-books before and after taught lessons. This would help to increase their knowledge and understanding, and could be used as the basis of a group discussion.

Online/remote/distance learning

Courses can be taught online (either at, or at a distance from the training venue) where learners can access a program via a specialist website or a *platform*. A platform is the device and operating system which runs the software, such as on a computer, tablet or smartphone. This is ideal for learners who might have difficulty attending a particular venue or wish to learn at times and places convenient to them. It's sometimes referred to as *remote* or *distance learning*, as the learner is not present at the venue. However, this type of learning doesn't always occur online. Correspondence courses can be entered into where learning materials are paper-based and sent and returned via a delivery service.

If you want your remote learners to work together as part of an online community, you could carry out online activities as though you are with the group in person. This could include introductions, carrying out an icebreaker, agreeing ground rules, and encouraging them to interact with each other and yourself. Good interpersonal skills, approachability, enthusiasm, and a strong commitment to supporting learning will help you to establish and maintain motivation and interaction with your learners.

Activity

What do you consider the issues are for teachers and learners regarding the use of digital and online technology? What impact might these have on the teaching and learning process for your subject?

Synchronous and asynchronous learning

Online learning can be *synchronous* i.e. the learner and the teacher are online at the same time, or *asynchronous* i.e. at different times.

Synchronous learning

This is where the teacher and learners can communicate in real time. However, everyone needs to decide to log onto their computer or device at an agreed time. It's like arriving to attend a class, but it's a virtual environment rather than a physical environment. A reliable internet connection is required, and ideally, the teacher and learners should be in a quiet place where they won't be interrupted by others.

The advantages of a synchronous learning environment are:

- attendance is automatically tracked: a record is made of when the learners log on and off

- teachers can choose from a variety of technologies to teach the subject i.e. slide presentations, a shared whiteboard, audio and video conferencing

- learners can work together in pairs or groups and the teacher can see how they are communicating to achieve a task

- that there is live interaction with the learners during a discussion. A learner can indicate when they want to *speak* (either verbally, raising a virtual hand, or by keying in a message). Most programs enable learners to see and speak to each other and the teacher. Learners will need to have switched on their audio and video facilities in advance i.e. speakers, a microphone, and a webcam. If a learner wishes to communicate something in confidence, they can ask to go to a private chat forum.

- teachers can use online questions and quizzes which are automatically assessed

- that assessment and feedback records are maintained and are trackable.

Asynchronous learning

This is where learning can take place anywhere and at any time. Learners can log on when they have time, and can interact with the various tasks and resource materials which have previously been uploaded. They can leave messages for their peers and their teacher, which will hopefully have been responded to by the next time they log in. Discussion *threads* (virtual conversations) are a great way to gain and share knowledge. However, the teacher will need to check what is being discussed in case anything inappropriate is posted.

The advantages of an asynchronous learning environment are:

- learning can take place at a time and place to suit each learner

- many learners can participate

- learners from different areas or countries can take part, enabling a wide variety of knowledge to be shared.

Virtual learning environments (VLEs)

These are often referred to by the acronym VLE and are like a virtual classroom where learners can participate in an online course. Learners can also access materials and resources to support a course they are attending in person. VLEs include a range of online collaboration and tracking tools, as well as a variety of assessment tools. They can be accessed via an organisation's intranet or stored in the cloud and accessed via the internet.

VLEs are useful to support traditional in-person courses or for purely online courses. For online learning, they can be used for learners to work through course materials, interact with their teacher and peers, and upload completed work for assessment and feedback. Some ground rules (in Chapter 3) will need to be agreed.

VLEs are a useful way for learners to access (in alphabetical order):

- assessment information and assignments

- chat forums for communicating with peers

- course information

- feedback from their teacher, which has been verbally recorded or written

- individual live tutorials

- learning materials, resources, and activities

- message facilities to communicate with their teacher

- projects for collaboration

- synchronous or asynchronous discussion forums

- video and audio clips, images, and sounds.

Theory into practice

Create an activity for your learners to carry out using digital and/or online technology. Use it with your learners and then evaluate how effective it was and why.

Artificial intelligence

'Artificial intelligence, or AI, refers to machines or computer systems that are designed to perform tasks that typically require human intelligence. These tasks can include things like learning, reasoning, and problem solving. In simpler terms, AI is like giving machines the ability to think and make decisions similar to how humans do, but using algorithms and programming instead of biological processes. It's about creating smart machines that can mimic certain aspects of human intelligence to make our lives easier and solve complex problems.'

That text was generated by AI in answer to the question: *'Explain what AI is in simple terms'.* The question was entered into the website ChatGPT which stands for Chat Generative Pre-trained Transformer. When ChatGPT was asked: *'What does Chat Generative Pre-trained Transformer mean?'* the response was:

'Chat Generative Pre-trained Transformer describes an AI model that has been pre-trained on a large dataset to generate conversational responses using a transformer architecture.'

These examples show how AI can generate answers to questions in just a few seconds. Generative AI refers to technology that can be used to create content or make predictions. However, this can only be based on what has been pre-programmed into it i.e. large volumes of data and information. The results can also include audio, code, images, text, simulations, and videos. ChatGPT can hold online text conversations. You might think that you are talking to a human being, but you are not. Think of AI as an alternative to searching for something online; just ask a question and you will receive an answer. You can then ask more questions to keep the conversation going. However, you have to be careful to verify the responses you receive, as some things might not be true, particularly if it's been trained on false information.

AI has actually been around for many years. If you have a smartphone and you message someone, text predict will generate words that it thinks you want to use. The process will improve further with use, as it learns from the way you construct your sentences. Word processors use spelling and grammar checkers. Online customer service chats are often just AI-generated answers based on the customer's choice from a list of pre-prepared questions.

Helpful hint

Once you start using AI you might want to use it instead of internet search engines to find what you are looking for. However, you cannot rely on the authenticity of the responses as they are generated artificially, not by human beings.

AI can be used in positive ways to help your teaching role. For example, by creating learning resources such as handouts and lesson plans, preparing tests, and supporting personalised learning. This would help to save time, but you will need to be specific with the criteria you want addressed when asking your question. You will also need to verify that the response is accurate and relevant. If you use AI to produce resources, the quality and content of the final document remains yours and your organisation's responsibility. You will need to find out what your organisation's policy is regarding the use of AI by teachers and learners.

Activity

Search for a ChatGPT website (you might have to register with them, but many are free) and ask it to create a handout for a particular topic. You might be surprised just how good it is, and how much time it can save you. However, make sure you read the full response if you plan on using it, to ensure it is fit for purpose, valid, and reliable.

Using AI responsibly

AI should be used responsibly by both teachers and learners. It would be helpful for learners to use it during a lesson to carry out research, but you will need to inform them that if they use it to answer any questions, it will be considered as cheating. Do be careful, as not all answers will be correctly generated and learners might use it instead of thinking for themselves. However, how would you know whether a learner has used AI to generate their responses? You could ask yourself the following questions:

☐   was their work handed in ahead of the deadline, which might be unusual for a particular learner?

☐   is the consistency of style and layout different to that which is normally used by the learner?

☐   does the language used seem inconsistent with other typical responses to questions, or the way that the learner normally speaks to you?

☐   is the response very complex, to a point of including what wasn't asked for?

☐   is there a lot of technical jargon used, which isn't necessary to answer the question?

☐   are specific details not addressed i.e. is the response very generic?

☐   was knowledge demonstrated which is beyond your learner's level at the time?

☐   were references used which are not relevant?

This of course is extra work for a teacher to check; however, if you get to know your learners, you will soon learn their style of talking and writing, and be able to differentiate. There might be some plagiarism software which your organisation has to detect the use of AI. Alternatively, you could key in the question to ChatGPT to see if its response is similar to your learner's. You could also inform your learners that you will randomly choose several of their responses to talk to them about. This will let them know that you will be verbally checking the content of their answers. If they can respond to you in a way that they would normally speak, and you can ascertain that they can answer the same question again without referring to their written work, then this should confirm that it's theirs. If not, you will need to challenge your learner as to how they ascertained their answers. This is a problem which will increase as technology develops further. Your organisation should have a policy in place for cheating and plagiarism and you will need to find out what to do if you experience it.

Example

Anika was marking a question she had set as homework to her group of history learners (all aged 16). The question was: **Who was the first king of England and how did they come to the throne?** *She noticed that one of her learners, Jimmy, had produced a lengthy response using words like* attributed, concept, unifica-tion, *and* incorporated. *Anika had never heard Jimmy use these words during lessons before, and was therefore concerned that he might have used AI. She asked him to clarify what the words meant, and he wasn't able to answer. He then confessed that he had used a chat generator to produce his answer. As it was only a homework activity, and not a formal assessment question, she warned him not to do it again. She also carried out a workshop with the full group as to how they should research and generate their own responses.*

AI can also be used in ways which cause distress, such as email scams, images which are made to look like and talk like someone in authority to deliver fake news, or social media posts designed to interfere with elections or promote propaganda. There is a lot of mis-information and disinformation available which can be made to look genuine. It would therefore be useful to conduct a lesson with your learners as to how to use social media responsibly, and how to identify fake and false news. Unfortunately, the saying *seeing is believing* is not always true nowadays. AI encompasses deep learning and machine learning, and can process things faster than humans. This means that computers or apps can predict things, make decisions for themselves, and create answers or images in a matter of seconds. The term deep fake is used for videos and images which appear to be real, but are not. Some chat tools can remember a person's internet provider (IP) address, may be able to access their browser history, and collect data which they have provided as part of using it. It's best to discuss all the negative as well as the positive benefits of AI with your learners.

The Department for Education (in England) have produced a policy paper regarding the use of generative artificial intelligence in the education sector. It gives opportunities and limitations, as well as how to use it effectively. Your organisation should already have embraced this, and it might be worth finding out how it's being implemented.

Theory into practice

Look at the Department for Education's policy paper: Generative artificial intelligence (AI) in education (2023) at http://tinyurl.com/DfEPolicyPaperAI and the Generative AI in education: Educator and expert views (2024) at: http://tinyurl.com/DfEExpertViewsAI. Read how AI will impact on you, your learners, and your job role. Find out if your organisation has embraced the content and if not, how they intend to. If the link is no longer live, just search for the document name.

Social networking, social media, and online safety

Social *networking* is about connecting and communicating with friends, family, and other people who share an interest (i.e. a network of people). It can be used to build up contacts with other professionals and future employers. Social *media* is about using technology to turn communication into an interactive dialogue. However, you might consider some networking sites to be social media sites and vice versa, depending upon the situation in which they are used. Both can be used by teachers and learners, providing everyone is aware of how to stay safe online. Most social networking and social media sites are free to join; however, you might need to pay for additional facilities.

Learners might already belong to a social networking site and/or access social media on a regular basis. They might therefore expect to have access to these during lessons.

Helpful hint

If your learners have access to the internet during lessons, agree some ground rules with them. This could include not accessing personal social media accounts during lessons.

Some learners might struggle with speaking in front of their peers but might feel comfortable communicating via social network or social media sites. This can be useful if particular learners are shy or feel intimidated to ask questions or respond to others verbally. When using social media, some learners might key in words as abbreviations or miss out vowels (e.g. B4 for before). If you can make sure that they are not doing this when using them for educational purposes, it can help improve their spelling and grammar.

Your learners might want to find out more about you, and therefore search the internet to see if you have an online presence. Do be careful with any information you post about yourself which can be accessed in the public domain. It's best to politely decline any requests from learners to join their personal social networking sites. You are not their *friend*; you are their teacher.

Social networking

There are many social networking sites available which teachers and learners can join to discuss their interest in a particular subject area. To join a social network, you will need to go to the relevant website and create an account. This will involve writing a bit about yourself, known as a *profile*, and uploading a photo. Some people join under an assumed name, and/or use a photo which is not of themselves. It's always wise to be careful when communicating with anyone you don't know, and to be cautious of what people are talking about. Once joined, you can choose to *follow* people or organisations by updating your settings to be notified when they post anything. Alternatively you can just view what has been posted in the public areas. You can choose to respond to discussions other people have started, or start a discussion yourself. You might find it useful to set up a social network purely for your learners to access, which is based on your subject, and is only used for educational purposes.

With most social networking sites, there is usually an option to communicate privately rather than publicly. Again, be careful of what you say to people you don't know. When you post text and images, they can easily be taken out of context and be accessible for many years. If you are ever unsure, don't post anything in a public forum which you would not willingly say or show to a total stranger. This is also useful to tell your learners. You could ask them to carry out an online search for their own name using different search engines. They might be surprised what they find, and this information could also be found by current and future employers, as well as family members.

There are some negative sides to social networking sites, besides people who join with an assumed name. Sometimes people post nasty or untrue comments which is a form of online bullying. This can be very hurtful to the person on the receiving end. Social networking sites can also be a target for others to steal personal information and identities to use them immorally. A positive side is that social networking enables people to keep in touch and to receive information quickly.

Online communities

An online community is a virtual community consisting of a group of people with a common interest, for example, a particular educational subject. Communication is via the internet, often using social networking or social media to post questions and discuss various topics.

There are many educational online communities which you will be able to search for and join. These might relate to your particular subject specialism, or to teaching, training, and assessment in general. You can post a question and receive responses from people who are in a similar situation to yourself. Some forums are open to anyone to join, others you will need to request to join.

Example

Daniel has been teaching his subject of geography for many years. He felt his lessons were becoming a bit repetitive. He decided to find out how other geography teachers incorporated the use of technology with learners. He joined a professional networking site and searched the 'groups' section for 'teaching geography'. Once he had found and joined a group, he was able to post a question to start a discussion, and then received some very helpful responses from other teachers.

Social media

Media relates to information which is accessible via newspapers, magazines, radio, and television. Social media relates to information and materials which are accessible via the internet. Using social media is a way of transmitting information very quickly to a lot of people. This can include text, videos, images, documents, blogs, and vlogs. A blog is a succession of written posts about various topics, a bit like a diary. The term comes from using the last letter of *web* before the word *log*. A vlog is a video version of a blog. The term *going viral* is often used when people spread the message that they have seen it, and it then gets viewed by thousands of people very quickly.

There are lots of social media sites available which can help support your subject. These can help your learners to communicate with each other, and for you to upload learning materials, videos, and images for them to access. You might consider the use of social media sites for personal use; however, they can be used in imaginative ways for teaching and learning purposes.

Activity

If you have access to the internet, carry out a search for various social networking and social media sites. You could join some to use for professional networking, and then get involved in relevant discussions for your subject specialism.

Some educational organisations block access to certain sites. However, some of the sites they block can actually be a really good source for your subject, such as videos regarding various topics. However, if you do have access to and plan on showing any videos to your learners, you are best watching them first, as you can't always trust the source. Not all the information which is posted online is genuine. If it's being used to support educational purposes, the origins will need to be verified.

Online safety

When using digital and online technology, both you and your learners need to be aware of how to stay safe. You will need to remember that as a teacher, you are in a position of authority and trust. As such, you have a responsibility to make sure your learners are safe when using it, and that they are not vulnerable in any way to the acts of others. Your organisation might have a *digital strategy*, a *code of practice*, or an *acceptable use policy* which states how ICT should be used to good effect. There should also be policies and procedures in place regarding the safeguarding of learners when using the internet. You will need to make sure that both you and your learners are aware of them and adhere to the content.

Staying safe online is not something that occurs automatically. Everyone needs to take responsibility for what they do and don't do. If your organisation is inspected by Ofsted (in England), they will be looking at how learners are able to stay safe online, and that they understand the potential risks and dangers of using and misusing technology. The Online Safety Act (2023) applies in the United Kingdom and provides a regulatory framework. The Act requires providers of services (who are regulated by the Act) to identify, mitigate, and manage the risks of harm (including risks which particularly affect individuals with a certain characteristic) from: illegal content and activity, and content and activity that is harmful to children (i.e. anyone under the age of 18).

Teachers and learners can contribute to staying safe online by (in alphabetical order):

- backing up documents and data

- being aware of scams (a dishonest scheme or fraud)

- being careful when using wifi networks, as others might be able to access their device and its contents

- changing passwords regularly, making them complex, and not revealing them to anyone

- checking the privacy settings on social networking sites so as not to reveal anything personal to strangers

- covering a webcam when it's not in use

- following relevant policies, procedures, codes of practice, and legislation

- keeping personal and professional networking accounts separate

- not accessing insecure or untrusted websites

- not getting friendly with strangers online; they might not be who they seem

- not meeting strangers in real life who you have met online; they might not be who they say they are

- not posting anything in a public forum which you would not willingly say to a stranger

- not purchasing anything from an insecure site

- not uploading images or videos of yourself unless you are happy that other people can access and use them for purposes you might not have intended

- only using the communication channels provided by your organisation i.e. a secure email account, VLE, or intranet

- thinking before you post: once your text/images are online, they might be accessible for many years, even though you have deleted them

- reporting sites or users which you are seriously concerned about

- using anti-virus and/or anti-spyware software and a firewall to stop unauthorised access to a computer or a device and its contents.

A further aspect to consider when using computers, devices, keyboards, and other items which are shared among others is hygiene. Germs can linger and then be caught and spread by everyone who uses them. Washing hands regularly and/or using cleansing wipes or antibacterial liquid can help to prevent this. Having good hygiene is something to be aware of, particularly in times of coughs and colds.

Theory into practice

Locate and read your organisation's policies and/or relevant codes of practice which relate to using ICT and the internet. You will probably find they are quite detailed and might contain a lot of jargon. If you are unsure of the content, ask someone for clarification. If you don't understand something, your learners probably won't either.

Summary

This chapter has explored:

- The role of digital and online technology in education
- Pedagogical skills and knowledge
- Artificial intelligence
- Social networking, social media, and online safety

7

Excelling when assessing learning

Putting theory into practice to assess learning

Introduction

Carrying out assessment activities with your learners enables you to ascertain if they have gained the required knowledge, skills, understanding, and behaviours at a given point in time.

Excelling when assessing learning will enable you to support your learners to be the best they can be. This includes confirming their achievement, providing constructive and developmental feedback, and identifying opportunities for them to progress further.

At the end of the chapter you will find a comprehensive table of assessment methods and activities, along with their strengths and limitations.

This chapter will introduce you to the following topics:

- Principles of assessment
- Assessment planning, types, and methods
- Making decisions and providing feedback
- Quality assurance

Occupational Standards covered in Chapter 7

Duties	Knowledge	Skills	Behaviours
D1, D2, D3, D4, D5, D7, D8, D9	K5, K7, K9, K11, K14, K18	S4, S8, S9, S11, S12, S14, S17, S25	B1

Principles of assessment

Principles of assessment are the processes and practices which you will use to assess that learning has taken place. They will enable you to check what your learners have achieved so far, and what still needs to be done. Assessment is a measure of learning at a given point, and the results should not be influenced by anything other than the learner's ability towards what is being assessed. If you don't plan for and carry out any assessment activities with your learners, you will not know how well, or what, they have learnt.

Before you can carry out any assessment activities with your learners, you will need to have taught the required course material, and know what you are going to assess. Usually, this information will be provided in an awarding organisation's (AOs) qualification specification. It will contain all the aspects which need to be taught prior to assessment, and give advice as to how to assess it. This might be listed as units or topics, which can be assessed independently, or standards which can be assessed holistically. Some AOs provide resources such as assignments or questions, or you might need to create your own. If it's the latter, make sure you are only assessing what is relevant and has been taught. If you create your own assessment resources, you might need to check their use with your AO beforehand.

If you see your learners regularly, you can assess that learning is taking place each time you are with them. This is called *informal* assessment. It could simply be by watching what your learners are doing and/or asking questions to check their knowledge and understanding. *Formal* assessment will count towards the achievement of something, such as a unit or a qualification, whereas informal assessment is to check progress.

Helpful hint

When preparing your scheme of work to teach your subject, work out when you will assess various aspects either informally or formally. Try to space out the assessment activities throughout the course.

Assessment for learning and assessment of learning

There is a difference between assessment *for* learning (AfL) and assessment *of* learning (AoL). Assessment *for* learning is usually a *formative* process and is often informal. It will ascertain the progress that a learner has made in order to plan for further learning and development. It's called formative assessment because it's ongoing throughout the learning process. It's also a chance for a learner to make a mistake, or to get something wrong and to learn from it. Assessment *of* learning is usually *summative* and often formal. It confirms whether learning and achievement have taken place (or not). It's called summative assessment because it occurs at the end of an aspect of learning. This could be *modular* i.e. after a module, unit or topic has been taught or *linear* i.e. when the whole course has been completed.

If your learners are working towards a qualification, there will be *formal summative* methods of assessment that you will need to carry out, such as an assignment or an observation of practice. However, you can devise *informal formative* methods to use at any time, such as discussions, role plays, or quizzes. Assessment, whether informal or formal, should always focus on improving and reinforcing learning as well as measuring progress and achievement.

Example

Jim has devised an informal formative quiz based on a popular television game show. He uses it to ask questions with his group of learners at the end of each theory lesson. Using this method also introduces an element of fun to his subject. The quiz is to assess knowledge and understanding towards the Level 1 Motor Vehicle Studies qualification. Jim then uses the formal summative activities provided by the awarding organisation to assess each learner's achievement at the appropriate time.

The assessment process can help your learners by (in alphabetical order):

- acknowledging what progress has been made
- addressing issues where there are gaps in learning
- ascertaining areas for development and progression
- checking for inaccuracies e.g. spelling or grammar errors in a written task, or mistakes during a practical task
- confirming achievements
- diagnosing any areas of concern to enable support to be arranged
- encouraging discussions and questions
- ensuring that they are on the right course at the right level
- identifying what is yet to be learnt
- maintaining motivation.

Activity

Look at the previous bullet list and consider other examples of how the assessment process can help your learners. How might the assessment process (informal or formal) hinder your learners?

If you assess group work, such as presentations or role plays, you will need to assess each individual's contribution towards the assessment requirements. Otherwise you could be passing the whole group when some learners may not have contributed much at all.

Minimising risks

There are risks involved when carrying out assessment activities. Being aware of these will help you to minimise or prevent them from occurring. The risks apply not only with regard to the health, safety, and welfare of all concerned, but what might occur for your particular subject. For example, a learner plagiarising another's work, a teacher providing hints or answers, or malpractice by a member of staff. When you plan and carry out assessment activities, just ask yourself if anything could go wrong, and if so, there is a risk.

There are also risks on your part, for example, pressure to pass learners quickly due to funding and targets. This might lead you to allowing something that you normally wouldn't. There is also the risk that you might unknowingly offer favouritism or bias towards some learners over others. You must never do something which you know to be wrong. If pressure is being put on you, then you must inform someone either where you work, or at the relevant awarding organisation. If you are related to or know personally the learners that you will assess, you might need to notify your organisation of any conflict of interest. They may also need to notify the relevant awarding organisation.

Plagiarism and authenticity

When assessing written work, you will need to be aware that some learners, intentionally or not, might plagiarise the work of others. Plagiarism is the wrongful use of someone else's work. Authenticity is the rightful and confirmed use of your own work. Learners should take responsibility for referencing any sources used in all work submitted, and may be required to sign a declaration or an authenticity statement to this effect. If you suspect plagiarism, you could type a few of your learner's words into an internet search engine or specialist software to see what appears. Or perhaps key in the question to ChatGPT (in Chapter 6) to see if the response is similar to your learner's. If you discover plagiarism, you would need to challenge your learner as to whether it was intentional or not, and follow your organisation's plagiarism procedure. The Copyright, Designs and Patents Act (1988) is the current UK copyright law. Copying the work of others without their permission would infringe the Act. Learners may be in breach of this Act if they plagiarise or copy the work of others without making reference to the original author. Therefore it might be useful to inform your learners about this.

Theory into practice

Your organisation will have assessment policies and procedures for you to follow. Find out what these are, and how they will impact on your role. They should relate to the full assessment process as well as what to do in the event of cheating and/or plagiarism.

Assessment planning, types, and methods

Assessment planning is a fundamental part of the assessment process. If it is not carried out correctly and comprehensively, problems may occur which could disadvantage your learners, or prevent them from achieving. There is a lot to think about, and you will need to take into account aspects such as: health and safety, differentiation, safeguarding, equality, diversity and inclusion.

You will need to know when your learners are ready to be assessed. There's no point in assessing them if they haven't learnt everything, as you will be setting them up to fail. If a learner has been absent for any reason, you will need to make sure that they are up to date regarding what they have missed. Carrying out a formative assessment well before a summative assessment can help both you and your learners ascertain how ready they are.

The timing of assessments can make a difference to learners: if you plan to assess on a Friday before a holiday period, your learners might not be as focused, equally so first thing on a Monday morning. However, this is difficult if you only see your learners on these particular days. If you are planning a schedule of assessments throughout the year, you will need to consider any public or cultural holidays. There is no point in planning to assess only on Mondays if the majority of these fall on public holidays. Some formal assessment dates might not be able to be changed, for example, a national test which must be taken by all learners on the same day and at the same time.

Most qualification specifications use terminology such as: *assessment criteria*. These include action verbs such as: list, describe, explain, demonstrate, analyse, and evaluate. A level one learner would struggle to evaluate, and a level seven learner would find a list too easy. Knowing the level of your learners will help you to create assessment activities to suit. It's just like writing objectives when creating a scheme of work (in Chapter 4). You might also need to explain to your learners what each action verb means in practice, to give them an idea of what they must do and how they can achieve it.

To help with planning, you could start by devising a rationale using the *five Ws and one H* format of *who, what, when, where, why*, and *how*. This information should always be discussed with your learners beforehand, so that everyone is aware of what will happen and when. Whether you are assessing on an individual basis (i.e. an observation in the workplace) or in a group (i.e. a test in a classroom or workshop), the assessment planning process should be formalised and agreed with your learners. They need to know what they are working towards, the criteria that will be used to assess them, how they will be assessed, and the date, time, and place of assessment. You should also plan how and when you will provide feedback to your learners. This could be verbally immediately after the assessment activity, the next time you see your learner, by email or another means. However, the sooner the better so that nothing is forgotten. Sometimes, teachers focus so much on the assessment process and the record keeping that they forget to tell their learners if they have passed.

Activity

Locate a qualification specification for your particular subject via an awarding organisation's website. Look at the terminology used for the criteria which will be assessed, and consider how you could use the five Ws and one H *format to help with planning.*

To effectively plan how you will assess your learners, you will need to use methods which are ethical, safe, and fair.

- Ethical: the methods used are right and proper for what is being assessed and the context of assessment. The learner's welfare, health, safety, and security are not compromised.

- Safe: the learner's work can be confirmed as valid and authentic. There should be little chance of plagiarism, confidentiality of information should be taken into account, and learning and assessment should not be compromised in any way, nor the learner's experience or potential to achieve. (Safe in this context does not relate to health and safety but to whether the assessment methods are sufficiently robust to make a reliable decision.)

- Fair: the methods used are appropriate to all learners at the required level, taking into account any particular needs. All learners should have an equal chance of an accurate assessment decision.

Example

If you provide your learners with the information to answer questions, this is unethical. If you allow your learners to copy text from the internet without quoting their sources, it will be deemed unsafe. If you provide some learners with more help than others, this is unfair.

Assessment planning should always be SMART.

- **S**pecific – the activity relates only to what is being assessed and is clearly stated.

- **M**easurable – the activity can be measured against the assessment requirements, allowing any gaps to be identified.

- **A**chievable – the activity can be achieved at the right level.

- **R**elevant– the activity is suitable and realistic, relates to what is being assessed, and will give consistent results.

- **T**ime bound – target dates and times are discussed and agreed.

SMART is a useful acronym to refer to when planning learning and creating assessment activities.

Assessing in different contexts and environments

Assessment activities can take place in any context and environment which is suitable and appropriate. This might be *on-the-job* if you are assessing vocational learners, employees, and apprentices in their place of work. Alternatively, it might be *off-the-job* if you are assessing academic learners in a classroom. Some courses might be a mixture of vocational and academic subjects, with assessment taking place in workshops or a realistic working environment (RWE). An example of an RWE is a commercial hairdressing and beauty salon within a college. Members of the public can visit, and to the learners, they are real customers. However, the learners are supervised and the public know that they are in a training environment. Other courses might have a mixture of on-the-job and off-the-job assessment.

Assessing off-the-job

If you are not assessing competence in the work environment or an RWE, you will probably be assessing a non-vocational course or an academic qualification, perhaps in a college or a private training provider.

If you are assessing off-the-job, the most commonly used methods are:

- assignments
- case studies
- essays
- observations
- peer-assessments
- professional discussions

- projects
- puzzles and quizzes
- questions: written and oral
- simulations
- tests.

Your learners will need to know what they are working towards, when they will be assessed, and how e.g. by assignments or professional discussions. This information could be in the form of an *assignment brief*. This is a way of formally stating what your learners need to do to achieve certain objectives or criteria. It could be an essay question, a case study, or a long-term project. The brief should clearly state what is to be assessed i.e. the assessment criteria from the qualification specification, and what needs to be met for the learner to be successful (and grades, if applicable). If you need to create an assignment brief, your organisation should provide you with a template to ensure that you include all the relevant details. Some assignments or tests might be graded, and you will need to check with the qualification specification as to what these are, and what is required by the learners to meet a particular grade (e.g. distinction, pass, refer, fail).

If learners are aiming towards an exam, you could use past exam papers as a formative assessment activity. This is good revision and will help to check the progress of your learners beforehand.

If your learners are working towards a qualification, you will need to ensure that they have been registered with the relevant awarding organisation. It might not be your responsibility to carry out this task, but you should communicate with the appropriate person in your organisation. If learners have not been registered, the awarding organisation is not responsible for them, and the results of their assessments will be deemed invalid.

Assessing on-the-job

If you are going to assess learners on-the-job i.e. in the workplace or an RWE such as a college training restaurant, you will need to arrange a suitable date and time to visit. You may need to gain approval from the employer to enter the premises, and you might need to wear appropriate personal protective equipment (PPE). Assessment in the workplace will usually be on a one-to-one basis and will need to be planned so that your learner knows what will be happening and when.

If you are assessing on-the-job, the most commonly used methods are:

- asking questions

- examining work products and evidence

- observation

- professional discussions

- recognising your learner's prior learning and achievements (RPL/A)

- reviewing expert witness testimonies

- written statements and reflective accounts.

On-the-job assessment will need to confirm that the learner has the required skills and behaviours, as well as knowledge and understanding. Having knowledge does not imply understanding. For example, you know that water evaporates in the sun, but do you know why? When assessing knowledge, it might be sufficient for a learner to know enough to get by, such as knowing certain historical dates and facts, but not the reasons why.

Helpful hint

Your learners might have particular needs that they have not disclosed to you. Always ask them beforehand if there is anything that you can do to help make their assessment experience a positive one. For example, using written or online questions instead of oral questions (or vice versa), if acceptable by the awarding organisation.

Assessment types and methods

Assessment *types* are different from assessment *methods*. The *method* is how the *type* is used. For example, a *type* of assessment is *formative* and the *method* used could be *questions*. You might have all the information provided for you regarding which types and methods of assessment to use. If not, you will need to carefully plan which informal and formal types and methods to use, to suit your subject, the situation, and your learners.

Assessment types

Five frequently used assessment types are:

- initial
- diagnostic
- formative

- summative
- holistic.

Initial assessment will help you to find out about your learners' prior knowledge and experience, and identify any particular aspects which might otherwise go unnoticed.

Diagnostic assessments can be used to ascertain strengths and areas for development in a particular area at a certain level. Diagnostic tests can also be used to ascertain competence regarding English, maths and digital skills.

Formative assessment should take place continually and is usually carried out informally to check progress, identify any support requirements, and inform further development.

Summative assessment usually occurs at the end of something, for example, a lesson, course, unit, qualification, or set of standards. It is a measure of achievement rather than progress. Awarding organisations often allow reasonable adjustments to be made to formal assessments; however, you will need to agree any changes with them beforehand. For example, using assistive resources (in Chapter 5) and digital technology (in Chapter 6).

Holistic assessment enables learners to demonstrate several aspects from different areas or units at the same time. You might be able to observe naturally occurring situations in addition to what had originally been planned. Holistic assessment is beneficial to all concerned when assessing occupational competence towards a vocational qualification, particularly in a work environment as it can save duplication and repetition.

Assessment methods

There are many different assessment methods and activities which you could use with your learners. The terms are very similar, and for the purpose of this book, they are used interchangeably. However, a method is a broader category in which activities are used. For example, a *method* of assessment could be an exam, but it will include *activities* such as questions and case studies. Examples of assessment methods and activities, along with their strengths and limitations, are listed in Table 7.1 at the end of this chapter.

If you are responsible for devising your own assessment activities, you might decide to choose ones which are easy for you to mark, for example, multiple-choice questions (depending upon the level of your learners). There's no point making assessment activities complex unless it's a requirement of the qualification, or if you need to challenge higher level learners further. Equally, lower level learners can easily become demoralised if the activities are unattainable. Using a variety of different assessment methods and activities can help to engage, inspire, motivate, and enthuse your learners. Don't just stick to one approach because you find it easy to manage.

Subjective and objective assessment activities

Subjective assessment activities enable learners to provide answers which relate to their own experiences, opinions, and/or interpretations of something. They are therefore subjective as the answers are qualitative. For example, questions, projects, and professional discussions.

Objective assessment activities are more specific, and enable learners to give a precise answer. They are therefore objective as the answers are quantifiable. For example, multiple-choice tests, questions with a single answer, and assignments based on set criteria.

Peer-assessment and self-assessment

Peer-assessment involves a learner assessing another learner's progress. Self-assessment involves a learner assessing their own progress. Both methods encourage learners to make decisions about what has been learnt so far, to take responsibility for their learning, and become involved with the assessment process.

For peer-assessment and self-assessment to be effective, your learners will need to fully understand what needs to be assessed, how to be honest with their decisions and how to provide feedback to their peers. Not all learners will be able to do this; therefore you might need to provide some training beforehand.

Examples of peer-assessment activities include:

- assessing each other's work and providing feedback

- holding group discussions before collectively agreeing a grade for something

- producing a written statement of how their peers could improve and/or develop their practice in certain areas

- providing written or verbal feedback regarding peer presentations.

Examples of self-assessment activities include:

- awarding a grade for their own presentation

- suggesting improvements regarding their knowledge, skills and behaviours

- compiling a written statement of what they could do differently, or how they could improve

- higher level learners judging themselves against certain criteria.

Questioning techniques

Questions are a really useful formative assessment method to ensure your learners are acquiring the necessary knowledge and understanding at a given point in time. They can also be used as summative assessment at the end of a course, perhaps as part of an online test or an exam.

Questions can be written, oral, or online and can be *open*, requiring a full answer, or *closed*, requiring a 'yes' or 'no' answer. They can be aimed at one learner i.e. directly using their name, or to a group i.e. indirectly to everyone. If you are asking questions to a group of learners, ensure that you give each learner the chance to respond. Don't just let the keen learners answer first, as this gives the ones who don't know the answers the chance to stay quiet. You could inform your learners that you are going to use a particular questioning method beforehand. For example, pose a question, pause for a few seconds, and then pick a learner to answer the question. This way, all learners are included and are thinking about the answer as soon as you have posed the question. They are therefore ready to speak if their name is picked. This is referred to as *pose, pause, pick* (PPP). *Pick* is also known as *pounce*.

To save something being missed when asking questions, try and only use one question in a sentence, as more than one may confuse your learners. For example, '*What plants will grow in arid conditions, in which countries, and how much rainfall do they need?*' This is three questions, and your learner might not remember what you have asked, or only address one part of the question.

Try not to ask '*Does anyone have any questions?*' as often only those who are keen or confident will ask. This doesn't tell you what has been learnt. Try not to use questions such as '*Does that make sense?*' or '*Do you understand?*', as your learners will often say 'yes' as they feel that's what you expect to hear, or they don't want to embarrass themselves. However, if you find yourself doing this, follow it up by asking *why* it makes sense, or *how* they understand it, to gain clarification.

When questioning, try to (in alphabetical order):

- allow time for your question to be processed by your learner

- allow time for your learner to answer without interrupting

- ask open questions i.e. those beginning with *who, what, when, where, why*, and *how*

- avoid complex or trick questions

- be aware of your posture, gestures, and body language so that you don't appear threatening

- be conscious of your dialect, accent, pitch, and tone of voice, particularly if your learners' first language is not English

- don't ask more than one question in the same sentence

- if you must use closed questions to your group, you could generate a fun practical activity by asking learners to stand up for a yes answer (or vice versa)

- know that some learners might be shy; therefore direct your question to a few learners or a pair to help encourage their input – just allow time for them to discuss their answer

- make sure your learners understand the language and terminology being used

- use active listening skills to show that you are concentrating on hearing what they have to say, for example, by using eye contact and nodding

- try not to say *erm, yeah, okay, you know*, or *does that make sense?*

- try not to use a lot of jargon or acronyms, or if you must, make sure your learners understand them – they could create a glossary of terms as they progress through the course

- use eye contact when talking to an individual learner, or use eye contact as you ask a question to a group by alternating looking at each learner for a split second as you speak

- use learners' names when possible

- watch your learners' reactions and body language for signs of not understanding the question.

You may need to rephrase some questions if your learners are struggling with an answer, as poor answers are often the result of poor questions. If you are using the same questions with different learners at different times, be careful as they may collude and share their answers with each other. For essay and short-answer tests you should create sample answers to have something with which to compare. If there are several assessors involved, you could all answer the questions beforehand and then compare the responses. This will help ensure the questions have been interpreted correctly, aid the standardisation process between assessors, help you to mark quickly, and provide consistent marks to learners.

Theory into practice

Look at Table 7.1 at the end of this chapter. Choose three and devise an activity for each which you can carry out with your learners. If possible, use them during a lesson and evaluate how effective they were and why.

Making decisions and providing feedback

Once assessment has taken place, a decision needs to be made and feedback provided to your learners. This will inform them what has or has not been achieved, and what will happen next. It is quite a responsibility to confirm an achievement (or otherwise) as it can affect your learner's personal and professional development. Feedback therefore has to be meaningful to the learner, and not just something that you have to do. Praise should not be used at the cost of being honest, or if you are concerned that you might upset a learner. What you say should always be truthful, and you might have to foster your learners' resilience to manage any negative points. Your learners need to know how well they have or have not done, and what they still need to do: not that everything is perfect all the time.

Making decisions

Decisions should be in accordance with the requirements of what has been assessed i.e. the qualification specification or a set of standards. This should give guidance as to what the learner must have done to achieve a pass. Often, it's a case of the learner has or has not achieved something. However, some AOs provide guidance as to what would also constitute a merit or a distinction, or a grade e.g. A, B, C. Marking and grading can be quite complex, and you may need to seek advice from an experienced colleague about this. You could use *blind marking* for some activities, which means you don't know who has submitted what. Learners could add a number or a key word to their work which only they know. You can then ensure that your marking is not influenced by anything other than what is being assessed.

Helpful hint

*Always remain **objective** i.e. make a decision based on your learner's competence towards the required criteria. You should not be **subjective** i.e. make a decision based on your own opinions, or other factors such as your learner's personality.*

When making a decision, you will need to ensure that all assessed work is VARCS:

- **V**alid – the work is relevant to what has been assessed and is at the right level.
- **A**uthentic – the work has been produced solely by the learner.
- **R**eliable – the work is consistent over time.
- **C**urrent – the work is still relevant at the time of assessment.
- **S**ufficient – the work covers all of the requirements.

If the above are not ensured, you might make an incorrect judgement and a learner might appeal against your decision.

Example

Meena wanted to follow the VARCS principle when observing her learner, Olive, towards an aspect of the Level 2 Hairdressing qualification in the college hair and beauty training salon. During the observation, Meena was able to see that Olive was performing what was required at the right level (V). As it was only Olive involved with her client, Meena knew what was being done was authentic (A). This particular hairstyle was one Olive had demonstrated before; therefore her work was reliable and consistent over time (R). What Olive demonstrated was current as the activity was performed live (C). When Olive had finished with her client, Meena asked her a few questions to confirm that her knowledge and understanding was sufficient to meet the requirements (S).

Providing feedback

Providing feedback to your learners will help them to understand how they are progressing and what they have achieved so far. Feedback can be informal i.e. during a lesson to inform a learner how well they performed in an activity, or formal i.e. based on course-work for the achievement of a qualification. Feedback can help to encourage, reassure, boost confidence, and motivate learners, as well as help them to learn and develop further. It should aim to improve, and to have an impact upon learning by identifying any additional requirements and/or areas for progression. If you are providing feedback regarding the very first piece of work a learner has submitted, try not to be too harsh. You should want to keep your learner's motivation, but yet remain honest in a supportive way.

If you are present with your learner, you could ask them how they felt they did. This gives your learner the opportunity to recognise their own mistakes (rather than you telling them). It also helps them to reflect on what they could have done differently. You could then build on what they say throughout your feedback, and discuss what needs to be improved and/or achieved next.

Activity

What are the strengths and limitations of providing feedback to learners? How would you deal with a learner who had not met the assessment requirements?

When providing feedback, try to:

- own your statements by beginning with the word 'I' rather than 'you'.

- start with something positive, for example, "*I really liked the confident manner in which you delivered your presentation*"

- be specific about what you have seen, for example, "*The way you explained that topic was really interesting due to your knowledge and humour*" or "*I found the way that you explained that topic was rather confusing due to the changes you made part way through*"

- offer constructive and specific developmental points, for example, "*I would have understood it better if you had broken the subject down into smaller stages*"

- end with something positive or developmental, for example, "*I enjoyed your presentation. You had prepared well and came across as very organised and professional.*" Or, "*I enjoyed your presentation; however, issuing a handout summarising the key points would prove helpful for everyone to refer to afterwards.*" Using the word '*however*' sounds much better than '*but*' and helps to ensure that your learner remains focused on what you are saying.

If you don't have any follow-on points, then don't create them just for the sake of it. Conversely, if you do have any negative points or criticism, don't say "*My only negative point is ...*" or "*My only criticisms are ...*" It's much better to replace these words and say "*Some areas for development could be ...*" or "*I'm sure that you will improve once you take into account what we have discussed.*"

Ongoing constructive feedback which is developmental and has been carefully thought through is an indication of your interest in your learner, but it does take practice.

Feedback styles

There are several feedback styles you can use to provide feedback to your learners and each should include the opportunity to ask questions, even if this is just '*what would you do differently next time?*'

There are many different feedback styles, and you might like to carry out further research regarding them. Some are better than others, and you will need to find out what works for you, your learners, and your subject.

Feedback styles include being:

- descriptive – gives examples of what was achieved, what could be improved, and why

- evaluative – gives a statement such as *well-done* or *good*. This method does not offer helpful or constructive advice

- directive – gives advice with ideas for direct ways of problem solving

- indirective – gives guidance for the learner to solve things for themselves

- constructive (or positive) – gives specific and focused information to confirm a learner's achievement and/or to provide developmental points in a helpful way

- destructive (or negative) – gives damaging or unhelpful comments which could demoralise the learner. However, negative feedback given in a constructive way can be helpful, such as a learner using a piece of equipment incorrectly

- objective – gives facts regarding what has and has not been achieved

- subjective – gives a personal opinion which can be biased or vague

- informative – gives specific information regarding how a learner could improve upon what they have done, and signposts them to ways of doing this

- confirmative – gives minimal information, such as a tick or a cross next to a learner's answer.

Record keeping

It is important to keep records of assessment planning, decisions, and feedback. This will provide an audit trail of what has taken place, and prove what progress and achievement your learners have made and when. You will also need to satisfy any organisational, quality assurance, awarding organisation, or regulatory authorities' audit requirements. Record keeping can be manual or electronic, and you will need to find out what the requirements are at your organisation.

You may need to communicate certain information to other professionals involved in supporting learner achievement, for example, learning support assistants, and administrators. You might also need to produce reports and data regarding learner achievements for relevant managers and other stakeholders such as funding agencies.

Records will usually need to be kept for a set period, for example, three years. They should be the original records (if hard copies are used), not photocopies. It's fine to give copies to your learners, as it is harder to forge a copy than an original. Unfortunately, there are some learners who might do this; therefore keeping the originals will ensure your records are authentic. You should also maintain an overall tracking system which shows at a glance what each learner has achieved and when. This could be manual or electronic.

Keeping full and accurate factual assessment records is also necessary in case one of your learners appeals against an assessment decision you have made. If this happens, don't take it personally. As long as you have been objective, they will be appealing against your decision, not you as a person. You will need to find out what the appeals procedure is at your organisation.

Assessment data should be used regularly to review the progress of your learners. For example, if several learners fail an activity, is this your fault? It could be because of how you worded a particular question, or perhaps you didn't teach everything required beforehand for your learners to respond effectively. Monitoring the data also helps you to track the progression and achievement of your learners over time, as well as helping to review and develop your own practice. All records should comply with your organisation's procedures, such as confidentiality, as well as any relevant legislation and guidelines.

Theory into practice

Ask a colleague or your mentor if you can observe an assessment activity that they are due to carry out. Observe how they communicate with their learners, what materials they use, and how they reach their decisions. Listen carefully to their feedback and see how they complete their records.

Quality assurance

Quality assurance is a system of checks which should take place to ensure that assessment has been carried out correctly. If it does not take place, there could be risks to the accuracy, consistency, and fairness of assessment practice, which might disadvantage the learners. Quality assurance should be a continual process which is carried out by someone other than the assessor. It can be internal and/or external, depending upon whether the course or qualification is externally accredited.

Helpful hint

Finding out who will quality assure your assessment practice at your organisation, and getting to know them, will help to build up a good working relationship. Never be afraid to ask for their help and advice. If you don't understand something, it's highly likely your learners won't either.

Internal quality assurance (IQA)

This relates to monitoring the process your learners go through during their time at your organisation. It helps to ensure that assessors make correct judgements, and don't pass a learner who hasn't met all the requirements.

As a minimum, the internal quality assurer should:

- plan what will be monitored, from whom and when

- observe teacher and assessor performance, provide developmental feedback, and follow up on any action points

- sample assessment records, learners' work, and assessors' decisions

- meet with or talk to learners and others, for example, witnesses from the workplace

- facilitate the standardisation of assessor practice

- support teachers and assessors with any concerns, and with their continuing professional development (CPD, in Chapter 9).

- maintain relevant sampling and tracking records.

Activity

- *What are the advantages of IQA for your subject? How will the internal quality assurance process impact upon your role?*

External quality assurance (EQA)

This is a similar process to internal quality assurance, but the EQA process is carried out by a representative from the awarding organisation for your subject. The EQA role is not just about monitoring; it's also about supporting IQAs, teachers, and assessors, and providing advice and guidance to help them get things right. A report will be completed by the EQA and any action points must be carried out; otherwise a sanction could be put in place.

Standardisation of practice

Standardising practice between teachers and assessors helps to ensure the reliability and fairness of assessment planning, decisions, materials and resources, feedback, and record keeping. The process enables staff to work as a team rather than on their own, and to give an equitable and consistent service to all learners. It is also an opportunity to ensure that all staff are interpreting the qualification and course requirements accurately. It's a good way of maintaining professional development, and ensuring compliance and accountability with awarding organisations' and regulatory authorities' requirements. Assessors should also discuss the content of what is being taught as well as what is being assessed, to ensure that they are all interpreting the content in the same way.

Example

Jon was a new assessor, and was not very familiar with the content of the qualification he was due to assess. The full team of assessors met once a month to

(Continued)

(Continued)

discuss each unit. This ensured they were all interpreting the requirements in the same way, and making correct and consistent decisions. Jon attended the next meeting and was given the opportunity to reassess a unit which had already been assessed by someone else. This activity helped him to understand the content of the unit as well as the assessment requirements. He was also able to see how the assessment documentation was completed.

Attending a standardisation activity will give you the opportunity to share good practice and to compare your assessment decisions with those of your colleagues. You can then discuss your findings as a team. This will ensure that you have interpreted the requirements accurately, that the learners' work is appropriate, and that the assessment records are completed and stored correctly. Even if you don't learn anything new, it will hopefully confirm that you are doing things right.

Theory into practice

Find out who else at your organisation is involved with the qualification/subjects that you teach, and when the next standardisation activity is. Attend the activity and see how other members of staff discuss and interpret various aspects. How do they standardise their practice, decisions, and record keeping? What changes to the standardisation process would you recommend and why?

Summary

This chapter has explored:

- Principles of assessment
- Assessment planning, types, and methods
- Making decisions and providing feedback
- Quality assurance

Table 7.1 Examples of assessment methods and activities

(See Table 4.2 in Chapter 4, as some teaching and learning activities can also be used for assessment)

Method/activity	Description	Strengths	Limitations
Assignments	Can be practical or theoretical tasks to assess various aspects of a subject or qualification over a period of time	Consolidates learning Several aspects can be assessed at once Might be set by an awarding organisation who will provide clear marking criteria Learners could add to their work if they don't meet all the requirements first time	Everything must have been taught beforehand, or be known by the learner Questions can be misinterpreted Can be time consuming for learners to complete Must be individually assessed, and written feedback given Assessor might be biased when marking
Blended assessments	Using more than one method of assessment, usually including technology	Several methods of assessment can be combined, making the assessment process more interesting	Not all learners may have access to the required technology, or know how to use it
Case studies	Can be a hypothetical situation, a description of an actual event or an incomplete event, enabling learners to explore a particular scenario	Can make topics more realistic, enhancing motivation and interest Can be carried out individually or in a group situation Builds on current knowledge and experience	If carried out as a group activity, roles should be defined and individual contributions assessed Time should be allowed for a debrief afterwards Must have clear outcomes Can be time consuming to prepare and assess
Checklists	A list of criteria which must be met to confirm competence or achievement	Can form part of an ongoing record of achievement or a job profile Assessment can take place when a learner is ready	Learners may lose their copy and not remember the details of what they have achieved Assessors might be tempted to 'tick all the boxes' when a learner hasn't fully met everything Not suitable for higher level learners
Cloze sentences (also known as gapped handouts)	Key words are missed out of sentences for learners to input	A quick way to test knowledge and vocabulary A clue can be given of how many letters are in each of the missing words Alternatively, several similar words could be given as options for the learner to choose from	Learners might guess the word rather than base it on their knowledge and understanding Learners might get the word correct but spell it wrongly Not suitable for higher level learners

(Continued)

Table 7.1 (Continued)

Method/activity	Description	Strengths	Limitations
Discussions	Learners talk about a relevant topic either in groups or pairs	Allows freedom to express different viewpoints Promotes questions and discussions Can contribute to meeting certain criteria	Easy to digress Assessor needs to keep the group focused A time limit should be set Some learners may not get involved, others may dominate Assessor needs to manage the contributions of each individual and know what has been achieved by whom Can be time consuming Learners may need to research a topic in advance Can lead to arguments
e-assessments/ online assessments	*Electronic assessment* – assessment using information and communication technology (ICT) *Synchronous* – assessor and learner are simultaneously present, communicating in real time *Asynchronous* – assessor and learner are interacting at different times	Teaching, learning, and assessment can take place in a virtual learning environment (VLE) Assessment can take place at a time to suit learners Participation is widened Results and feedback can be instantly generated Less paperwork for the assessor Improves computer skills Can be blended with other assessment methods Groups, blogs, forums, and chat rooms can be set up to improve communication	Learners need access to a computer or suitable device Learners need to be computer literate Reliable internet connection needed Self-discipline is required Clear targets must be set Authenticity of learner's work may need validating Technical support may be required
End-point assessment (EPA) activities (synoptic assessment)	The term refers to apprenticeship programmes where assessment takes place at the end of the programme, and will include several methods	Assessment is usually by someone who has not been involved with the learner's training; therefore they will be objective with their judgements Allows the apprentice to demonstrate their skills and knowledge independently; therefore the EPA process can be seen as more important, raising the value of apprenticeships	Assessment is only a snapshot of what has been learnt; therefore the learner might do well with what is assessed, but not do well with what is not assessed (or vice versa) Learners may struggle in exam conditions (if used) and perform badly The learner might be demoralised if they don't pass first time EPAs are expensive and any resits must be paid for by the employer Some apprenticeships only have one EPA organisation who can carry out EPAs; therefore waiting times can be long Administration around EPA can be arduous and time consuming

Method/activity	Description	Strengths	Limitations
Essays	A formal piece of written text, produced by a learner, for a specific topic	Useful for academic subjects Can check a learner's English skills at specific levels Enhances a learner's knowledge and understanding by using research and reading	Not suitable for lower level/lower ability learners Marking can be time consuming Plagiarism can be an issue Doesn't usually have a right or wrong answer, therefore can be difficult to mark Learners need good writing skills
Examinations	A formal activity which must be carried out in certain conditions	Can be open book, or open notes, enabling learners to have books and notes with them Some learners like the challenge of a formal examination and cope well Examinations are often perceived to have greater rigour than some other assessment methods Can be externally created and assessed by an awarding organisation, saving the assessor time If externally created but internally assessed, the awarding organisation should provide sample answers, ensuring marking is consistent	Invigilation or online proctoring is required Security arrangements must be in place prior to and afterwards for examination papers Learners may have been taught purely to pass expected questions by using past papers; therefore they may forget everything afterwards Some learners may be anxious Can be closed book or closed notes, not allowing learners to have books and notes with them Results might take a while to be marked and processed (if external) If a learner fails, they may have to wait a period of time before a re-take
Holistic assessment	Enables learners to demonstrate several aspects of a course or qualification at the same time	Similar aspects from the full course or qualification can be assessed at the same time Makes evidence collection and demonstration of achievement and competence much more efficient Can incorporate a range of assessment activities Helps learners link knowledge to practice	Could confuse the learner if aspects were assessed which were not planned for

(Continued)

Table 7.1 (Continued)

Method/activity	Description	Strengths	Limitations
Homework (self-study time)	Activities carried out between lessons, for example, answering online questions or completing a project	Learners can complete work at a time and place that suits them Maintains interest between lessons Encourages learners to stretch themselves further Consolidates learning so far Learners could peer-assess each other's work Learners could collaborate for a group task	Clear targets and time limits must be set Learners might not do it, or get someone else to do it for them Must be marked/assessed and individual feedback given Might not count towards an apprentice's off-the-job hours
Independent assessment	An assessment process carried out by someone who is independent of the learner i.e. has not been involved with their training	The decision will be objective as the assessor does not know the learner	If the learner is not ready for assessment, time will be wasted and the learner might be demoralised if they don't pass first time It might occur in a place the learner is unfamiliar with
Interviews	A one-to-one discussion	Enables the assessor to determine how much a learner knows Enables the assessor to get to know each learner as an individual, and to discuss any issues impacting upon their learning	Not all learners may react well when interviewed Needs careful planning and timing Detailed records need to be kept
Learner statements	Learners write how they have met certain criteria	Enables learners to take ownership of their achievements	Learners might misinterpret the criteria and/or write too much or too little Another assessment method should also be used to confirm practical skills
Learning journal/diary or reflective account	Learners keep a record of their progress, their reflections, and thoughts, and reference these to certain criteria	Helps assess English skills Useful for higher level courses Can be paper-based, digital, audio, or video-based to suit the learner and their course	Should be specific to the learning taking place and be analytical rather than descriptive Content needs to remain confidential Can be time consuming and/or difficult to read/watch or hear

Method/activity	Description	Strengths	Limitations
Observations	Watching learners perform a skill and/or demonstrate a change in knowledge and behaviour	Enables skills to be seen in action Learners can make a mistake (if it is safe), enabling them to realise their areas for development Learners could be observed again if they didn't fully achieve the requirements Can be used as a starting point to generate the content for a professional discussion or question and answer session Can assess several aspects at the same time (holistic assessment) Ensures authenticity (providing the assessor knows the learner)	Timing must be arranged to suit each learner Communication needs to take place with others (if applicable e.g. in the workplace) No permanent record unless visually recorded Questions must be asked to confirm knowledge and understanding (either during or after the observation depending on the task i.e. if the learner is in the workplace with customers, it would be intrusive and inappropriate for the assessor to interrupt) Assessor might not be objective with their decision Learner might put on an act for the assessor which isn't how they normally perform (for better or worse)
Panel discussion	Learners are asked questions by a panel of assessors	Gives learners a chance to explain what they have achieved and what they understand	Learners might feel intimidated
Peer-assessment	Learners provide feedback to their peers after an activity	Promotes learner and peer interaction, involvement, and teamwork Learners may accept comments from peers better than those from the assessor Enables learners to assess each other Activities can often correct misunderstandings and consolidate learning without intervention by the assessor	Everyone needs to understand the criteria being assessed Needs to be carefully managed to ensure no personality conflicts or unjustified comments Assessor needs to confirm progress and achievements as it might differ Some peers may be anxious about providing feedback, perhaps if their peer has not done well Should be supported with other assessment activities Needs careful management and training in how to provide feedback
Piece of work	Learners create a piece of work of their choosing, which demonstrates their skills and/or knowledge	Enables learners to choose a relevant activity which they excel at e.g. case study, painting, model creation, video, blog or vlog, written work	Authenticity needs to be checked if the assessor has not seen the learner producing the piece of work Learners might get carried away and produce too much; therefore, clear guidance must be given

(Continued)

Table 7.1 (Continued)

Method/activity	Description	Strengths	Limitations
Portfolios of evidence (also see showcase)	A formal record of evidence (manual or electronic) produced by learners and apprentices to meet professional or qualification requirements	Ideal for learners who don't like formal tests and exams Can be compiled over a period of time to reflect ongoing performance and knowledge Learner-centred, therefore promotes autonomy and ongoing reflection Evidence can be left in its natural location to be viewed by the assessor	Authenticity and currency to be checked Computer access required to assess electronic portfolios Tendency for learners to produce a large quantity of evidence (it should be quality not quantity) All evidence must be cross-referenced to the relevant criteria Can be time consuming to assess Confidentiality of documents within the portfolio must be maintained
Presentations	Learners present a topic, often using information and communication technology	Can be individual or in a group Can assess skills, knowledge, understanding, and behaviour Develops presentation skills and equips learners with skills for the workplace, such as communication	If it's a group presentation, individual contributions must be assessed Some learners may be nervous or anxious in front of others
Products	Evidence produced by a learner to prove competence, for example, paintings, models, video, audio, photos, documents	Assessor can see what the learner has done Learners feel a sense of achievement, for example, by displaying their work in an exhibition, or producing a portfolio of paper-based or digital evidence	Authenticity needs to be checked if the assessor has not seen the learner producing the products Learners might forget to document and evaluate the process, losing opportunities for the submission of further evidence
Professional discussion	An in-depth two-way conversation between the assessor and learner based around certain criteria	Ideal way to assess aspects which are more difficult to observe, are rare occurrences, or take place in restricted or confidential settings Useful to support observations to check knowledge and understanding Learners can describe how they carry out various activities Can fill in any gaps not seen by an observation Develops communication skills	A record must be kept of the discussion, for example, audio/digital/visual along with notes Needs careful planning as it's a discussion, not a question and answer session Learners need time to prepare Assessor needs to be experienced at using open and probing questions, and listening carefully to the responses, to ensure the learner has met the requirements

Method/activity	Description	Strengths	Limitations
Projects	A longer-term activity enabling learners to provide evidence which meets certain criteria, or to consolidate their learning and experiences	Can be interesting and motivating for the learner Can be individual or group-led Encourages research and creativity skills Learners could choose their own topics and devise tasks which interest them Can involve real life problem-solving opportunities	Clear outcomes must be set, along with a time limit Must be relevant, realistic, and achievable Progress should be checked regularly If a group is carrying out the project, be aware of each individual's input, don't let one person dominate Thorough feedback should be given
Puzzles, quizzes, wordsearches, crosswords	A fun way of assessing learning in an informal way	Fun activities to test skills, knowledge, and/ or understanding Useful way to assess progress of lower level learners Good for assessing retention of facts Can be quickly created online	Can seem trivial to mature learners Does not assess a learner's level of understanding, or ability to apply their knowledge to different situations Can be time consuming to create and assess if not created digitally
Questions	A key technique for assessing understanding, either verbally, written, or online Questions can be: open, closed, probing, prompting, clarifying, leading, hypothetical, reflective, rhetorical, or multiple-choice	Can be short answer or long essay style Can be informal or formal, written, or verbal Can challenge and promote a learner's potential A question bank can be devised for certain topics (and standardised with other assessors) which could be used again with different learners and different groups Can test critical arguments or thinking and reasoning skills Verbal questions suit some learners more than others e.g. a learner who has dyslexia might prefer to talk through their responses to written questions	Closed questions only give a yes or no response which doesn't demonstrate knowledge or understanding Questions must be devised carefully i.e. be unambiguous, and can be time consuming to prepare If the same questions are used with other learners, they might talk and share their answers Written responses might be the work of others i.e. copied or plagiarised Expected responses or grading criteria need to be produced beforehand to ensure consistency and validity of marking May need to rephrase some questions if learners are struggling with their answer

(Continued)

Table 7.1 (Continued)

Method/activity	Description	Strengths	Limitations
Recognition of prior learning (RPL) Recognition of prior achievement (RPA)	Assessing what has previously been learnt, experienced, and achieved to find a suitable starting point for further assessments	Ideal for learners who have achieved certain aspects already No need for learners to duplicate work, or be reassessed Values previous learning, experiences, and achievements	Checking the authenticity and currency of the evidence provided is crucial Awarding organisation approval might be required if it's towards an accredited qualification Previous learning, experiences, and achievements might not be relevant in relation to current requirements Can be time consuming for the learner to provide the relevant evidence, and for the assessment process
Reflective account	Learners reflect upon how they have put theory into practice, and link this to the criteria being assessed	A type of self-assessment Can be formally assessed, therefore can count towards achievement as well as progress Useful for higher level learners Learners can include photos to illustrate their points, and provide further evidence and links to work saved elsewhere	Can be time consuming to assess Learners need the skills of reflective writing and cross-referencing Learners might feel they have achieved more than they have
Reports, research, and dissertations	Learners produce a document to inform, recommend, and/or make suggestions based on certain criteria	Useful for higher level learners Promotes critical and analytical skills Encourages the use of research techniques	Learners need to know how to carry out research, and to use academic writing skills Can be time consuming to assess Plagiarism and authenticity could be an issue
Self-assessment	Learners decide how they have met certain criteria, or how they are progressing at a given time	Promotes learner involvement and personal autonomy Encourages learners to check their own work Encourages reflection Learners can digitally record themselves carrying out a task, then view it and critically reflect on their progress	Learners may feel they are doing better or worse than they actually are Assessor needs to discuss progress and achievements with each learner to confirm their decisions Learners need to be specific about what they have achieved and what they still need to do Could be difficult for the learner to be objective when making a decision

Method/activity	Description	Strengths	Limitations
Showcase	A way of enabling a learner to show what they have achieved over a period of time e.g. via a report, presentation, or professional portfolio of evidence	Often used during the end-point assessment of apprentices for them to evidence the relevant occupational standards Learners can justify their evidence in an interview, if part of the showcase	Learners might not perform at their best during an interview/presentation if they are nervous
Skills tests	A way of finding out the current level of a learner's skill or experience towards a particular subject or vocation	Could be online or computer-based to enable a quick assessment, for example, maths Results can be used as a starting point for learning or progression	Learners might be apprehensive of formal tests Feedback might not be immediate If electronically generated, feedback might not be useful or developmental, or be misunderstood
Simulation	An imitation activity carried out when the real activity would be too dangerous For example, the evacuation of a building when the fire alarm goes off: there's no need to set fire to the building for a simulated evacuation	Enables learners to demonstrate what they might do in a real situation Learners may realise things about themselves they were not aware of	Careful planning is needed Can be time consuming Specialist equipment may be needed Not all learners may be able to participate fully May not be taken seriously by some learners Thorough debrief needed
Team building exercises/ energisers	A fun and light-hearted way of re-energising learners after a break	A good way for learners to work with each other Can revitalise a flagging lesson Can be used to informally assess skills, knowledge, and behaviours	Not all learners may want or be able to take part Some learners may think the activities are insignificant and time-wasting Careful explanations are needed to link the experience to the topic being assessed Can be difficult to evidence in terms of sufficiency and learner involvement

(Continued)

Table 7.1 (Continued)

Method/activity	Description	Strengths	Limitations
Tests (and multiple-choice tests) *Also see skills tests*	A formal approach to assess knowledge and understanding	Cost-effective method as the same test can be used with large numbers of learners Some test responses can be scanned into a computer for marking and analysis Other tests can be taken at a computer or be online, which gives immediate results Questions can be randomly generated to prevent different learners taking the same test	Needs to be carried out in supervised conditions or via a secure platform/website Time limits usually required Can be stressful to learners Feedback might not be immediate if assessed manually or externally Learners in other groups might find out the content of the tests from others Identity of learners must be confirmed Electronic feedback from multiple-choice tests might not be developmental enough to help the learner improve in certain areas
Tutorials	A one-to-one or group discussion between the assessor and learner with an agreed purpose, for example, reviewing progress so far	A good way of informally assessing a learner's progress and/or providing feedback An opportunity for learners to discuss any issues A chance for informal tuition to take place	Needs to be in a comfortable, safe, and quiet environment, as confidential issues might be discussed Time may overrun Records should be maintained and action points followed up
Video/audio	Recorded evidence of actual achievements – often digital	Direct proof of what was achieved by a learner i.e. eliminates issues of proving authenticity Can be reviewed by the assessor and internal quality assurer after the event Digital facilities are more easily accessible i.e. by using different devices and smartphones	Can prove expensive to purchase the equipment and storage media Can be time consuming to set up and use Technical support may be required Storage facilities are required If recorded in the workplace, confidentiality of content/people may be needed, and a declaration signed Privacy might be compromised Large files might exceed the maximum upload size for an e-portfolio

Method/activity	Description	Strengths	Limitations
Viva	A formal oral discussion between the assessor and learner to confirm whether certain criteria have been met	Gives the opportunity for the learner to explain the content of their work e.g. an assignment answer, or the contents of a professional practice portfolio	The assessor needs to have reviewed the learner's work/portfolio beforehand, and prepared relevant questions A digital recording may need to be made as proof of the discussion
Walk and talk	A spoken and visual way of assessing a learner's competence	Enables a learner to *walk and talk* through their product evidence within their work environment Gives an audit trail of the evidence relating to certain criteria Useful where sensitive and confidential information are dealt with	Can be time consuming Can be difficult for the assessor to appreciate all the evidence in the time they have Difficult for quality assurers to sample the evidence
Witness testimonies/statements	A statement from a person who is familiar with the learner and/or an expert in the same subject area	The witness can confirm competence or achievements for situations which might not regularly occur, or which include confidential and security aspects If the witness spends time with the learner, they could observe aspects which are more difficult to plan for i.e. dealing with a difficult customer or dealing with an emergency situation Witness testimonies can be recorded in written or digital format	The assessor must confirm the suitability of the witness and check the authenticity of any of their testimonies Learners could write the statement and the witness might sign it not understanding the content Assessors may need to spend time with the witness in advance, to ensure that they understand how to write a good testimony, and how to link learner achievement to certain criteria
Worksheets	Interactive handouts to check knowledge and understanding (can also be electronic/online) Can contain text and images, followed by questions	Informal assessment activity which can be carried out individually, in pairs, or groups Useful for lower level learners Can be created at different degrees of difficulty to address differentiation	Mature/higher level learners may consider them inappropriate Too many worksheets can be boring Learners might not be challenged enough

8

Succeeding with professional pedagogical practices

Putting theory into professional practice for your subject

Introduction

Professional pedagogic practice is about having the opportunity to teach your subject specialism to your learners. You must succeed with your teaching practice and non-teaching practice to achieve the Learning and Skills Teacher Occupational Standards. In turn, you will meet the requirements of the teaching qualification or apprenticeship programme.

This chapter will introduce you to the following topics:

- Micro-teaching
- Teaching practice
- Observed practice
- Professional practice portfolio

Occupational Standards covered in Chapter 8

Duties	Knowledge	Skills	Behaviours
D1, D3, D4, D5, D6, D7, D8	K1, K3, K5	S1, S4, S9, S10, S11, S18, S19, S22, S23, S24	B2, B4, B5

Micro-teaching

Micro-teaching is about delivering a short lesson to a group of learners. It's a great opportunity to demonstrate your teaching skills, and subject specialism skills and knowledge. This might take place as part of a teaching qualification or apprenticeship programme you are working towards, for example teaching a short lesson to your peer group. You should be able to demonstrate the use of a range of teaching, learning, and assessment approaches, as well as the use of resources. You will also have the opportunity of being a learner during lessons taught by your peers. This is an excellent way of seeing how they plan and teach their subject. You should have the opportunity of providing feedback to your peers, which might be verbal and/or written. This can help with your own development, as you will know what it's like to be a learner, and will see things from a different perspective. You might also be able to deliver micro-teach lessons to your current learners if you are in-service. This means you will be in your own teaching environment rather than a learning environment.

Your micro-teach lesson should be based on your subject specialism, and an observation (formal or informal) will take place. The length of the lesson, date, time, and place should be agreed in advance. Your observer will provide you with feedback at the end of the lesson. The feedback is designed to help you to improve and develop your pedagogical practices. Your mentor might also carry out observations and will be in a good position to give you guidance regarding your subject specialism.

Helpful hint

You may feel nervous about your first micro-teach lesson, particularly if you are new to teaching. However, try to imagine you are acting a role and this might help to boost your confidence and calm your nerves.

Prior to your micro-teach lesson

There are certain things that you will need to know prior to your micro-teach lesson taking place. You might find it useful to ask your observer the following questions.

- How long will my lesson be?

- When and where will it take place, and at what time?

- How many people will I be teaching?

- How can I find out any individual needs?

- Can I find out in advance what prior knowledge and/or experience my learners have of my subject?

- Who will observe me and will they (or can I) make a visual recording?

- Is it an informal observation or will it count towards my qualification/apprenticeship?

- Will you need to see my lesson plan in advance?

- How should I dress?

- What if I need personal protective equipment (PPE)?

- What equipment and resources are available for me to use?

- Can I show a video clip? If so, how long can it last?

- What will I need to bring with me e.g. board markers, clock, pens, and paper?

- Will I have time beforehand to set up the area e.g. move tables, check my resources and equipment?

- Will I have internet access if I need it?

- If I use an electronic presentation, should I email it to you or bring it on a memory stick or card?

- Is there somewhere I can get handouts photocopied in advance?

- Do I have to explain the housekeeping information e.g. fire exits and toilets?

- Should I start with an icebreaker and ground rules?

- What kind of assessment activities can I use?

- How will I receive feedback afterwards?

- Should I complete a reflective learning journal?

Planning your micro-teach lesson

You will need to plan and prepare in advance. Don't underestimate how much time this may take you. Make sure your lesson can flow logically through the introduction, development, and conclusion stages (beginning, middle, and ending, in Chapter 4). You could rehearse your lesson in front of family or friends. This would help with your timings, and any questions which might be asked. Keep things simple; don't try to achieve too much too soon. You know your subject, but your learners don't. They will need time to assimilate new knowledge.

You might find it useful to formalise what you want to achieve, and what you want your learners to achieve. The former is your aim (what you will do), and the latter is your objectives (what your learners will do).

Example

Aim: To introduce learners to non-verbal communication skills.

Objectives:

1. *State two methods of non-verbal communication.*

2. *Identify aspects of good and bad body language.*

3. *Discuss experiences regarding assumptions made from body language.*

This can help to create your lesson plan (in Chapter 4) which will also state the activities and resources that you will use with your learners, along with timings for each.

Delivering your micro-teach lesson

You could start by welcoming everyone to your lesson and introducing yourself, the aim and objectives. If you are teaching your peer group, you will probably know them already; however, do remain professional and treat them as your learners. Refer to your lesson plan as you progress, and use a variety of teaching, learning (in Chapter 4) and assessment activities (in Chapter 7).

You could ask a question such as *'what knowledge, if any, do you have of this subject?'* This is a great way to engage your learners from the start, and to carry out an initial assessment. You can then build on and include their experiences as you progress through your lesson.

Try to relax, but stay focused on what you are doing, and above all try and enjoy yourself. If you are passionate about your subject and excited to pass on your skills and knowledge, your enthusiasm should help the lesson to go well.

The timing of your activities needs to be followed carefully; if you are only teaching a 20-minute lesson, you may not have time for group activities. If you use practical activities, think what you will be doing while your learners are busy i.e. moving around them and observing or asking questions shows that you are in control.

Longer lessons i.e. 30 minutes or more, benefit from a mixture of teaching and learning approaches and the use of different assessment activities. If you have taught a practical task, you will need to observe that your learners have the skills to demonstrate it. If you have taught theory, you will need to assess that your learners have gained the required knowledge and understanding.

It's useful to have a spare activity in case you have time i.e. a few questions which you can ask your learners. It's also useful to know what you can remove in case you are running out of time.

The following are some short assessment activities which you could use to check that learning has taken place (in alphabetical order):

- completing gapped handouts or wordsearches

- designing a poster to address a question

- discussions in pairs or small groups

- questions – written, oral, online, or multiple-choice

- observation of a practical task

- puzzles and quizzes

- role plays.

Don't forget to tell your learners whether they have been successful at achieving the objectives, and if not, what they can do to improve. If you are unsure how to end your lesson, you can repeat your aim and objectives and then say *Thank you, I've enjoyed my lesson with you today*. This will indicate to your group that you have finished. Try and refrain from saying things like '*I'm glad that's over*', or '*I'm finished now*'. Just remember that you are a professional and, as such, you should end your lesson in a professional way.

Activity

What do you consider would contribute to a good micro-teach lesson? For example, careful planning and timing, and demonstrating confidence. Make a list of points and discuss them with a colleague or your mentor.

Evaluating your micro-teach lesson

Evaluating your lesson is an important aspect of your own learning and development. You could think that you have done really well, but you might have received some helpful feedback afterwards from your observer and your peers to help you improve. Listen to them carefully, and ask questions to clarify any points you are unsure of. Try not to interrupt or become defensive when you are receiving feedback, and don't take anything personally.

When evaluating your lesson and reflecting on your practice (in Chapter 9) it's helpful to consider:

- your strengths

- areas for development

- any action and improvements required, from both a teaching perspective and of your subject specialism.

You might need to complete a reflective learning journal to formalise the above, or you could just make notes to help with your development. The micro-teach lessons are a chance to try things out in a safe space, and to consider what you would change or do differently next time. If you made mistakes, such as struggling to keep to your planned timings, try not to be annoyed, but learn from it.

Create a 45-minute micro-teach lesson plan based around an aspect of your subject specialism. Make sure that you have a clear aim and objectives, and a variety of teaching and learning approaches. Think carefully about what resources you will use and how you will assess that learning has taken place. What could you add in if you have spare time, and what could you remove if you are short of time?

Teaching practice

Teaching practice is about demonstrating your skills and knowledge as a teacher, as well as those of your subject specialism. It will give you actual experience of what it's like to be a teacher, in a real teaching and learning environment. It's a great way for you to try out everything you have been learning about during your time working towards a teaching qualification or apprenticeship programme. It's also a chance to try out new things. If something doesn't work, you just need to reflect as to why, and consider what you could do differently next time. No situation is ever the same, as you will be teaching different learners on different occasions in different environments. What works for one learner or group might not work with others.

Activity

Find out how many teaching practice hours you will need to carry out and when and where they might occur. Who will be your contact person to arrange them?

Effective teaching practice should include:

- teaching in different locations, settings, or contexts

- teaching across more than one level of learning

- teaching a variety of learners and age ranges (14+)

- teaching individuals and groups

- engaging and inspiring learners

- adapting lessons to reflect the needs of learners

- acting in a manner which is ethical, fair, consistent, and impartial

- valuing equality, diversity and inclusion

- putting subject and pedagogic knowledge into practice, based on evidence-informed research.

Specific details regarding teaching practice and observed practice for achievement of the teaching qualification or apprenticeship programme are in Chapter 1. However, you will need to find out the exact requirements which relate to you from your course tutor.

Helpful hint

Observing your mentor will prove valuable to gain ideas regarding how they teach their particular subject. If possible, arrange to do this and ask to use the observation report which they will use when observing you.

Placement log

You will need to keep a log of the amount of time spent undertaking your teaching and non-teaching practice, as in Table 8.1, along with a list of supporting evidence. For example, schemes of work, lesson plans, and learning journals. The log and evidence will form a major part of your professional practice portfolio. The evidence must be cross-referenced to the Occupational Standards (OS, in Chapter 1). You might be given a template to complete for this, you could design your own, or you could use an electronic method. You should give each piece of evidence a number, which will refer to where it's filed in your professional practice portfolio (either manually or electronically). Your evidence could be used several times, for example, one scheme of work might cover several OS, and therefore it will keep the same reference number.

If you are working towards a qualification or an apprenticeship programme, you will be required to evidence a certain number of teaching hours and administrative hours (in Chapter 1). Non-teaching hours might involve: observing other teachers, attending meetings, interviewing learners, and carrying out other activities which support your teaching role such as administration, standardisation activities, preparation, and planning.

Theory into practice

Create a placement log and start keeping a record of what you have done so far regarding your teaching and non-teaching practice. Give each piece of evidence a number, bearing in mind that you can use it several times. You might also wish to complete a learning journal after each lesson you have taught to consider your strengths, areas for development, and any actions or improvements required.

Table 8.1 Example placement log

Date	Details	Location	Teaching practice	Non-teaching practice	Evidence reference
9th September	Preparation of schemes of work and lesson plans	Staff office Annexe building	n/a	6 hours	1 – scheme of work 2 – lesson plan 6 – lesson plan 10 – scheme of work 11 – lesson plan
3rd October	Preparation of lesson plans	Staff office Annexe building	n/a	2 hours	2 – lesson plan 6 – lesson plan 11 – lesson plan
5th October	Level 2 Certificate in Customer Service – 15 in group	Room 7 Main building	2 hours	n/a	1 – scheme of work 2 – lesson plan 3 – group profile 4 – handout 5 – learning journal
9th November	Level 2 Certificate in Customer Service – 15 in group	Room 7 Main building	2 hours	n/a	1 – scheme of work 6 – lesson plan 7 – handout 8 – copy of electronic presentation 9 – learning journal
10th November	Level 1 Award in Health and Safety – 10 in group	Room 1 Main building	1.5 hours	n/a	10 – scheme of work 11 – lesson plan 12 – group profile 13 – handout 14 – group activity 15 – assessment activity 16 – learning journal 17 – observer's report (covers one hour)
11th November	Team meeting	Meeting room Annexe building	n/a	1 hour	18 – agenda 19 – own notes 20 – minutes of meeting

Observed practice

You will be observed several times throughout your work placement. Some will be informal, perhaps by colleagues and mentors, and some will be formal. The latter will count towards achievement of your teaching qualification or apprenticeship programme.

The observations are designed to:

- provide developmental feedback as to how you can improve your practice

- establish that you are teaching at the level expected to meet the Occupational Standards (in Chapter 1).

Earlier observations will predominantly be developmental as you are still learning how to be a teacher. You will be able to build upon the feedback you receive from your observer, and your competence will improve over time. As you near completion of the course, you should be fully meeting the requirements of the Occupational Standards.

There might be an occasion when you will teach an observed lesson but your observer will not be present in the same room. For example, they might be observing you live via the internet. If this is the case, make sure you find out in advance what the procedure will be and how you can obtain feedback afterwards.

Activity

Prior to an observation taking place, make and watch a visual recording of yourself to look for aspects you do well, and areas you could develop and improve upon. It's useful to inform your learners that you are making a recording and that it's to help with your development as a teacher. You will need their permission if they are included, and it's best to check with your organisation to make sure you are allowed to do this.

All observers will want to satisfy themselves that you are using teaching, learning, and assessment approaches effectively. They will want to see that learning is taking place, that you are including all your learners during the lesson, and differentiating your materials/activities for any particular learner needs. Make sure that all the materials you have prepared are of good quality, are varied, address inclusivity and differentiation, and are free from spelling, grammar, and punctuation errors. Don't try and prepare too much at the risk of showing off, or use any equipment you are not totally comfortable with. Make sure that you have a spare activity in case you have extra time available, and activities to stretch and challenge learners when necessary. You might also be required to embed aspects of English, maths and digital skills (in Chapter 4).

You should have a lesson plan which shows a clear aim (what you want to achieve) and objectives or tasks which your learners will carry out. You should also state how you will check that learning will take place i.e. the different assessment methods and activities you will use. Your observer may also want to see your group profile, record of attendance/register, and other relevant administrative documents. These might be electronic rather than hard copies, but they should still be accessible.

If possible, it would be useful to ask your mentor to comment on your lesson plan beforehand. They might be able to give you some valuable advice, perhaps regarding your timings. It's useful to have hard copies of an electronic presentation in case of an equipment malfunction. You could also consider which activities you could reduce or remove if you are running out of time. Check the environment and equipment beforehand, and complete any health and safety checks and/or risk assessments. Make sure you have enough of everything for the number of learners you expect.

Example

Reena was due to be observed next week and wanted to make a good impression. She had a lesson plan showing a mixture of teaching and learning activities, and a group profile showing how individual needs would be met. She had several handouts and books, and she would use the interactive whiteboard. She showed her plan to her mentor, who reminded her to include some checks that learning was taking place. She hadn't allocated any time to assessing learning. She was just so focused on demonstrating her teaching skills that she had forgotten about this.

Try not get too focused on what you will be doing; it should be about the learning that's taking place. Above all, don't panic; keep calm and don't try to do too much. You are still learning, and you will need to work at things over time. If you make a mistake, it's fine and it shows you are human. Just be honest with yourself and learn from it. However, don't bluff your way out of something as your learners will probably notice.

You might find the following checklist useful to help you to prepare for an observation.

Checklist for being observed

☐ Confirm the date, time, and location with your observer.

☐ Ask to see the observation report that will be used. It's useful to see what your observer is looking for.

☐ Inform any other staff such as your supervisor and/or mentor.

☐ Inform reception of your observer's name; you might need to reserve a parking space for them, inform them about public transport, and/or confirm directions to the venue. Your observer might also need to sign in and out of the building, wear a name badge, and be informed about relevant health and safety procedures.

☐ Inform your learners that you will be observed, and that it's about you, not them.

☐ If your observer is due to arrive prior to your lesson, arrange to meet them beforehand.

☐ If you will have started your lesson before your observer's arrival, make sure they know where to go, and prepare yourself/your learners to be interrupted when they do arrive.

☐ Check that you have the necessary documents and resources. These might include your scheme of work, lesson plan, group profile, handouts, and other resources. Your observer might ask for electronic or hard copies.

☐ Check beforehand that all the equipment which you plan to use is in working order.

☐ Wear appropriate clothing for the subject you will teach.

☐ Prepare your room so that there is somewhere for your observer to sit. They will need a position away from you and your learners, but where they can see what is going on. They might also need to wear some specialist clothing if applicable, for example, a laboratory coat, face mask, or safety goggles.

During the lesson

Being observed, even if you are an experienced teacher, can be a bit worrying or stressful, as you will want to deliver a perfect lesson. However, you are being observed every time you deliver a lesson by your own learners; it's just that they don't give you formal feedback afterwards. If you are nervous, don't let your learners know, as they probably won't notice.

Helpful hint

If you make a mistake, your observer will be watching to see that you put it right. Always have a contingency plan in case anything could go wrong.

You could introduce your observer to your learners and state they are observing the lesson, not them as individuals. Having a stranger in the room might lead to some behaviour issues if you haven't forewarned your learners. If so, you must deal with these as soon as they arise, and do it in a professional manner. Try not to look at your observer while they are with you; they are not part of your group and will not participate in any activities. Don't embarrass them by trying to involve them. They will be making lots of notes throughout the lesson. Therefore try not to be concerned if they don't appear to be watching you all the time; they will still be listening to what's going on.

Don't worry if you don't follow your lesson plan exactly. As your lesson progresses you will naturally adapt the timings and activities to meet the needs of your learners. Your observer will not mind if you don't keep to your timings as it will show that you are being flexible to meet the needs of your learners. Try and use a variety of teaching and learning approaches and activities to stretch and challenge your learners. If possible, use technology at some point during the lesson. Above all, check that learning has taken place. If you are not using formal assessment activities, make sure that you use informal activities which will enable your learners to demonstrate the progress they have made during the lesson.

After the lesson

If your observer stays until the end of your lesson, they should be able to provide you with verbal feedback when your learners have left. If this is not possible, make sure you ask your observer when you will receive their feedback, which might be oral, electronic, or paper-based. Ideally, the feedback should be given in a quiet area which will enable you to listen and focus upon what is said. You might also like to make some notes. Hopefully, the feedback you receive will reassure you that you are teaching correctly, and that learning is taking place. However, if you receive some negative feedback, don't take it personally, but learn from it. Your observer has only seen a snapshot of what you are capable of, and will be observing you on several occasions.

You might be given a copy of your observer's completed report, which you should read carefully. It would be useful to refer to this when evaluating your lesson. Your observer might have identified some points for your further training and development which you hadn't considered. As part of your teaching qualification, you might be required to keep a learning journal (in Chapter 9). This will help you to reflect upon what you did or did not do over time, and can be placed in your professional practice portfolio.

Theory into practice

Ask your mentor to carry out an informal observation of your teaching practice. Make sure that you have a detailed lesson plan, group profile, and relevant resources. Inform your learners why you will be observed and ask them to behave in their normal way. After the observation, ask your mentor for feedback. This can help with your pedagogic practice as well as knowledge of your subject.

Professional practice portfolio

This is a file (manual or electronic) which contains evidence of your teaching and non-teaching practice (which you have listed in your placement log), to prove that you have met the Occupational Standards (OS). It must be compiled in an organised and efficient manner, and all the evidence should be accessible to your assessor when they ask to see it.

Helpful hint

If you save anything electronically, use reference numbers as file names, make sure everything is safe and secure, and make backup copies.

Evidence might also include items of equipment or models you have used or made. Therefore reference can be made as to where they are located, and a photo placed in your file.

A professional discussion will take place towards the end of your course, based around the contents of your portfolio, often referred to as a *viva*. It will usually be carried out by your assessor and your placement provider, and will be to decide if you have met the OS.

Activity

If you haven't already obtained a copy of the Occupational Standards for Learning and Skills Teachers, download it at this link: http://tinyurl.com/ LSTTeacher. If the link doesn't work, just search for the title. Take a look at the duties, knowledge, skills and behaviours with a view to cross-referencing your evidence towards them. You could use the document as a checklist to ensure that you don't miss any.

A cross-reference matrix should be used to match all your evidence to the relevant duties, knowledge, skills and behaviours of the OS. Several pieces of evidence could be grouped, or you could list the evidence individually. The matrix might be supplied for you as a template, or you could create your own, as in Table 8.2. An alternative method would be to list all the OS first, and then match your evidence to them (as in Table 8.1). This method ensures that none will be missed. You could also adapt your placement log to include the cross-references. Whatever method you use, you must be able to justify to your assessor how you have met a particular OS when asked.

Table 8.2 Example cross-referencing matrix

Evidence reference	Duties	Knowledge	Skills	Behaviours
1, 10 – schemes of work	D1, D2, D3	K1, K3	S1	n/a
2, 6 – lesson plans	D1, D2, D3, D4, D5, D6, D7, D8	K1, K5, K9	S1, S4, S10, S19, S25	B5
3, 12 – group profiles	D1, D2, D5, D9	K1, K6	S4	n/a
4, 7, 13 – handouts	D3, D5	K4	S1, S8	n/a
5, 9, 16 – learning journals	D1, D2, D3, D4, D5, D7, D8	K1, K5, K9, K10, K16	S1, S9, S18, S19, S24	B2, B4
21 – CPD log	D3, D4, D6, D9	K1, K2, K5, K13, K15, K19, K20	S1, S14, S21, S22, S25	B2, B3
22 – Assignment One	D1, D2, D3, D4, F5, D7, D8, D9	K1, K2, K3, K4, K5, K6, K9, K10, K17	S1, S4, S8, S9, S10, S11, S19, S20, S24	B1, B2, B6

Evidence

Your evidence should include everything which you have listed in your placement log (which can go at the front of your portfolio), and other items such as coursework, completed assignments, and your observer's and mentor's observation reports. Everything must be cross-referenced to and fully meet the OS. If you don't meet them all, you will not pass.

Examples of evidence which you could provide includes:

- teaching practice documents such as: initial and diagnostic results, group profiles, schemes of work, lesson plans, learning support records, handouts

- personal development plan (PDP)

- continuing professional development (CPD) log and supporting documents

- learning journals

- logs of meetings with mentors such as the date and time, what was discussed, and how you have met any identified action points

- notes/emails showing liaison and communication with others

- observer's reports and feedback (with a statement of how you have met any identified action points)

- records of micro-teach lessons (if applicable)

- your own coursework e.g. assignments, research projects, and reports – all cross-referenced to the Occupational Standards

- witness testimonies from someone who is an expert in your area.

When producing your portfolio, consider quality not quantity. It's not the amount of work (quantity) that matters; a small amount could cover many criteria if it's done well (quality). If you have had to redo any work, it's best to include your original work as well as your revised work to show progression, for example an assignment which you resubmitted.

Theory into practice

Create a professional practice portfolio (either manual or electronic) and a cross-reference matrix. Start cross-referencing your evidence to the Occupational Standards.

Summary

This chapter has explored:

- Micro-teaching
- Teaching practice
- Observed practice
- Professional practice portfolio

9

Evaluating and improving professional practice

Putting theory into practice using evaluation and self-reflection

---

Introduction

Evaluation is about measuring the effectiveness of something with the aim of improving it. To help you improve your professional practice you can obtain feedback from learners and others. This feedback, whether positive or negative, can be used not only to help you improve your own practice, but the experiences of your learners.

Self-reflection is an important aspect of the evaluation process. It can lead to relevant continuing professional development, enabling you to remain up to date with your job role and your subject specialism.

This chapter will introduce you to the following topics:

- Evaluation
- Self-reflection
- Theories of reflective practice
- Continuing professional development

Duties	Knowledge	Skills	Behaviours
D3, D4, D8	K19	S1, S14, S21, S22	B2, B3

Evaluation

Evaluation is a way of obtaining data and feedback to help you to improve your practice and the overall learner experience. Evaluation should be an ongoing process throughout all aspects of the course, from the application process to when learners leave. The process can be informal by talking to others or formal by using a questionnaire or survey. Either way, the process should help you to realise how effective things were, and what you could change or improve. It will also help you to identify any problem areas, enabling you to do things differently in the future.

Helpful hint

Never assume everything is going well just because you think it is. There is always room for change and/or improvement.

Your job role might only require you to evaluate your own teaching practice, or it might involve you evaluating several other aspects which contribute to curriculum development. Your organisation will be able to inform you what's required.

Carrying out evaluation activities can help to ensure:

- a professional service is given to learners and others

- the teaching, learning, and assessment process is fair to all

- you are meeting organisational and regulatory requirements

- you are meeting any performance targets

- you can learn from any incidents

- changes and improvements can be made where necessary.

The best feedback you can obtain to help improve your lessons will be from your learners. This can range from informally asking questions at the end of a lesson, to formally issuing a survey at the end of a course. You could even ask your learners to design their own questions to put to their peers. Depending upon their age range and maturity, this might be a fun activity for them to participate in. They could analyse the responses and compile a report of recommendations. Make sure you keep your learners updated with how you have or have not implemented the recommendations; otherwise the process has no value.

Feedback can also be obtained from your peers, your mentor, colleagues, employers, and stakeholders. Your organisation might have a systematic programme regarding evaluation and who to obtain feedback from. There will be different activities which should be carried out at certain points throughout the course or the year. The feedback received from evaluations should lead to productive changes for you, your learners, and the organisation.

Examples of aspects which could be evaluated include (in alphabetical order):

- appeals and complaints
- assessment data
- budgets and funding
- data such as enrolment, retention, achievement, destinations, and progression
- equality, diversity and inclusion
- embedding English, maths and digital skills
- induction and initial assessment
- internal policies and procedures
- marketing and recruitment activities
- observations of teaching and learning
- quality assurance reports (internal and external)
- staff recruitment and retention
- staff training and development
- standardisation of practice
- sustainability
- the demand for curriculum content
- the quality of resources used
- teaching, learning, and assessment approaches and activities.

Obtaining data and feedback

Obtaining data and feedback is a crucial part of the evaluation process. This information will help you to deal with any problems or issues as necessary. Even if this is not part of your role, it's useful to know how data and feedback can be used to have an impact upon performance. For example, positive feedback can be used in publicity and promotional materials. Negative feedback should be acted upon as soon as possible.

The process of obtaining feedback could be carried out face to face, online, via the telephone, text messages, the internet or be paper-based via the postal service. Depending upon the type of feedback you wish to obtain, you will need to consider what method you will use; how you will use it; and who you will choose e.g. your learners or others (known as respondents). Afterwards, always inform your respondents how their feedback has led to changes and improvements. If the latter have not yet taken place, let them know what will happen and when.

There are many different ways of asking questions and of designing a questionnaire or a survey. Your organisation might already have a procedure for this and it's useful to find out what methods are used and why. For example, using open or closed questions. Open questions give the respondent the option of adding their own response and gives you *qualitative* information. This gives you something of *quality* to work with. Closed questions only give an option such as 'yes' or 'no', or a numbered response, which gives you *quantitative* data. This gives you *quantities* i.e. 25 said yes, 15 said no. You will need to be careful as to how you word your questions so that they are objective i.e. not personal or leading, and only relate to what you need to find out at the time. Short questions and short questionnaires or surveys are better than long ones, as people might be put off if it's too time consuming.

When using questionnaires or surveys, make sure that you set a date for their completion (and for their return). Always inform your respondents why you are asking them to take part and what the information will be used for. If it doesn't have any meaning or benefit for them, they might not get involved. If you are designing the questions, you will need to be careful of the level of language you are using. You will also need to consider aspects such as equality, diversity and inclusion, those whose first language is not English, and learner needs such as those who are neurodivergent (in Chapter 3).

Anonymity for those completing a questionnaire or survey could lead to you gaining more truthful responses if the person knows they will not be identified. However, if the respondent works closely with you, or you are interviewing in person, this might not be the case. The same goes for telephone, text message, or face-to-face questioning. Electronic surveys that are emailed back will denote who the respondent is; however, postal ones will not (unless a reference code has been added). There are lots of online programs which can be used that will guarantee anonymity and will also analyse the results of quantitative data. Some of these offer a free basic service such as www.surveymonkey.com. You could carry out a small scale survey with just a few learners to see how it works first. This is called a *pilot* and allows you to make any changes before a full survey is carried out.

Activity

Research different ways of devising questions to gain responses using questionnaires or surveys (online or paper-based). What would be the best method to use with your learners and why?

Try not to be disappointed if you don't get as many responses as you had hoped for. However, if you give people time to complete them, perhaps towards the end of a lesson, they can hand it in straight away rather than take it away and forget about it.

Analysing data and feedback

Analysing data can prove useful for the evaluation process, such as obtaining statistics about: enrolment; retention; pass rates; achievement; destinations; progression; appeals and complaints.

You will need to find out from your organisation what they expect you to do in relation to obtaining and analysing data. Some aspects of data analysis might be automatic via the organisation's online management systems. This might be quantitative data i.e. statistics, percentages, bar charts, or graphs (quantity), as opposed to qualitative data i.e. statements and general feedback (quality).

Example

Quantity – this is the number of respondents who took part (e.g. 18 out of 24) and how many of those 18 chose the different options which were offered for each question. This is quantitative data and can give an at-a-glance statistical view. It can be automatically analysed with a computer or online program.

Quality – this relates to the statements which are made by the respondents in answer to questions. You will need to read through them and perhaps summarise them according to any relevant themes which occur. This is qualitative information, which can be very useful.

If you haven't used a computer or online program, you will need to count up all the responses to any closed questions, and then summarise the responses to any open questions. You could use a blank survey form which was the same as the one issued to mark how many responses you received. Once you have analysed your responses, you may need to write a report with a supporting action plan and subsequent target dates. This might go to managers and/or others involved in the learning process. Make sure you follow up any action points. Informing the respondents of the results and subsequent action keeps them up to date with developments and shows that you take their feedback seriously.

Theory into practice

Design a short questionnaire or survey which you could use with your learners, either now or in the future. Ensure that it is inclusive, taking into account any learner needs and levels of learning. Consider what information you would like to obtain and why, and then devise your questions carefully. You could use a free online program such as Survey Monkey® at www.surveymonkey.com. If you have the opportunity, use it with a small group of learners and remember to set a target date for the return. You can then analyse the results and create an action plan with target dates if necessary.

Self-reflection

Reflective practice is about becoming more self-aware of what you do and how you do it. This should give you increased confidence and improve the links between the theory and practice of teaching, learning, and assessment. It should become a part of your everyday activities, enabling you to analyse and focus on things in greater detail. All reflection should lead to relevant changes and an improvement in practice. However, do be careful not to over-analyse or be too critical of yourself or your actions, as this could lead to you losing confidence as a teacher. Your mentor should be able to help you with the reflective practice process.

Helpful hint

There might be events you would not want to change or improve as you felt they went well. If this is the case, reflect as to why they went well.

Self-reflection is a way of continually thinking and analysing your own practice to ensure that you are carrying out your role effectively. You will need to consider how your own behaviour has impacted upon others, what you could do to improve, and then put this into practice. The word *self* would make you think that you need to do it on your own. However, what you think and what others think might be quite different. If you self-reflect that you have taught a fantastic lesson as all your learners appeared actively engaged, this might be very different to what they actually experienced. When you carry out the self-reflection process, you could consider the perspectives of other people besides your learners. This will help you to become more objective with your judgements of yourself, rather than being subjective i.e. only taking your own viewpoint into consideration.

Self-reflection could take place after each lesson you teach, if you have time. This will enable you to consider your strengths, areas for development, and any action required. One way of doing this is to write a reflective account or maintain a learning journal. It's like keeping a diary or a log of your professional practice. It's a chance to write down what you have done, what was good about it, what you would change and why. You can also add notes as to any training or action points which you feel are required.

Aspects which you could ask yourself as part of the self-reflection process include:

- ☐ how effective was my planning and preparation?
- ☐ how well did I communicate with my learners and others?
- ☐ how effective were the teaching, learning, and assessment approaches I used?
- ☐ how did I stretch and challenge my learners?
- ☐ how well did I meet the needs of my learners?
- ☐ how effective were the resources, equipment, and materials I used?
- ☐ were the learners able to successfully answer my questions and carry out the activities I gave them?
- ☐ how efficient was my record keeping i.e. did I keep records of my learners' progress and achievements?
- ☐ how well did the learners perform i.e. did they achieve what they should have?

Activity

Reflect on other aspects of your job role, such as how you communicate with others, how you manage your time, and how you take care of your health and wellbeing. What would you change and why?

A straightforward method of self-reflection is to use the EDAR process as in Figure 9.1. This enables you to have the *experience*, *describe* it, *analyse* it, and *revise* it (Gravells 2017). This method incorporates the: *who, what, when, where, why,* and *how* approach, and should help you to consider ways of changing and/or improving your practice.

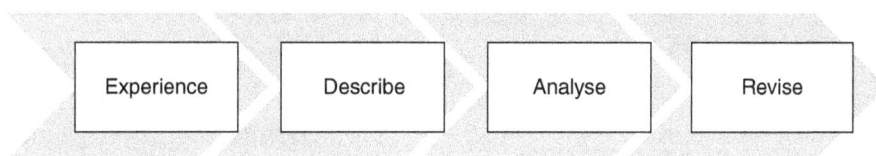

| Experience | Describe | Analyse | Revise |

Figure 9.1 The EDAR process

Example

- *Experience: a significant event or incident you would like to change or improve.*

- *Describe: aspects such as who was involved, what happened, when it happened and where it happened.*

- *Analyse: consider the experience more deeply and ask yourself how it happened and why it happened.*

- *Revise: think about how you would do it differently if it happened again, and then try this out if you have the opportunity.*

It could become a habit to reflect, for example, by mentally running through the EDAR points after a significant event. As you become more experienced and analytical with reflective practice, you will progress from thoughts of *I didn't do that very well*, to aspects of more significance such as *why* you didn't do it very well and *how* you could change something as a result.

If you can take reflective practice seriously, embrace change, and maintain your personal and professional development, you should see an improvement in your practice. This will hopefully result in a positive impact upon your learners' progress and achievement, as well as your own practice.

Theory into practice

Write a reflective account after the next lesson you teach. You could use the EDAR approach to help you focus. What was good about the lesson and why? How did you react and respond to certain situations? Identify areas for your improvement and/or development.

Theories of reflective practice

There are many reflective practice theories which have been based on ideas, thoughts, experiences, and research. Unfortunately there isn't room in this book to explore them all; therefore you will need to research others for yourself. You could even create your own theory which suits you best, based on your experiences and/or after carrying out further research.

Brookfield (1995)

Brookfield identified the importance of being *critical* when reflecting. He advocated four points of view when looking at your practice, which he called *critical lenses*, as in Figure 9.2. These lenses are from the point of view of:

- the teacher (T)
- the learner (L)
- colleagues (C)
- theories and literature (T&L).

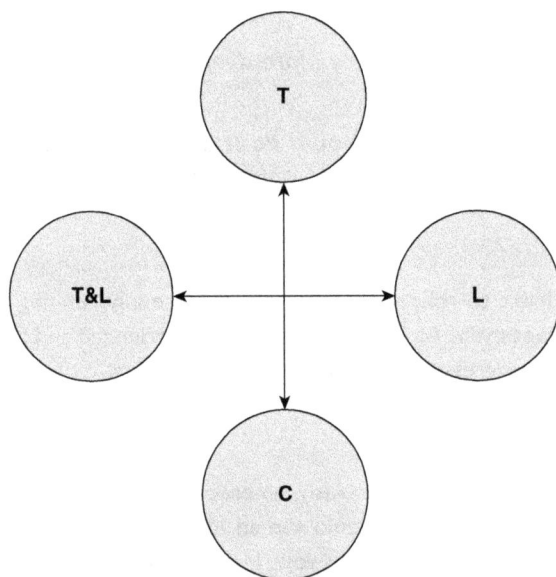

Figure 9.2 Brookfield's (1995) critical lenses

Using these points makes the reflection critical by first looking at it from your own point of view; secondly, how your learners perceived your actions and what they liked and disliked; thirdly, the view from colleagues e.g. your mentor is taken into consideration. This enables you to have a critical conversation about your actions which might highlight things you hadn't considered. Fourthly, you should link your reflections to theories and literature, comparing your own ideas with others.

Helpful hint

Reflection can be helped by a critical friend who is willing to question, challenge, and offer support and advice to overcome any problems or issues.

It's useful to discuss all aspects of your progress with your mentor. They could become your critical friend. You could also pair up with a colleague to question, challenge, and support each other. This support can be useful in establishing actions to overcome barriers. However, you do need to be open to receiving criticism and to be able to act on it.

Activity

Consider something that you could do with your learners which is different to what you would normally do, such as a role play activity. Carry it out and then evaluate the activity based on Brookfield's critical lenses. What could you do differently and why?

Kolb (1984)

Kolb proposed a four-stage theory, known as the *Experiential Learning Cycle* as in Figure 9.3. Part of reflection is about knowing what you need to change. If you are not aware of something that needs changing, you will continue as you are until something serious occurs.

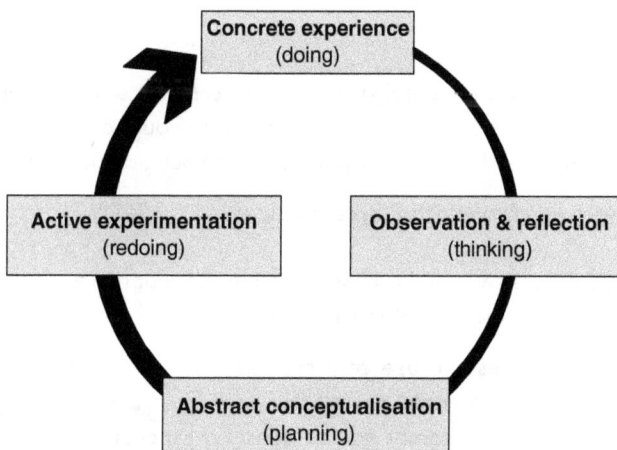

Figure 9.3 Kolb's (1984) Experiential Learning Cycle

The cycle is a way by which people can understand their experiences, and as a result, modify their behaviour. It is based on the idea that the more often a person reflects on a task, the more often they have the opportunity to modify and refine their efforts. The process of learning can begin at any stage and is continuous i.e. there is no limit to the number of cycles which can be made in a situation. This theory suggests that without reflection, people would continue to repeat their mistakes.

- Concrete experience is about experiencing or immersing yourself in the task and is the first stage in which a person simply carries out the task assigned. This is the *doing* stage.

- Observation and reflection involve stepping back from the task and reviewing what has been done and experienced. Your values, attitudes, and beliefs can influence your thinking at this stage. This is the stage of *thinking* about what you have done.

- Abstract conceptualisation involves interpreting the events that have taken place and making sense of them. This is the stage of *planning* how you will do it differently.

- Active experimentation enables you to take the new learning and predict what is likely to happen next, or what actions should be taken to refine the way the task is done again. This is the *redoing* stage based upon experience and reflection.

Example

Wang is working towards an accounting course which has an examination at the end. If he fails, he will not know why, and he will need to wait another three months before a resit. During the course, he could experience the learning process, but not reflect upon what he might be doing wrong that may lead to failure. He is not therefore able to modify his behaviour and try again. If he took a course with ongoing assessment instead of an examination at the end, he would have the opportunity to go through the full cycle. He would have the experience, reflect upon it due to ongoing feedback, think how he could improve, and then experiment to try again.

You are probably familiar with the saying *you learn by experience*. You might find that doing a task, then thinking about it, leads you to plan how you would do it differently next time. Redoing and reflecting on tasks should help to improve your practice.

A few other theories (in chronological order) include:

- Schön (1983) suggests two methods of reflection: reflection *in* action and reflection *on* action i.e. during a situation or after a situation.

- Gibbs (1988) advocates the use of a reflective cycle with headings to generate thought processes. For example, description, feelings, evaluation, analysis, conclusion, action plan. The headings prompt you to consider aspects such as: What happened? What was I feeling at the time? What could I have done differently? What can I do now?

- Griffiths and Tann (1992) introduced a cycle of reflection with different timeframes. They state that without a conscious effort, the most immediate reactions to experiences can overwhelm the opportunity for deeper consideration and learning.

- Tripp (1993) advocates *critical incident analysis*. A critical incident is something you interpret as a problem or a challenge in a particular context, rather than a routine occurrence. The guiding principle is to change the incident into a question to reflect upon it.

- Ecclestone (1995) advocates that there is a danger of reflective practice becoming nothing more than a *mantra*, a comforting and familiar wrap as opposed to a professional tool for exploration.

- Johns (2006) uses structured reflection to look inwards (your thoughts and feelings) and outwards (your actions in a certain situation). Questions can be posed and answers written in a reflective journal.

Theory into practice

Choose two of the above theories and research them further. Which one would you prefer to use for your own self-reflection and why? Next time you complete your learning journal, make reference to one or more of the theories.

Continuing professional development

Continuing professional development (CPD) can be anything that you do that helps you to improve your practice, and keeps you up to date with your subject specialism. It can also be a way of taking control of your health and wellbeing, by participating in activities to support this, such as mindfulness and stress management.

There are constant changes in education; therefore it is crucial to keep up to date and embrace them. Examples include changes to the qualifications or standards you teach, changes to policies and procedures within your organisation, updates to regulatory requirements and government policies. It's useful to regularly reflect upon how you are meeting relevant professional or occupational standards for your subject and your teaching role. It can enable you to identify gaps in your learning and then plan ways to meet them.

You could carry out a SWOT analysis to help you understand where you are at the moment regarding your teaching role, and what you need to do as part of the CPD process. SWOT stands for **s**trengths, **w**eaknesses, **o**pportunities, and **t**hreats.

Strengths and weaknesses can be considered as internal (i.e. within the organisation) whereas opportunities and threats can be considered as external (outside of the organisation). Strengths and opportunities can be helpful, whereas weaknesses and threats can be harmful. A SWOT analysis is useful for identifying your own strengths and weaknesses, as well as the opportunities available and the threats faced. These could be from a personal as well as a professional perspective.

Complete the SWOT boxes below regarding your current job role and your knowledge of your subject specialism. Once completed, consider what CPD you can do to improve your practice.

SWOT analysis – your current role

	Helpful	Harmful
Internal	**S**trengths	**W**eaknesses
External	**O**pportunities	**T**hreats

Listing your strengths and weaknesses while identifying opportunities and threats is of no use if you don't use the results for a purpose. You will need to decide what that purpose is, and whether it's for yourself and/or others you work with. Once identified, you can apply the strengths and take advantage of the opportunities. You will also need to minimise the weaknesses and threats or get rid of them altogether. This might be a long-term project and you may need to work with others to achieve it.

Personal development plan

A personal development plan (PDP) is a way of formalising what you are going to do as part of your CPD. Your organisation should discuss the PDP process with you, and inform you as to what records you will need to maintain. You might like to cross-reference what you want to do (your goals or aims) to relevant professional or occupational standards. A PDP plan is usually a template with headings such as:

- goals or aims: short and long term
- activity or actions to meet the goals or aims
- start date
- completion date
- review date.

To help you with your plan, you could follow the Society for Education and Training's (SETs) CPD cycle as in Figure 9.4. Please note, the SET might have changed their name since this book was published.

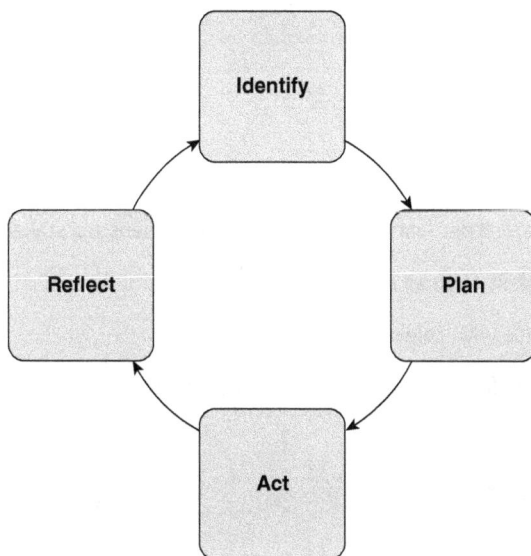

Figure 9.4 CPD cycle

Example

- *Identify: consider where you are now and what goals you want to achieve.*

- *Plan: consider which CPD activities can help you to achieve your goals, and how and when they can be achieved.*

- *Act: carry out the CPD activities and update your CPD plan if necessary.*

- *Reflect: think about how the CPD activities have helped you to achieve your goals, and what impact they have had on your performance. You can then start the cycle again and identify further CPD activities as necessary.*

You can regularly review how you are progressing and update and amend your plan as you progress.

Continuing professional development (CPD) activities

There are many CPD activities you could carry out. Some might be during work time, or others during your own time. Some activities might only take a short while, such as internet research, or some might take hours or days. However, whatever you do should have a real impact upon your professional practice, and be done to meet an identified need. For example, changes to educational policies which impact upon your role, or emerging pedagogical trends for your subject.

CPD activities could include:

- attending events and training courses

- attending meetings

- blogs/vlogs and podcasts
- collaborative working
- communities of practice
- e-learning and online activities
- evaluating feedback from learners, peers, managers, mentors, stakeholders, and others
- improving own skills such as English, maths and digital skills
- keeping up to date with relevant legislation
- membership of professional associations or committees
- mentoring or coaching new staff
- observing colleagues
- networking (online and in person)
- researching developments or changes to your subject
- secondment
- self-reflection
- standardisation activities
- studying for relevant qualifications
- team-teaching
- updating subject skills and knowledge
- using social media to follow/inform others of relevant information
- using new and emerging technologies
- voluntary work in your subject specialism
- work experience placements
- writing, reading, and/or reviewing text books and journal articles.

Prior to planning or undertaking any CPD, you might like to ask yourself the following questions:

- ☐ Why am I doing it and what will I gain as a result?
- ☐ How will others benefit, such as my learners or colleagues?
- ☐ Is it really relevant and/or necessary that I do it?
- ☐ Is there any funding available for me to do it?
- ☐ How much of my own time and/or money will I need?
- ☐ How can I apply the CPD I have done to my professional practice?

☐ Can I share what I've learnt with others? If so, who?

☐ Who can support me and give me advice while I undertake it?

☐ What will the role of my manager/mentor be?

☐ Are there any organisational implications as a result of my undertaking CPD?

☐ When is the best time to review my progress, and update my personal development plan and CPD record?

Helpful hint

All CPD should have an impact on your professional role and the teaching of your subject. It should not just be something you do because you think you should, or someone tells you to. You could cross-reference your activities to a set of occupational or professional standards.

Continuing professional development (CPD) log

A CPD log is a way of formalising what you have done and when, and helps you to reflect upon your progress and development. Your organisation should discuss the CPD process with you, and inform you as to what records you will need to maintain. It is usually a template with headings such as:

- date

- activity undertaken

- reflective comments and impact upon job role

- action required

- target date for achievement.

You could add a reference number to any documentation which supports your CPD, in case you need to provide it to funding bodies, awarding organisations, professional associations or regulatory bodies. You could also cross-reference your evidence to relevant professional or occupational standards.

You might carry out various CPD activities over time to support your job role and your subject specialism. They might not always be on your PDP, but it's useful to add them to your CPD log.

A good point to remember is that failure is not when you get something wrong, but when you stop trying to get it right. Aim to be the best you can be. The demands of your job might affect what you do and how you feel. However, when you are with your learners you should remain professional and give them a learning experience which they will remember and benefit from.

Theory into practice

Make a list of several CPD activities which you can undertake to benefit both your professional role and your subject specialism. Create a PDP and a CPD log (if none currently exist at your organisation). If possible, carry out some of the activities, reflect on them and complete your CPD log.

Summary

This chapter has explored:

- Evaluation
- Self-reflection
- Theories of reflective practice
- Continuing professional development

AAO	Apprentice Assessment Organisation
ACL	Adult and Community Learning
ADD	Attention Deficit Disorder
ADHD	Attention Deficit and Hyperactivity Disorder
ADS	Adult Dyslexia Support
AELP	Association of Employment and Learning Providers
AfL	Assessment for Learning
AI	Artificial intelligence
AO	Awarding Organisation
AoC	Association of Colleges
AoL	Assessment of Learning
AP	Action Plan/Assessment Plan
APL	Accreditation of Prior Learning
ASD	Autism Spectrum Disorder
ATS	Advanced Teacher Status
BYOD	Bring Your Own Device
CA	Classroom Assistant
CertEd	Certificate in Education and Training
CL	Community Learning
CLA	Copyright Licensing Authority
COSHH	Control of Substances Hazardous to Health
CPD	Continuing Professional Development
DBS	Disclosure and Barring Service
DfE	Department for Education
DiT	Diploma in Teaching
DSO	Designated Safeguarding Officer
EBD	Emotional and Behavioural Difficulties
EDAR	Experience, Describe, Analyse, Revise
EDI	Equality, Diversity and Inclusion
EDIP	Explain, Demonstrate, Imitate, Practise
EHCP	Education, Health and Care Plan
EI	Emotional Intelligence
EMD	English, maths and digital skills
EPA/O	End-Point Assessment/Organisation
EQA	External Quality Assurance or Assurer
ESD	Education for Sustainable Development
ESFA	Education and Skills Funding Agency
ESOL	English for Speakers of Other Languages
ETF	Education and Training Foundation
FAQ	Frequently Asked Questions

FE	Further Education
FES	Further Education and Skills
FELTAG	Further Education Learning Technology Action Group
FHE	Further and Higher Education
FHEQ	Framework for Higher Education Qualifications
GDPR	General Data Protection Regulation
GLH	Guided Learning Hours
H&S	Health and Safety
HE	Higher Education
HEA	Higher Education Authority
HEI	Higher Education Institution
HSE	Health and Safety Executive
IAG	Information, Advice and Guidance
IAC	Independent Assessment Centre
IAO	Independent Assessment Organisation
IAP	Individual Action Plan
ICT	Information and Communication Technology
IDP	Individual Development Plan
IfATE	Institute for Apprenticeships and Technical Education
ILA	Individual Learning Account
ILP	Individual Learning Plan
ILT	Information and Learning Technology
IT	Information Technology
ITE	Initial Teacher Education
ITP	Independent Training Provider
ITT	Initial Teacher Training
KSB	Knowledge, Skills and Behaviours
LA	Local Authority
LAR	Learner Achievement Record
LDD	Learning Difficulties and/or Disabilities
LLN	Literacy, Language, and Numeracy
LRC	Learning Resource Centre
LSA	Learning (or Learner) Support Assistant
LSTA	Learning and Skills Teacher Apprenticeship
MLD	Moderate Learning Difficulties
MOOCs	Massive Open Online Courses
MOODLE	Modular Object-Oriented Dynamic Learning Environment
NAS	National Apprenticeship Service
NEET	Not in Education, Employment, or Training
NLP	Neuro Linguistic Programming
NOS	National Occupational Standards
NQF	National Qualification Framework
NQT	Newly Qualified Teacher
NTA	Non-teaching Assistant
NVQ	National Vocational Qualification
NYA	Not yet achieved
OHP	Overhead projector
OER	Open Education Resources
Ofqual	Office of Qualifications and Examinations Regulation

Ofsted	Office for Standards in Education, Children's Services and Skills
ODD	Oppositional Defiant Disorder
OS	Occupational Standards
OU	Open University
PAR	Present, Apply, Review
PCK	Pedagogical Content Knowledge
PDBW	Personal Development, Behaviour and Welfare
PDP	Personal Development Plan/Portfolio
PGCE	Post/Professional Graduate Certificate in Education
PGDE	Post Graduate Diploma in Education
PLP	Personal Learning Plan
PLTS	Personal Learning and Thinking Skills
PPE	Personal Protective Equipment
PPP	Pose, Pause, Pick
PSHE	Personal, Social, and Health Education
QIP	Quality Improvement Report
QSR	Qualification Success Rates
QTLS	Qualified Teacher Learning and Skills (FE and Skills Sector)
QTS	Qualified Teacher Status (Schools)
RLJ	Reflective Learning Journal
RoC	Rules of Combination
RPL/A	Recognition of Prior Learning/Achievements
RQF	Regulated Qualifications Framework
RWE	Realistic Working Environment
SAR	Self-Assessment Report
SEND	Special Educational Needs and Disabilities
SET	Society for Education and Training
SMART	Specific, Measurable, Achievable, Relevant, and Timebound
SoL	Scheme of Learning
SoW	Scheme of Work
SSB	Standard Setting Body
SSC	Sector Skills Council
STEM	Science, Technology, Engineering, and Maths
SWE	Simulated Working Environment
SWOT	Strengths, Weaknesses, Opportunities, and Threats
T&L	Teaching and Learning
TA	Transactional Analysis or Teaching Assistant
TAQA	Training, Assessment, and Quality Assurance
TEL	Technology Enhanced Learning
TLA	Teaching, Learning, and Assessment
TQT	Total Qualification Time
TNA	Training Needs Analysis
ULN	Unique Learner Number
VARCS	Valid, Authentic, Reliable, Current, Sufficient
VARK	Visual, Aural, Read/write, Kinaesthetic
VET	Vocational Education and Training
VLE	Virtual learning environment
WBL	Work-Based Learning
WWWWWWH	Who, What, When, Where, Why, and How

References and further reading

Allen, CR (1919) *The Instructor: The Man and the Job: A Handbook for Instructors of Industrial and Vocational Subjects.* USA J B Lippincott Company.

Bates, B (2016) *A Quick Guide to Special Needs and Disabilities.* London: Sage Publications Ltd.

Bates, B (2023) *Learning Theories Simplified.* London: Sage Publications Ltd.

Berne, E (1964) *Games People Play: The Psychology of Human Relationships.* London: Penguin Books.

Bloom, BS (1956) *Taxonomy of Educational Objectives: The Classification of Goals.* New York: Mckay.

Brookfield, SD (1995, 2017) *Becoming a Critically Reflective Teacher.* San Francisco CA: Jossey-Bass.

Brune, JA (1960) *The Process of Education.* Cambridge MA: Harvard University Press.

Coffield, F (2008) *Just Suppose Teaching and Learning Became the First Priority.* London: Learning and Skills Network.

Crawley, J (2018) *Just Teach! in FE.* London: Sage Learning Matters.

Dale, E (1969) *Audio Visual Methods in Teaching* (3rd Edition). New York: Holt, Reinehart and Winson.

Dewey, J (1963) *Experience and Education.* New York: Collier Books.

Duckworth, V (2014) *How to be a Brilliant FE Teacher.* Abingdon: Routledge.

Ecclestone, K (1995) The Reflective Practitioner: Mantra or Model for Emancipation. *Studies in the Education of Adults,* 28 (2).

Fischer, K and Immordino-Yang, H (2008) *The Brain and Learning.* San Francisco: Jossey-Bass.

Fleming, N (2001) *Teaching and Learning Preferences: VARK Strategies.* Honolulu: Honolulu Community College.

Fleming, N and Mills, C (1992) Not Another Inventory, Rather a Catalyst for Reflection. *To Improve the Academy,* 11:137.

Gagne, R (1985) *The Conditions of Learning* (4th Edition). New York: Holt, Reinehart and Winson.

Gibbs, G (1988) *Learning by Doing: A Guide to Teaching and Learning Methods.* Oxford: Further Education Unit.

Gravells, A and Simpson, S (2012) *Equality and Diversity in the Lifelong Learning Sector.* London: Sage Learning Matters.

Gravells, A (2015) *Principles and Practices of Assessment.* London: Sage Learning Matters.

Gravells, A (2016) *Principles and Practices of Quality Assurance.* London: Sage Learning Matters.

Gravells, A (2017) *Principles and Practices of Teaching and Training.* London: Sage Learning Matters.

Gregson, M and Hillier, Y (2015) *Reflective Teaching in Further, Adult and Vocational Education.* London: Bloomsbury.

Griffiths, M and Tann, S (1992) Using reflective practice to link personal and public theories. *Journal of Education for Teaching.* Vol 18 (1): 69–84.

Harvey, B and Harvey, J (2013) *Creative Teaching Approaches in the Lifelong Learning Sector.* Maidenhead: OU Press.

Hill, A, Watson, J, Rivers, D, and Joyce, MD (2007) *Key Themes in Interpersonal Communication.* Maidenhead: McGraw Hill Education.

Honey, P and Mumford, A (1992) *The Manual of Learning Preference* (3rd Edition). Maidenhead: Peter Honey Associates.

James, W (2000) (edited by Giles Gunn) *Pragmatism and Other Writings.* London: Penguin Books.

Johns, C (2006) *Engaging Reflection in Practice: A Narrative Approach.* Oxford: Blackwell Publishing.

Kirkpatrick, DL (1994, 2006) *Evaluating Training Programs.* Oakland: Berrett-Koehler Publishers.

Knowles, M (1975) *Self-Directed Learning: A Guide for Learners and Teachers.* New Jersey: Prentice Hall.

Kolb, DA (1984) *Experiential Learning: Experience as the source of learning and development.* New Jersey: Prentice Hall.

Lewin, K (1951) *Field Theory in Social Science.* New York: Harper and Row.

Malthouse, R and Roffey-Barentsen, J (2013) *Academic Skills: Contemporary Education Studies.* London: Thalassa Publishing.

Mansell, S (2019) *50 Teaching and Learning Approaches.* London: Sage Learning Matters.

Mansell, S (2019) *50 Assessment Approaches.* London: Sage Learning Matters.

Martin, K (1996) Critical Incidents in Teaching and Learning. *Issues of Teaching and Learning,* 2 (8).

Maslow, AH (1987) (edited by Frager, R) *Motivation and Personality* (3rd Revised Edition). New York: Pearson Education Ltd.

Ofqual (2009) *Authenticity – a Guide for Teachers.* Coventry: Ofqual.

O'leary, M (2020) *Classroom Observation: A Guide to the Effective Observation of Teaching and Learning.* Abingdon: Routledge.

Pavlor, IP (1927) *Conditioned Reflexes: An Investigate of the Physiological Activity of the Vertebral Cortex.* London: OU Press.

Petty, G (2009, 2014) *Evidence-Based Teaching: A Practical Approach.* Cheltenham: Nelson Thornes, Ltd.

Piaget, J (1959) *The Language and Thoughts of the Child* (Vol. 5). Sussex: Psychology Press.

Rogers, C (1959) A Theory of Therapy, Personality and Interpersonal Relationships as Developed in the Client-centered Framework. In Koch, S (ed.) *Psychology: A Study of a Science. Vol. 3: Formulations of the Person and the Social Context.* New York: McGraw Hill.

Rogers, C (1994) *Freedom to Learn.* New York: Prentice Hall.

Rogers, B (2015) *Classroom Behaviour* (4th Edition). London: Sage.

Roffey-Barentsen, J and Malthouse, R (2013) *Reflective Practice in Education and Training* (2nd Edition). London: Learning Matters.

Shannon, C and Weaver, W (1949) *Mathematical Theory of Communication.* Champaign Ill: University of Illinois Press.

Scales, P et al (2011) *Continuing Professional Development in the Lifelong Learning Sector*. Maidenhead: Open University Press.

Schön, D (1983) *The Reflective Practitioner*. London: Temple Smith.

Scott, D (2022) *Digital Learning, Teaching and Assessment for HE and FE Practitioners*. Northwich: Critical Publishing Ltd.

Sellars, M (2017) *Reflective Practice for Teachers*. London: Sage Publications Ltd.

Siemens, G (2005) *Connectivism: A Learning Theory for the Digital Age*. Ontario: International Journal of Instructional Technology and Distance Learning.

Skills for Jobs (2021) *Lifelong Learning for Opportunity and Growth*. DfE.

Skinner, BF (1974) *About Behaviourism*. San Francisco, CA: Knopf.

Stewart, I and Joines, V (2012) *TA Today; A New introduction to Transactional Analysis*. Kegworth: Lifespace Publishing.

Stufflebeam, DL (2007) *Evaluation Theory, Models and Applications*. San Francisco: Jossey-Bass.

Sweller, J (1988) Cognitive Load during Problem Solving: Effects on Learning. *Cognitive Science*, 12: 257–85.

Tripp, D (1993, 2012) *Critical Incidents in Teaching: Developing Professional Judgement*. London: Routledge.

Vygotsky, LS (1962) *Thought and Language*. Cambridge MA: MIT Press.

Wallace, S (2017) *Motivating Unwilling Learners in Further Education: The Key to Improving Behaviour*. London: Bloomsbury.

Watson, JB (1928) *The Ways of Behaviourism*. New York: Harper & Brother.

White, J (2015) *Digital Literacy Skills for FE Teachers*. London: Sage Learning Matters.

Wood, J and Dickinson, J (2011) *Quality Assurance and Evaluation in the Lifelong Learning Sector*. Exeter: Learning Matters.

Websites

The following were current at the time of publication.

Ann Gravells – www.anngravells.com

Copyright – www.gov.uk/copyright

Department of Education – https://tinyurl.com/DeptForEducation

Department of Education – Keeping children safe in education 2023 – https://tinyurl.com/DfEKeepingChildrenSafe

Department for Education – Promoting and supporting mental health and wellbeing in schools and colleges – http://tinyurl.com/MentalHandW

Department for Education – Generative artificial intelligence (AI) in education (2023) – http://tinyurl.com/DfEPolicyPaperAI

Department for Education's Sustainability and Climate Change Strategy for Education: Progress Update 2023 – http://tinyurl.com/DfESustainability2023

DfE Sustainability and Climate Change Strategy: Evaluation Framework – http://tinyurl.com/DfEEvaluationFramework

Education and Training Foundation (ETF) – www.et-foundation.co.uk

Essential Teaching UK – www.essentialteaching.uk

ETF Digital Teaching Professional Framework – http://tinyurl.com/DigitalTPFramework

ETF Education for Sustainable Development – http://tinyurl.com/esdETF

ETF Professional Standards – http://tinyurl.com/ETFPSTeachers

Equality Act 2010 – https://tinyurl.com/GovUKEqualityAct2010

FE Advice – www.feadvice.org.uk

Federation for Industry Sector Skills and Standards – http://fisss.org

Gavin Lumsden – www.essentialteaching.uk/the-teacher-coach

Guide to using research evidence – https://educationendowmentfoundation.org.uk/

Harvard Referencing – http://tinyurl.com/HarvardRefGuide

History of Further Education – https://tinyurl.com/FEHistory

Home Office: Prevent Guidance – https://tinyurl.com/PDGuidance

Icebreaker and energiser examples – https://tinyurl.com/IcebreakerEnergiser

Institute for Apprenticeships – http://tinyurl.com/InstForApps

Joint Information Systems Committee (JISC) Guides for using digital technology – www.jisc.ac.uk/guides

Learning and Skills Teacher Occupational Standards – https://tinyurl.com/LSTTeacher

Online surveys – www.surveymonkey.com and www.smartsurvey.co.uk

National Association for Numeracy and Mathematics in Colleges – www.nanamic.org.uk

Ofqual Guide to Authenticity – http://tinyurl.com/OfqualAuthenticity

Ofsted – www.gov.uk/government/organisations/ofsted

Online Safety Act (2023) – http://tinyurl.com/OnlineSafetyAct

Plagiarism – www.plagiarism.org

Prevent Duty Guidance: England and Wales (2023) – https://tinyurl.com/GOVPreventDutyGuidance

Sage Journals – Is learning styles-based instruction effective? – https://tinyurl.com/SageLearningStyles

SET Code of Ethics and Conduct – http://tinyurl.com/SETCodeOfEthics

Skills and Post-16 Education Act (2022) – http://tinyurl.com/SkillsPost16

Society for Education and Training (SET) – https://set.et-foundation.co.uk

Sustainability Exchange – http://tinyurl.com/FESustainabilityExchange

Teaching Assistants: Support in Action – https://tinyurl.com/OLTeachingAssistants

Teaching in Lifelong Learning Journals – www.teachinginlifelonglearning.org.uk

Transactional analysis – www.ericberne.com/transactional-analysis/

Tuckman's Group Formation theory – http://tinyurl.com/TuckmanGroups

UNESCO Sustainability – http://tinyurl.com/esdUNESCO

VARK – www.vark-learn.com

INDEX

Note: Page numbers in *italics* represent figures; page numbers followed by (t) refer to a table.